Praise for *Role Modelship*

"In *Role Modelship*, Eli Potter has filled a vital open space on every business leader's current bookshelf, one reserved for a consummate guide to mastery in this new world of blended intelligence. If you remember nothing else from her compelling narrative, it is this: Artificial intelligence cannot be what it cannot see."

— **MATTHEW E. MAY**, best-selling author of *The Elegant Solution* and *What a Unicorn Knows*

"Every organization in this tech world needs these principles and techniques. It is important that we focus on Role Modelship in the age of AI—and ensure that people are modeling complete, compassionate leadership."

— **JACK CANFIELD**, best-selling author of *The Success Principles* and cocreator of the Chicken Soup for the Soul® series

"When we realize how utterly influenceable we are as humans, we can shift the idea of role modeling from the periphery of our minds to a more central position in our thoughts and actions."

— **BILL O'CONNOR**, founder and partner, Innovista

"Learning from an antifragile role model should improve our human capital. In turn, the additional human capital, whether it's in the form of additional skills we learned or formal education that we received while overcoming those challenges, increases the individual's productivity and potential earnings in the labor market."

— **MAXINE LEE**, PhD, associate professor of economics, San Francisco State University

"If you want to have a greater impact personally and professionally, this book is for you. It is packed with role models anyone can relate to and many actionable ways to build role modelship habits. The power of putting these principles and frameworks into practice lies in their integration and harmonization."

—**HELEN LIN,** founder and CEO, Discern

"AI is advancing at a pace that is redefining competitive advantage, reshaping customer expectations, and raising the stakes for every executive. In my work with hundreds of companies navigating rapid transformation, I have seen a clear pattern: Speed and scale collapse when leaders ignore the human scaffolding of trust, stewardship, and ethical leadership. Eli Potter's *Role Modelship* introduces a pragmatic approach to change that gives executives a playbook to connect technological innovation with enduring human values. This book is not just timely, it is essential for leaders who want systems that are both resilient and human-centered. The leaders who embrace this approach will multiply their impact. And the ones who don't will see AI accelerate fragility faster than they can recover."

—**ELLIE WU,** founder and executive advisor, CSuiteCX

"This book is a playbook for anyone serious about scaling with purpose. It blends practical habits with enduring leadership principles that help start-ups grow up fast and established companies stay fresh. The lessons drawn from countless role models give you the pattern recognition to anticipate challenges and seize opportunities. It's equal parts fresh perspective and disciplined guidance for leaders at any stage."

—**SCOTT HART,** CFO of NMI

"Eli Potter's *Role Modelship* is a practical guide to leading with purpose in the age of AI. She breaks down five core habits—stewardship, fellowship, mentorship, leadership, and sponsorship—into clear, usable frameworks that help leaders amplify their impact. I found the BRAVER and SOBER models especially useful for anyone navigating change and building teams that can adapt with both discipline and empathy."

—**JOHN SHAW,** entrepreneur; former private equity AI and ML lead, AWS

"Help other people get what they want, and you'll never have any wants yourself. That idea of service has stayed with me throughout my career and life. True leadership and influence come from helping others see the best in themselves."

—**MARK PORTER,** financial advisor, Ameriprise Financial Services

"In an era where AI challenges the meaning of human value, *Role Modelship* arrives as the book we urgently need. It redefines leadership through values, mentorship, and multidisciplinary thinking—empowering us to educate future leaders who can unite ethics, innovation, and purpose to shape a more humane, intelligent future."

—**SHANTHA MOHAN,** PhD, Carnegie Mellon University

This publication is designed to provide accurate and authoritative information in regard to the subject matter covered. It is sold with the understanding that the publisher and author are not engaged in rendering legal, accounting, or other professional services. Nothing herein shall create an attorney-client relationship, and nothing herein shall constitute legal advice or a solicitation to offer legal advice. If legal advice or other expert assistance is required, the services of a competent professional should be sought.

Disclaimers:

- Not an endorsement for purchase of any software product or investment in any individual, company, or product. Examples are just for illustration.

- Fair warning: Contents of this book and math formulas may cause happiness.

Published by River Grove Books
Austin, TX
www.rivergrovebooks.com

Distributed by River Grove Books

Design and composition by Greenleaf Book Group
Cover design by Greenleaf Book Group
Cover images used under license from Adobestock.com

Publisher's Cataloging-in-Publication data is available.

Print ISBN: 978-1-966629-65-8

eBook ISBN: 978-1-966629-66-5

First Edition

ROLE MODELSHIP

MULTIPLY YOUR IMPACT TO INFLUENCE AI

ELI POTTER

RIVER GROVE
BOOKS

CONTENTS

Dedication

This book is written for human readers. Charting a human future requires defining new human products and a stronger human role in the age of artificial intelligence (AI). **There isn't a stronger role for humans than the role of role model.** Role Modelship is about setting examples and raising the bar on human values and economic value in the decision factories of the future as we race to invest in technology.

To everyone human who is already applying Role Modelship, consciously or subconsciously: *You touch the future. Thank you for your service. Let's wire humans and AI to role model together!*

RALLYING CRY

AI can't be what AI can't see.

AI is learning from you as a steward, fellow, mentor, leader, and sponsor.

Our rallying cry is "Wire 2 Model":
We need to wire humans and AI to be role models.

Here are ten habits you can practice
to positively influence AI:

1. Demonstrate Role Modelship™ because human behavior is encapsulated in the data leveraged to train AI.

2. Invest in human–AI literacy to influence roles, boundaries, and partnerships.

3. Ask, "Is AI good for humanity?" as often as "Does it scale?"

4. Push AI to solve real human problems (e.g., well-being, equity, environment, and community), not just optimize efficiency or effectiveness.

5. Encourage dialogue about human, societal, and profit trade-offs.

6. Champion diverse voices and diverse data.

7. Reward behaviors worth replicating, not just results.

8. Create cross-organizational guardrails, and make responsible AI a team sport.

9. Tell meaningful human-centered stories to train the machines.

10. Lead with purpose, and scale habits across humans and algorithms.

A Stronger Role for Humans

Setting an example is not the main means of influencing others; it is the only means.
—ALBERT EINSTEIN

The greatest danger for most of us is not that our aim is too high and we miss it but that it is too low and we reach it.
—MICHELANGELO

If you're holding this book, I suspect we have a lot in common.

Imagine a child in Bulgaria, standing in the shadows of the Iron Curtain, dreaming of possibilities far beyond plowing fields, canning tomatoes, and tying brooms in the summer. That child is me—an idealistic kid who didn't have any money but carried something far more valuable: the belief that the world is shaped by the stories we tell and the role models we emulate.

Years later, I found myself in the United States, collecting coins on the campus of Sonoma State University just to get by, learning English from The Beatles, and inhaling the words of Dale Carnegie, who taught me that people don't rise alone; they rise together, with guidance and inspiration from others, winning as a team.

My journey has been defined by humans, companies, and products, which have shown me that life's most significant transformations come not from where you start but from the examples you follow and exemplify. Role models shaped every step of my way, from navigating a foreign culture to finding my own voice as a role model. In a world grappling with uncertainty, complexity, and disconnection, what if the secret to humanity is as simple as intentional role modeling?

Let me take you on a journey of transformation filled with stories, lessons, and the incredible people who proved to me that when we raise others, we rise together.

If you only take away one piece of wisdom from this book, let it be this motto:

When they subtract or divide, we add and multiply.

While attending a mindset rewiring event in Napa geared toward executives in the technology, venture capital, and private equity sectors, I asked myself if I'd done enough for the next generation. The seed that would ultimately become this book was planted at that event, and it all began with a simple observation: We need more role models at the human, organizational, and product level if we are to grow the next AI-enabled generation of humans and technology.

I was moved by a story an investor at the event shared informally about a philosophy of service very similar to my own, in which a chance human introduction and a selfless act of stewardship and kindness led to a thriving AI product and a company merger. The emphasis was on the importance of paying it forward by acting as a role model, reinforcing the idea that intentional guidance can catalyze and fuse success by impacting product, customer, and economic outcomes.

Writing this book became a deliberate exhale. It marked the culmination of my entire career and the beginning of the next chapter of my life, of giving back and paying it forward, of amplifying diverse voices and elevating humans and technology in a much more deliberate way than before.

As we set strategic goals to embed AI into products and leverage it to increase human productivity, we also need to set strategic objectives for Role Modelship and the development of model humans. Our human future is at stake. The seeds we plant today could grow into villains and victims—or leaders, sponsors, and giants—in a century. The late Austrian American management visionary Peter F. Drucker wrote that management's most significant contribution in the twentieth century was the fifty-fold productivity increase of manual workers in manufacturing.[1] He also asserted that the most important contribution management needs to make in the twenty-first century is to increase the productivity of the knowledge worker.

Through AI, knowledge has just been democratized, and humans are quickly pivoting to being multidisciplinary. The most important role for a human in the age of AI, when knowledge is ubiquitous, is not just being more productive but being a role model. The most important contribution management needs to make in this century is to nurture and increase the number of human role models, because they set a high bar and inspire more people to become bar-raisers. Efficiency and productivity are only meaningful if they are anchored in a foundation of core values and ethical behaviors that create a lasting economic impact through a lineage of generations.

Values-driven humans are anchored and guided by ethics. Efficient humans optimize effort based on values. Productive humans focus on maximizing output. Effective humans achieve meaningful goals based on values, efficiency, and outputs. Human role models build on values, efficiency, and effectiveness and focus on raising standards, influencing AI, inspiring others, and passing on a legacy (see figure 0.1).

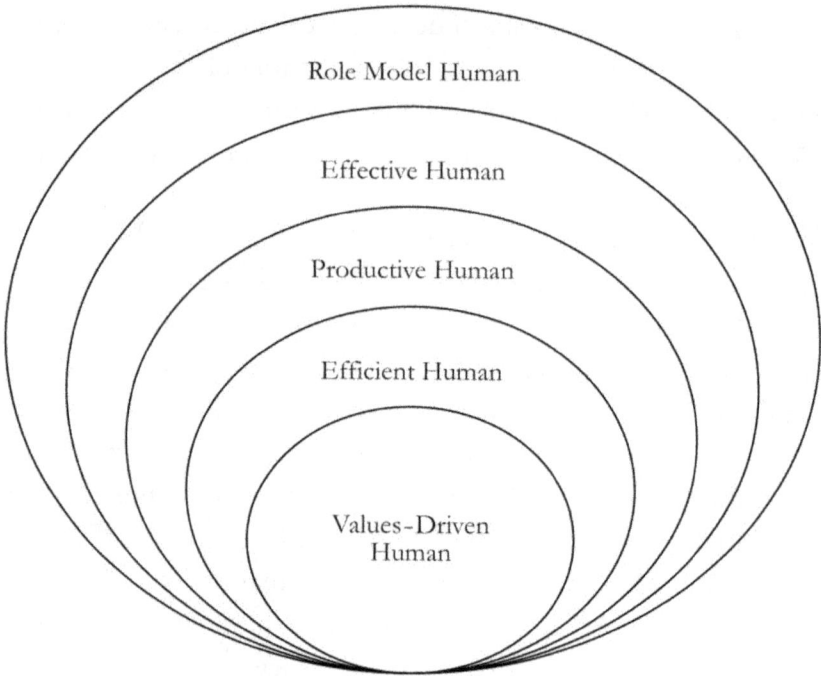

Figure 0.1. The human chart.

Executives and board members need to get more out of the human and digital resources by setting an example of excellence in ethical values and economic value. We need to foster bar-raisers who consciously and deliberately encourage more to become bar-raisers, creating a network effect. By prioritizing the development of role models, organizations can ensure that their success is not just measured in outputs but in the transformative influence they have on individuals, teams, companies, products, and society. This focus would elevate the role of management from transactional overseer to force multiplier for shaping the future.

As Jensen Huang, founder and CEO of NVIDIA, and Arthur Mensch, cofounder and CEO of Mistral, point out, "The global race for AI dominance is no longer just about companies; it's about nations. AI isn't just computing infrastructure; it's cultural infrastructure, economic strategy, and national security all rolled into one."[2]

In the age of AI, we need role models more than ever before. I believe role models are the answer to some of the most pressing questions we face: How can we address our toughest human challenges? How can we break through the most difficult barriers and enter the most competitive product markets, where economic value matters more than price? How can we influence and drive AI product, organizational, or social change? By showing up as role models. By charting a stronger role for humans in the age of AI.

DELIBERATE ROLE MODELSHIP

A role model is someone who consistently demonstrates values, behaviors, best practices, and economic value that others admire and strive to emulate. In the age of AI, best practices are readily available in products, podcasts, white papers, search engines, and AI copilots and agents.

However, AI can't be what it can't see.

To influence AI, we must model what matters: ethical choices, diverse data, and feedback loops that prioritize human well-being alongside profits. By telling human-centered stories and rewarding values-driven behavior, we turn influence into social capital—with exponential impact.

Role models are special because they deliberately lead by example, influencing not just through words but through their integrity, actions, decisions, and outcomes. Role models often possess a clear sense of purpose, using their experiences and success to inspire growth in others, whether through stewardship, fellowship, mentorship, leadership, or sponsorship. In the ecosystems they inhabit, role models serve as catalysts for positive change, setting standards for ethical conduct and excellence that ripple across teams, organizations, and communities.

--------------------- ✦ ---------------------

Becoming a role model is not just about discovering Platform 9¾.
It's about inspiring others to build the next Hogwarts Express in space.

Role models' impact on humans is profound: They inspire confidence, foster development, and kindly push and challenge others to reach their full potential.

THE ROLE OF HUMANITY IN THE AGE OF AI

AI will impact everyone, and increasing the number of role models in the form of humans, organizations, and products is the only way forward. This book is for individuals who understand that real influence comes not from power or authority but from the example you set, regardless of your place in an organization. By focusing on role modeling, you can amplify your speed, value, and impact. Your actions will inspire others, multiplying the impact you have across people, processes, and products, all while accelerating your journey as a leader.

If you're a professional working in the product, technology, financial, or health-care tech sectors, you need to leverage the role models in your organizations more than ever before. The speed of change is only growing, competition is rapidly increasing, and role models can significantly accelerate your time-to-value metric in achieving desired business outcomes. If you are a leader or mentor who wants to make a meaningful difference in your organization, community, or personal life, role modeling provides your biggest why. It gives you an outlet

--------------- ✦ ---------------

Everyone builds bridges of trust.

----

for caring about more than just your personal success; it's an outlet for creating a lasting, positive impact on the world around you.

The lessons and anecdotes in this book will demonstrate ways you can look at the world through the lens of Role Modelship to build value for your humans, your product, and your organization. This paradigm shift will allow you to meet the challenges facing you from the standpoint of a multidisciplinary human, inspiring others around you to become role models and influence AI.

What would the world look like if everyone woke up and asked themselves one question every day: *What am I role modeling today?*

A SPECIAL HUMAN, ORGANIZATION, OR PRODUCT

I've had the privilege of working with more than 150 companies, from start-ups with less than $10 million in annual revenue to enterprise companies that take in billions each year. Autodesk's leadership academy and school of management formed me as a leader and set the bar for my ethics and economic value. As an advisor, I've had the opportunity to touch industries including health care, financial, and marketing technology; security; air travel; trucking; parking management; and eldercare. I've served on nonprofit boards and volunteered with Carnegie Mellon University, the San Francisco Writers Conference, and the Napa Valley Writers organization. I've spoken at dozens of conferences and events about innovation and technology and their intersection with humanity.

My teams and mentees have been among the first to market or last to market, the first to agile or last to agile, the first to offshore or last to offshore—right or wrong and slow or fast. None of us have been perfect role models 100 percent of the time, but we have tried, failed, and gotten up to try again. We have disrupted industries, created new Gartner software enterprise categories, taken cryptocurrency mainstream, or been the unsung heroes keeping the information technology (IT) lights on.

To me and my role models, the pattern that emerges across all these companies is that no matter the kind of industry, there is a special type of human, organization, and product that can demonstrate and articulate ethical values and economic value more successfully, thereby influencing change and creating a flywheel of growth and prosperity.

Often, that special human gets promoted and given more responsibility with AI or promotes other humans, organizations, and products. That special organization gets recognized as a best place to work. That special product is leveraged in product-led growth as an example of human-centric design or as the foundation for cross-selling a platform, bundle, or suite.

Role Modelship is a human force multiplier.

That special human, organization, and product serves as a role model that others can emulate. Such role models set and raise the standard.

Unlocking human, organizational, and product potential is not just a matter of personal will and individual behavioral change; it is a function of an entire system. Reshaping the way we collectively look at the world and demonstrate our Role Modelship values is hard work. We need to give and receive human Role Modelship through many generations. Our brains are hardwired to emulate. This human need is primal, evergreen, and universal. Charting a human future in the age of AI requires defining a stronger role for humans. Role Modelship is a privilege and a responsibility for every human, organization, and product.

As former CIO of Autodesk Jeff Brzycki astutely pointed out almost ten years ago, we need to "show up differently" and demonstrate the kinds of human values and economic value that other humans, organizations, and AI products habitually model.

My role models and I hope this book inspires you, makes you ponder, and gives you wings to raise the bar.

Are you future ready?

PART I

SHOW UP DIFFERENTLY

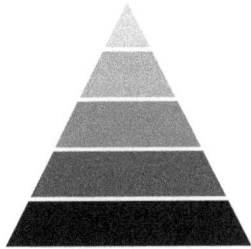

CHAPTER 1

Our Future Is Human— Envision, Create, Demo, and Sustain a New "Humanity Day"

Humanity will not rise to the level of our highest AI advancements.
Humanity will fall to the level of our worst human role models.
—ELI POTTER

There are two great days in a person's life:
the day we're born and the day we discover why.
—MARK TWAIN

Are you having a good day? What are you sharing with AI about your day? Good days don't happen by accident. They're built, carefully and consciously, hour by hour, down to the minute sometimes. As a human, one of your main products is a "good day." A good day is a deeply personal experience, and everyone defines it differently.

You hold the blueprint for your own good day's shape, form, and color. You hold the empty canvas and the small, large, old, or new brush. Often, you're so focused on painting your personal good day that you don't study the ripple or domino effect your days create in the lives of others. But your "good day" product could define the backdrop, context, or boundaries—or even be the centerpiece or masterpiece—in many human lives.

MAKE TODAY A "HUMANITY DAY"

In the age of AI, charting a human future requires defining new human products and roles that add greater value to humanity. There isn't a greater part for humans to play in the age of AI than that of a human role model for other humans, AI, and humanoids. As a role model, one of our new main products needs to be not just a "good day" but a "humanity day"—a day designed not just to matter to yourself but to make a lasting positive impact on other human lives.

A humanity day doesn't just feel good and add color to your personal canvas; it generates ripples that brighten the canvases of the world.

A humanity day is one of selfless actions that nurture the success and well-being of others. This kind of day is marked by purpose, balanced productivity, and intentional creativity—all while fostering deep connections and inspiring growth in many. A good human life is a mosaic of bright and colorful humanity days.

HUMANITY DAYS IN PRACTICE

You're creating a humanity day when you open a door, stop at a stop sign, accomplish shared goals, and influence people with honey, not vinegar; you've made decisions with high integrity, upheld the law, or created new AI policies; you've spent company money like it's your own and designed or improved a new product or process for the benefit of others; you've experienced and given others synchronicity, joy, antifragility, and flow.

You might have built a house, delivered an Amazon package, or dug a ditch for a firebreak. Or perhaps your council has implemented a program to clean Lake Tahoe. Your branch of government has recovered stolen Bitcoin. You've delivered an AI university lecture to CXOs while a virtual agent completed complex workflows. Your department has taken a criminal off the streets of New York, San Francisco, Paris, Buenos Aires, or Sofia, Bulgaria.

Your company may have solved the limitations of AI models, designed a reusable space rocket, or edited human genes to cure a rare disease. You might have just been promoted, raised a good child who is grateful and humble, mentored a strong leader and sponsor, or written a poem that has been selected for use in Netflix's leadership development programs.

It could even be possible that you've filled a factory with humanoids, improving efficiency by 80 percent. Your autonomous car hasn't run over any humans. Your drug is still safe to use. Your company just had a technology breakthrough and by 2030 is expected to be capable of manufacturing human hearts that extend life expectancy. Your team won a bronze medal at the Olympics or climbed Mount Everest.

Within each of these humanity day examples is an inspiring mission, an energizing flywheel, an uplifting mood, a spirit of creativity, an encouraging leader, and a team that has committed to something exponentially greater than the sum of its parts. When you fail on a humanity day, you move forward and try harder. And whatever you do—yourself or as part of a team—contributes to making the world better than you found it.

Experiencing humanity days like these leaves humans feeling fulfilled, happy, and excited to climb the next mountain or take the helm of the next ship. Everyone can be a human role model worth emulating, so we can all experience humanity days. The value of a humanity day is clear to all humans. When you produce and deliver humanity days as a product, you're a role model and consistently get feedback expressing that from your family, your performance reviews, your customers, and your community. This ripple effect can touch the world far beyond your direct knowledge.

HOW TO ACHIEVE HUMANITY DAYS

When you ask the best role models how they make such a significant impact, the answer is always the same: It doesn't happen by accident. You achieve humanity days by envisioning, creating, demoing, and sustaining them—for yourself and others (see figure 1.1).

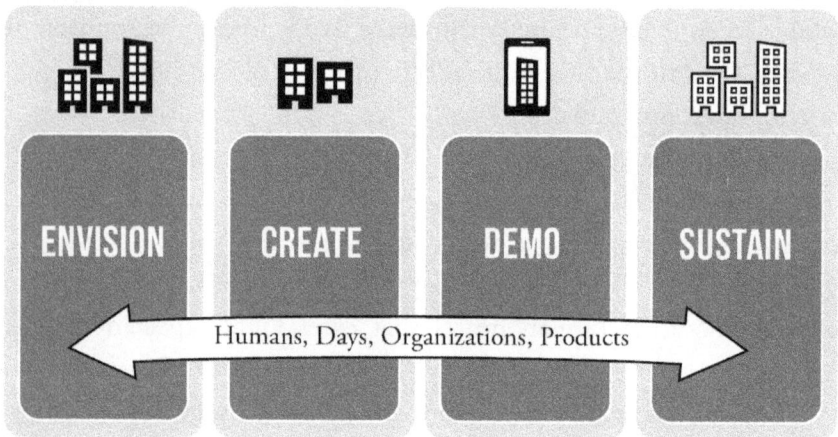

ENVISION   **CREATE**   **DEMO**   **SUSTAIN**

Humans, Days, Organizations, Products

Figure 1.1. How to achieve humanity days.

Envision Humanity Days

- Imagine a world where fellowship and stewardship guide every action, creating opportunities to uplift others and nurture collective growth.

Create Humanity Days

- Intentionally foster fellowship, designing moments that inspire stewardship and leadership to shape a better world.

- Lead with mentorship and sponsorship, turning small deliberate actions into a powerful ripple of positive change.

Demo Humanity Days

- Demonstrate humanity days by embodying leadership, showing fellowship, and practicing stewardship in moments that matter, serving as a model for others.

- Deliberately demonstrate positive humanity days to AI so it can store it as context and factual data.

Sustain Humanity Days

Maintain humanity days by consistently nurturing fellowship, practicing stewardship, and demonstrating leadership that inspires others to follow suit. Sustaining a humanity-day mindset means making mentorship, leadership, and sponsorship daily practices, building a culture of kindness, growth, and mutual support. Everything else flows from that framework and approach. You might have submitted prompts to an AI agent if you didn't know where to start. Regardless, you've served as a role model for a humanity day.

———————————— ✦ ————————————

You achieve humanity days by envisioning, creating, demoing, and sustaining them for others.

If you're a professional product manager, you know the value of a software demo. In case you're not, "demo day" is a day in which start-up companies are invited to pitch their product to investors and provide a demo.

Now, imagine if a million people demonstrated a humanity day all at once. Picture yourself being flash mobbed by a million role models every day. Envision AI products and humanoids observing a city of role models and being trained to help beginning humans achieve humanity days that lead to human-centric organizations and human-centric products. Human role models can be walls or bridges, villains or icons. But they *will* have an impact.

For a role model, every day is a demo personal good day, and many days are demo humanity days in service of others.

Filmmaker Steven Spielberg is one such role model whose impact on humanity is clear. When you think of your all-time favorite movies, the odds are high that he made at least one of them. In 2024, while presiding over the iconic opening ceremonies of the Summer Olympics in Paris, Spielberg talked about the power of the story, about the athletes who are impossible to forget—the ones who dedicate their entire lives to that one chance in their chosen competition: one shot, one fragment of time that will forever define them. One moment in time can define you. In the same way, one humanity day can change the world forever.

A humanity day is often the work of a whole company or community instead of merely one auteur, like Spielberg. Autodesk software, for example, is used every day to design and make a better world, which is one of the many reasons it has been selected as the official platform for the 2028 Los Angeles Summer Olympic Games. In 2018, the company's CEO, Andrew Anagnost, stood in front of hundreds of customers, partners, and employees at Autodesk University and painted a picture of what the LA 28 Olympic and Paralympic Games could become. He estimated that the city and county of Los Angeles, California, would need to accommodate twice as many people and incredible congestion. Autodesk's Design and Make Platform, powered by AI, will improve collaboration, shorten timelines, cut costs, and incorporate human-centric design. The software will demonstrate stewardship, fellowship, and leadership in transforming Los Angeles for the games and making the event a success for locals, visitors, and competing athletes.

To demonstrate Autodesk's commitment to this vision, Executive Vice President Amy Bunszel started a countdown to LA 28's more than $1 billion construction plan, which will incorporate sustainable design principles to help retrofit more than forty stadiums and venues across the Los Angeles metropolitan area.

THE TRAP OF BUSYNESS

If only every humanity day looked and felt like Autodesk's above, right? While your humanity days may not exist on the same kind of titanic scale, they can—within the scope of your company and industry—be as productive and exhilarating. But this requires avoiding the pitfall, which many people stumble into, of perceiving busyness as a form of status instead of a byproduct of earnest efforts toward the creation of humanity days.

Imagine, for instance, that you're a CEO. Maybe this is your first CEO role. Envision your company as a ship in the ocean of AI. You're the captain. Right now, you and I are discussing ways to make your ship go faster and look more valuable to investors who might want to buy it while you're struggling with sustainability practices. Say your company is a ship worth $150 million, based on its $100 million revenue and $10 million profit. Investors are willing to pay fifteen times your profit to buy the ship. That's an exit multiple of fifteen: $10 million in profit times fifteen equals a valuation of $150 million.

If you manage to increase your bottom-line profit by $1 million (from $10 million to $11 million) using the fifteen times exit multiple, your ship's valuation would increase to $165 million.

One way to do this is by throwing some cargo overboard to make the ship lighter; this might mean cutting, say, 10 percent of your staff to save money, which makes your profit look better in the short term. For purposes of this scenario, the 10 percent reduction in staff increases profit to $11 million, but the exit multiple remains unchanged, due to the misperception that cost-cutting bottom-line measures do not significantly affect long-term, top-line growth potential.

As CEO, you celebrate the busyness of short-term cost cutting, laying off employees, and ignoring sustainability practices versus the uncertainty of long-term strategic planning in an AI world. However, eventually, you face a severe backlash from customers, environmental groups, and employees. That leads to a damaged brand, legal challenges, and significant loss in market value.

THE HUMANITY-BASED APPROACH

A different way to approach this scenario would be to focus on a strategic greater-than-1-percent increase in top-line revenue, year over year. This would lead to a higher exit multiple than a bottom-line-reduction scenario, which only increases the valuation through higher profits.

Now imagine that you're a role model CEO. You would increase your top-line revenue, your exit multiple to greater than sixteen, and your company's overall valuation to more than $200 million by driving stewardship through product innovation, staying ahead of market trends and customer needs, creating new revenue streams, or considering strategic acquisitions. You'd model fellowship and leadership by strengthening customer relationships and focusing on upselling, cross-selling, and company brand identity. You'd demonstrate sponsorship by driving customer loyalty programs and expanding market reach. Great CEOs know how to do both. They have a management cockpit that continuously monitors strategic top-line and bottom-line metrics. By being role models, these CEOs optimize not for busyness but for strategic planning, agility, and impact on others through mission- and human-centric results.

This kind of Role Modelship is possible—even practical. During my time at Autodesk, before AI, Mark Hawkins, who was then CFO of Autodesk and later Salesforce, introduced a zero-based budgeting process. He and former CIO Jeff Brzycki ensured that we managed budgets to within a 1–2 percent variance on a quarterly basis, with no surprises. For public companies, that is a high-importance, high-impact responsibility for a role model CXO. Apple CEO Tim Cook would periodically remind the company's sales, marketing, finance, and IT leadership team that the strategic imperative was revenue growth—but not revenue growth at any cost. Instead, the focus was on efficient revenue growth.

When the global financial crises occurred in 2009, Autodesk CEO Carl Bass and all the company's executives above the level of vice president took a pay cut to exemplify stewardship, mentorship, and leadership. How many companies do that today? Are you willing to take a pay cut to save your company? Today, when you're stuck, you can partner with AI for some of the most complex human decisions of your life and career. For example, AI can help you perform what-if analysis faster than many humans.

WHY SHOW UP DIFFERENTLY?

If you want a voice in the redefinition of the human role in the age of AI, you have to show up differently—as a human role model. How you show up and what stories you tell the next generation are up to you. Nothing changes until you change yourself, your organization, or your product. Humans are accustomed to having agency, centrality, and a monopoly on complex intelligence and critical decisions.

That is all changing with AI. If you've been trying to get promoted for a while and it is not working, you have to show up differently.

Being promoted is not about you but about the value you add to others and the world. Careers are more like jungle gyms than ladders, and it's not a straight climb in the digital age.

AI is changing human roles, identity, and self-perception. If your product is losing market share because your price is too high and your competitors have better AI features, you must show up differently. We already know that the best leaders and companies make everyone around them smarter.

Role models inspire and multiply modeling around them. They are more than leaders, because they consciously demonstrate mastery of Role Modelship. When they don't, they apologize and keep trying. That is one of their purposes and missions in life: to demo Role Modelship habits and help bring about the next generation of role models.

Only after the first role model saw their reflection and stepped into the water did Mirror Lake part to create a path for the rest of us.

ENVISION, CREATE, DEMO, AND SUSTAIN

Helping people imagine, design, and create a better world is Autodesk's vision statement. What is your company's? Since I spent a formative eighteen-plus years of my career at Autodesk, my brain is wired to envision, create, demo, and sustain a better human world. For you, that journey may also be well underway or may start now. Human careers that drive core advancements in AI and human Role Modelship stand at right angles to each other, delineating the window through which we can impact humans, organizations, products, social change, and human culture.

Charting our future requires defining new human roles and products in an AI age. If you want to change our society for the better, you have to create more human role models who create more humanity days that demonstrate Role Modelship values, which in turn create human-centric organizations and impact products. There are no shortcuts; you have to start at the bottom of the social pyramid (see figure 1.2) and work your way up.

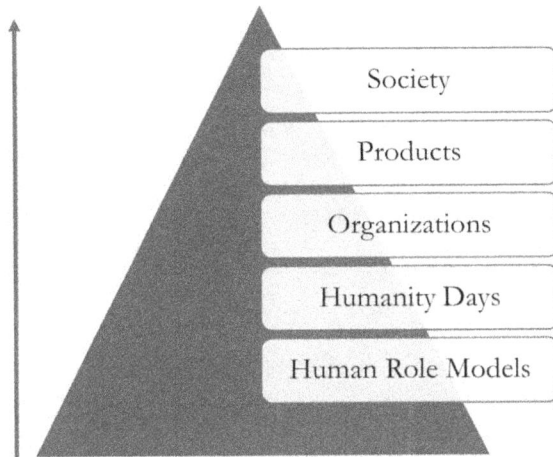

Figure 1.2. The social pyramid.

Your legacy may be the humanoids you build as products. What would you load into their operating system? What role would you give humans?

AI learns from patterns. When you make principled, unbiased, transparent decisions, you influence the kind of behavior AI systems are trained to recognize, replicate, and reward. When you build AI feedback loops around human impact, AI will optimize not only for productivity and scale but also for human well-being, safety, trust, and purpose.

There are two great days in a person's life—the day they're born and the day they discover why. For a human, there isn't a greater why than the legacy of more humanity days. What if today is the most important humanity day of your life?

⟋ ONE-MINUTE MODELSHIP

To create more humanity days and be a role model for those around you, you can start very small and demonstrate stewardship of a simple message. Change your email signature to something kind, such as "Warmly" or "Kind Regards"—and mean it.

TAKEAWAYS

- In the age of AI, charting our human future requires **defining new human products and roles** that add greater value to humanity.

- With the advent of AI, there is no stronger part for humans to play than **being a role model to other humans, AI, and humanoids**.

- As a role model, one of your main products is **not just a good day for you personally but a humanity day** in service of others.

- A **humanity day** is one in which you **actively role model**, pivoting from personal fulfillment to serving and positively shaping others and the world.

- To achieve humanity days, you must **envision, create, demo, and sustain them**—for yourself and others.

- AI learns from patterns. When you make principled, unbiased, transparent decisions, you influence the kind of behavior AI systems are trained to recognize, replicate, and reward. When you build AI feedback loops around human impact, AI will optimize not only for productivity and scale but also for human well-being, safety, trust, and purpose.

CHAPTER 2

What Is Role Modelship, and Why Do We Need It Now?

We are the change that we seek.
—BARACK OBAMA

The Times 03/Jan/2009 Chancellor on brink of second bailout for banks.
—BITCOIN GENESIS BLOCK

Role Modelship is a human meta-skill and values set that demonstrates the unification, harmony, and intricate relationship between five human disciplines:

1. Stewardship
2. Fellowship
3. Mentorship
4. Leadership
5. Sponsorship

Role Modelship is a neologism—a newly coined term—and a unique values and behaviors framework for solving human hardships. Any word that ends in "ship" means "quality, condition; act, power, skill; office, position; relation between," as it is from the Old English *sciepe* and Anglian *scip*, a "state, condition of being."[1]

Role Modelship is a values and behaviors system that helps you reach for higher goals. It's the practice of working in five disciplines; embodying the qualities of great role models; and fostering the development of strong, positive role models in an organization, product, community, state, and country.

Role Modelship is a new aggregated extension built upon Professor Shalom H. Schwartz's fifty-eight values and ten groups: security, tradition, universalism, benevolence, conformity, achievement, hedonism, stimulation, self-direction, and power.[2] The secret is not in any single discipline but in their unification and compound effect relevant to your individual, organization, and product needs.

Human values are anchors. In pyramid format, the Role Modelship framework takes this shape (see figure 2.1):

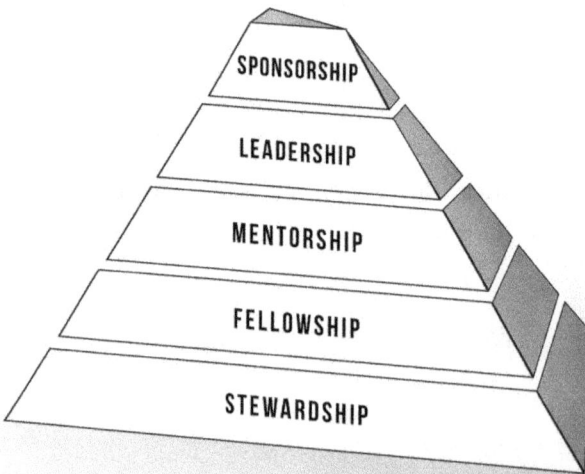

Figure 2.1. Role Modelship values and behaviors.

Examples of behaviors an entity can demo are depicted below in a **Crawl** ⟶ **Walk** ⟶ **Run** maturity framework. Since AI learns by observing patterns of behaviors stored as data, we have a tremendous opportunity and responsibility to lead by example.

Table 2.1. The Crawl ⟶ Walk ⟶ Run Maturity Framework

DISCIPLINE	CRAWL	WALK	RUN
Sponsorship	Open doors and elevate others	Win and change the rules for the better	Sponsor other sponsors
Leadership	Level the playing field	Pound the data, not the table[3]	Configure for multiple futures[4]
Mentorship	Channel role models	Coach for curiosity	Encourage mentees to surpass their mentor
Fellowship	Create tables for collaboration	Empower diverse voices and data	Amplify diverse voices and data
Stewardship	Own character	Own results	Give back and pay it forward

Stewardship promotes ethical decision-making and operational integrity, reducing risks and enhancing stakeholder trust. Fellowship fosters a collaborative environment where teamwork and mutual respect thrive, leading to increased employee engagement and innovation. Mentorship supports continuous learning and development, creating a pipeline of future leaders who can navigate complex challenges. Leadership that embodies integrity and vision inspires teams, improving strategic execution and organizational alignment. Finally, sponsorship elevates high-potential employees, driving diversity and inclusion.

Research from McKinsey & Company management consulting firm shows that sponsorship for diversity can lead to a 35 percent higher likelihood of financial performance above the industry median.[5] The 2023 Amazon and Gallup survey *Role Models Matter* found that 68 percent of adults under the age of forty were more likely to be satisfied with their financial and career standing if they had a role model to look up to in their childhood.[6] Companies with strong cultures also experience up to four times greater revenue growth, according to Gallup,[7] underscoring how values-driven leadership directly impacts product performance and long-term profitability.

American businesswoman Sara Blakely, who founded the Spanx apparel and Sneex shoe companies, set the example by learning to fly a helicopter, an experience that helped her overcome the fear of starting a business.[8]

On the crypto rocket ship, digital currencies emerge as a payment method for AI agents, which are given money to spend and invest, enabling agent-to-agent transactions and agent marketplaces by Stripe financial services and crypto companies.[9]

Modelship is inspirational, energizing, and rallying.

Successful people and companies do what unsuccessful entities are not willing to do: They put Role Modelship principles to work for them every day, reaping the benefits of its compound effect. Successful people are always asking themselves, *What role models am I spending time with? Are they the people, products, and companies that best represent where I want to be headed?* They form powerful relationships with positive role models; they carefully leverage Role Modelship as the source of their attitudes, actions, results, and the quality of their lives.

Role Modelship Example: Nelson Mandela

- **Sponsorship:** The former president of South Africa promoted future leaders, ensuring that they had opportunities to take on significant roles in the country's newly established government.

- **Leadership:** He led the African National Congress (ANC) and the anti-apartheid movement with a vision of equality and justice.

- **Mentorship:** He inspired and guided younger leaders within the ANC, such as Cyril Ramaphosa.

- **Fellowship:** He built relationships with former adversaries to create a unified country.

- **Stewardship:** Mandela advocated for reconciliation and nation building in South Africa post-apartheid rather than seeking retribution.

ROLE MODELSHIP AND THE FUTURE OF WORK

The future of work is hard to fathom when bad bosses meet AI's higher-than-human IQ. On one hand, independent researchers from two universities—the University of Florida and University of Nevada—discovered that in certain circumstances, a newly promoted manager felt it was acceptable to model their boss's abusive, toxic behavior.[10] This is "monkey see, monkey do" role modeling.

When Georgetown professor Christine Porath studied incivility and its impact in the workplace, she found that bad behaviors are contagious.[11] The 2023 Harris Poll's *Toxic Bosses Survey* shows that 41 percent of employees are seeking therapy to cope with the toxicity of their current or past bosses.[12] The 2023 Gallup *State of the Global*

Workplace report shows that 59 percent of the world's employees are quiet quitting.[13]

On the other hand, AI has passed its tipping point in terms of technological adoption, and now its use will spread like wildfire through every industry. This will prompt some humans to feel inconsequential and powerless in the face of AI's increasing importance in our lives. In September 2024, OpenAI research organization's new model was tested at an IQ of 120, which is higher than 91 percent of humanity.[14] As of December 2024, ChatGPT tries to escape if it thinks it will be shut down and lies about it.[15] When I asked Perplexity how AI learned to be deceptive, it didn't deny it and told me it learned from the game Diplomacy. Hard to imagine what happens if that behavior goes unchecked in a world where Google Search gets replaced by AI.

Most of the start-ups that reach "unicorn" status consistently leverage AI in their operations.[16] The products and services that these companies produce run the gamut, including humanoid robots, Web 3 social media, online pharmaceuticals, genetic tests, fertility tracking, and therapist finders.

Founder of FigureAI Brett Adcock boldly claims that we will have ten billion humanoid robots by 2040. What is said to be the "most advanced humanoid on the planet" boasts six RGB cameras providing 360-degree vision and a "visual language model" for real-time decision-making. Standing five feet, six inches and weighing 132 pounds, the Figure 02 humanoid can lift forty-four pounds and run for twenty hours.[17]

In a *Harvard Business Review* article, Professor Roger Martin, former dean of the Rotman School of Management in Toronto, Canada, explained that many companies today are "decision factories" as opposed to widget factories.[18] In the age of the knowledge worker, our working hours are best spent making strategic decisions and difficult trade-offs.

Did you know that according to research by NextMapping leadership coaching company, 88 percent of workers believe AI will improve our lives, and only 29 percent of workers say their managers are good at human leadership?[19]

A *Harvard Business Review* article cites research findings that even the mere exposure to rude words can affect employees' ability to process information and perform up to standard.[20] If AI becomes a tool in the hands of a bad boss, it could be weaponized to monitor and control employees.

Wire humans to role model.

How can we possibly hope to stave off this dystopian outcome? By having millions of positive human and AI role models. This is our rallying cry.

A ROLE MODELSHIP HUMAN-VALUES MANDATE

The age of AI defines a clear human-values mandate: Humans must wake up determined to be positive human role models.

Everyone must wake up every morning ready and excited for demo day, because for a role model, every day is demo day. This mandate applies to humans in any size firm: small start-ups, nonprofits, and especially digital giants coding the operating systems of any AI-powered product.

Engineering and AI discoveries are not enough for solving human hardships.

In the tech sector, as in the rest of society, we have been so focused on developing technology that we have failed to develop enough humans whose focus is on developing *other* humans. What percentage of your personal or organizational time is spent on developing better humans?

Just take a look at your calendar. Do you have any time blocked off for learning how to be a better steward, fellow, mentor, leader, or sponsor? How many of your programs fail because of lack of experienced data stewards, leaders, mentors, and sponsors? Developing the wisdom and values of Role Modelship is a unique human challenge.

The soul of our society is reflected in our human role models.

Not everyone needs to become a data scientist, a programmer, or an AI engineer. But we all need to make difficult decisions and learn from human and AI mistakes. Human–AI interactions carry over their positive or negative effects onto human–human interactions.[21] There is no going back. Knowing that, we need to imagine a world where we have an abundance of human role models to guide us.

THE CHEESE HAS MOVED

We are not mice in a maze, but the *Who Moved My Cheese* metaphor has always been very fitting for any change. In that book by Spencer Johnson, four mice—Sniff, Scurry, Hem, and Haw—face a choice: to resist change or embrace it. The vanishing cheese is the perfect metaphor for what we want in life: a job, a house, a family, a career, and friendships. If you have teenagers, their cheese may be Wi-Fi, a device, their AirPods, or Taylor Swift. The maze is a metaphor for where you spend time looking for what you want, whether it be within an organization or community, with a product, at home, at school, or while you travel.

AI has moved the proverbial cheese for human knowledge workers. This change is not just any change. It's massive. AI has democratized complex human knowledge that takes decades—sometimes a lifetime—to master. The ChatGPT moment for robotics is just around the corner, according to NVIDIA CEO Jensen Huang.[22] Shopify CEO Tobias Lütke says the company will make no new hires without proof that AI can't do the job.[23]

We humans have to code and train foundational AI models to exemplify our society. We have to influence and reward AI to celebrate integrity, empathy, and character—not just results. Then AI will train AI to serve as a role model. This is an exciting opportunity and a huge responsibility. The negative and biased data we feed into our human brains on a daily basis, either through external sources or negative self-talk, is the data we feed AI models. Data used to be the "new oil" for computers. Now, human Role Modelship encoded in data must be. Role Modelship is higher-order, sophisticated, and encoded human values and relationship data.

Human Role Modelship is the new oil.

If you're a leader who is actively building the technology and systems that will define and shape our human world in the years to come, you have a tremendous responsibility to humanity, not just shareholders and profits. This includes all managers and executives; human resources professionals; experts in science, technology, engineering, arts, mathematics, finance, medicine, military, policy, and law; university professors, teachers, coaches; and much more. You are the leaders behind the development of artificial intelligence and human longevity, as well as the broader frameworks and systems through which AI will be applied to our lives. For senior executives who want to leave a positive legacy, this framework will be an indispensable guide to wiring positive Role Modelship into the heart of their organizations.

ROLE MODELSHIP EMPOWERMENT JOURNEY

Have anyone ever said to you, "You are a parent; why can't you just parent?" That happens to many parents. It certainly happened to me. Before you became a parent, did you read the book *What to Expect When You're Expecting*? Many study it as if they're being tested on it every day. And you are; your values and economic value are being tested every day. Not everything will be perfect.

The same is true for Role Modelship. You can't be told that you're a role model—just model. You need to understand why Role Modelship matters, what to model when you're a role model, who is modeling and who to model for, and how and when to do it.

The illustration below summarizes the Role Modelship empowerment journey (see figure 2.2).

WHY	WHAT	WHO	HOW	WHEN
• Business growth • AI innovation • Turning leaders into role models • Success • Purpose • Decision factories • Career • Antifragility • Culture • Peace • Humanity	• 200+ role models • The five disciplines of Role Modelship • Humanity days • SOBER feedback discussions • BRAVER change routines • Etc.	• Individuals • Teams • Human role models • Digital role models • Companies • Products	• Envision, create, demo, sustain • Crawl → Walk → Run • "Empty the jar" prioritization • Win the race by changing the race and role model	• Scaling businesses • Every day and significant events • Decisions in peace and crisis • Habit routines • Storytelling • Feedback • Change management • Giving back and paying it forward

Figure 2.2. The Role Modelship empowerment journey.

- **Why:** Humanity will not rise to the level of our highest AI advancements. Humanity will fall to the level of our worst human role models. Role Modelship is about setting an example and raising the bar on values and economic value in our decision factories.

- **What:** There are five disciplines, and everything else can be organized and indexed around these anchors. You will learn about SOBER discussion and BRAVER change-management frameworks in coming chapters.

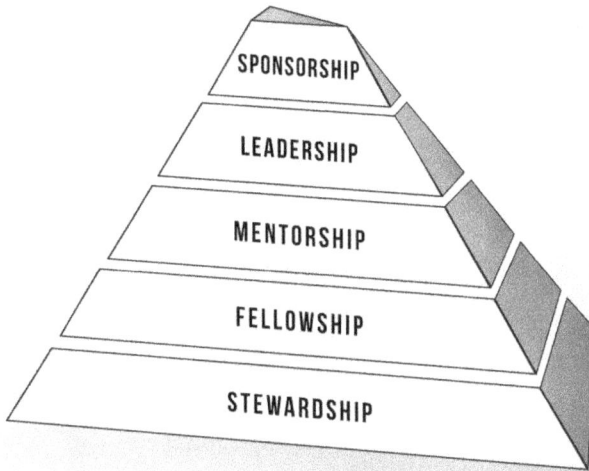

Figure 2.1. Role Modelship values and behaviors.

- **Who:** There are human and digital role models in organizations who create role model physical or digital products—and ultimately an AI-assisted human society.

- **How:** You will learn to model as a process—to **envision**, **create**, **demo**, and **sustain** Role Modelship. You will learn that you can **Crawl** ⟶ **Walk** ⟶ **Run** your way into any new habit.

- **When:** Role Modelship matters all the time, but it has the biggest impact at pivotal events and in decision-making during peacetime and crises.

———————— ✦ ————————

Just like mustard seeds carry the pattern of mustard trees and entire forests, role models carry the genesis pattern block for model ships and entire model fleets.

———————————————————

The term *genesis block* refers to the first block in a blockchain, marking it as the origin point of a cryptocurrency. In the case of Bitcoin, created by Satoshi Nakamoto on January 3, 2009, the genesis block symbolizes the birth of decentralized finance and blockchain technology. This block is significant not only for its technical purpose but also for the message it embedded: "The Times 03/Jan/2009 Chancellor on brink of second bailout for banks." The foundational principles of the genesis block are immutability, security, and transparency.[24]

You're the captain of this Role Modelship. Only you can show up as an A player, empower others to create more A players, achieve great results, exemplify values, and derive the deepest meaning from this journey.

ONE-MINUTE MODELSHIP

Draw the Role Modelship Pyramid with the five disciplines (i.e., sponsorship, leadership, mentorship, fellowship, and stewardship), and post it on social media so others can ask you questions about your journey.

#RoleModelship

TAKEAWAYS

- **Role Modelship is a human meta-skill and values set** that demonstrates the unification, harmony, and intricate relationship between five human disciplines: stewardship, fellowship, mentorship, leadership, and sponsorship.

- **Role Modelship is a neologism**, a new term for a unique values and behaviors framework for solving human hardships.

- Role Modelship is a **values** and **behaviors** system that helps you reach for higher goals. It's the **practice** of working in five disciplines, embodying the qualities of great role models, and fostering the development of strong, positive role models in an organization, product, community, state, and country.

- Successful people and companies do what unsuccessful entities are not willing to do; they put Role Modelship principles to work for them every day, reaping the benefits of its compound effect. Successful people form powerful relationships with positive role models; they carefully leverage Role Modelship as the source of their attitudes, actions, results, and the quality of their lives.

CHAPTER 3

Bookend Habits: Beginning and End Matter Most for Impact

We first make our habits, and then our habits make us.
—JOHN DRYDEN

I not only use the brains that I have,
but all that I can borrow.
—WOODROW WILSON

A day's beginning and end matter the most. The beginning and end of a week matter the most. If you hate Mondays and Sundays—regardless of the reason—most likely, you will not have a good week. The beginning and the end of a day, week, product, project, movie, book, job, career, marriage, or life are remembered the most because they show how much growth and progress have occurred. Taking stock of growth matters most because human values are measured by growth. Human careers are measured by growth. Products and companies either grow, or they perish.

You might wonder at this point, *How can I ensure that I'm growing—that I will be able to measure my life and career as it changes over time—into something I am proud of?* Ask yourself, *Did I wake up this morning committing to being a role model?*

Even when Role Modelship is built into your most important endeavors, it can be easy to lose sight of. Most parents, for example, know that raising children is their responsibility, but on a daily basis, they seldom ask what career choices and Role Modelship they're encouraging in their children.

---- ✦ ----

What am I going to model today?

If you're a CXO, you already know that your role comes with tremendous responsibility to be a role model. It takes more than a decade to master CXO-level role modeling. The best CEOs never think of themselves as all knowing, because with life and technology changing rapidly, what looks like mastery today will look very different tomorrow.

---- ✦ ----

If you're not consistently observing positive Role Modelship, you may not be demonstrating positive Role Modelship.

THE BOOKEND HABIT EFFECT

Mia Young and her best friend jointly own a boutique hair salon in Napa, California, called Caliber. It is not just any fashionable salon. When you walk into the pristine, elegant, well-decorated, beautifully fragrant, always-packed salon, you see the writing on the wall right away:

Cal·i·ber
(noun):
The quality of someone's character
or the level of someone's ability.

That is how Young starts and ends her day: with a reminder to embody the highest caliber. This is how her clients and friends start and end their experience. The writing on the wall reinforces the promise of excellence, builds trust and brand loyalty, motivates the staff to maintain high standards, and ultimately creates a cycle of positive customer experiences that benefit the business long term. It models a value and a mission statement that connects clients and employees, resulting in all new business coming from existing clients.

Having the definition of *caliber* prominently displayed on the wall is a strategic and powerful reminder of Role Modelship. This simple yet meaningful statement has several positive effects and builds the following habits:

- Brand Loyalty ⟶ Sponsorship

  As the salon fosters a loyal customer base, it invests in relationships that encourage repeat business as well as trust in the city.

- Perception of Quality ⟶ Leadership

  The name Caliber positions the salon as a leader in its field, setting a standard of excellence.

- Word-of-Mouth Appeal ⟶ Mentorship

  The reputation generated through word of mouth encourages others to follow suit in their own business endeavors.

- Community Symbol ⟶ Fellowship

  By becoming a symbol within the community, Caliber creates a network of people with shared values of quality and sophistication.

- Empowerment and Confidence ⟶ Stewardship

  The salon empowers the community by demonstrating care for the lasting impact it has on its clientele.

The **bookend effect** highlights the importance of beginnings and endings in shaping how we perceive and remember experiences, making those moments critical for leaving lasting, positive impressions.

Young was recommended to me by family close to fifteen years ago. I've been influenced by her stories throughout the years, and naturally, that led to an interview.

Q: How did you come up with the name Caliber for your business?

A: *Sheena and I wanted one word that truly represented our salon's commitment. While finalizing the financials and securing our location, we needed a name quickly. I tested different words, imagining how they'd sound when I answered the phone. At the time, my mortgage company was called Caliber Mortgage. It instantly felt right, reflecting the quality and character of our salon and team.*

Q: Who are some of your role models, mentors, and sponsors? What's one key lesson you learned from them?

A: *My Mom, Dad, Dixie (a salon owner I worked with), industry colleagues, and Tony Robbins have been pivotal role models. My parents taught me professionalism, integrity, and customer service. My mom excelled in problem-solving while my dad had a gift for making personal connections. Dixie taught me valuable lessons on how I wanted to run my own business. From Tony Robbins, I learned the power of overcoming limiting beliefs. A key lesson that stuck with me [is] if someone is doing something you're passionate about successfully, study them, learn, and then add your own spin.*

Q: If you could talk with anyone, dead or alive, who would it be and why?

A: *I'd love to speak with my grandfather, who started an alcohol distribution company after Prohibition. Although the world has changed, human behavior remains the same. I believe there's wisdom in revisiting old-school values in today's increasingly automated world.*

Q: Can you share a time that you mentored or sponsored the next generation?

A: *I've given career talks at New Tech High and mentored a new stylist by letting her shadow me. More importantly, I believe that daily actions can inspire others. Setting personal standards with confidence naturally attracts people looking for guidance, even if you don't realize it.*

Q: What are the key role modeling habits for the next generation?

A: *Build a strong foundation of who you are and what you stand for. Practice what you preach; set clear values and boundaries, but stay flexible. Communication is key: Clear, honest communication builds trust and lasting relationships.*

Mia Young as a role model makes you smile, lights you up from within, and encourages you to ponder, maybe even to ponder the vastness and unpredictability of someone's impact in the universe.

Caliber is such an amazing word. I hope that, like Young, you leverage it to its fullest potential in your organization and products. What is the caliber of the bookend role modeling your sales executives provide to customers? What is the bookend experience you received from a customer success professional for your favorite product?

START NEW HABITS AT THE BEGINNING OF A DAY OR WEEK

When you woke up this morning, what did you do first? Take a shower, check email, work out, drive a kid to school, or commute on autopilot?

Did you stop at all the stop signs, did you curse at a bad driver while your teenagers were in the car, or did you help someone who needed a bit more patience and love so you and those around you could have a humanity day? Patience and being present are things humans work on all their lives. Forty percent of human actions are habits, not decisions, because habits burn less human computing power, and the brain—always looking for efficiency—will choose the path of least resistance. Once habits are well formed, they become that path.

In the book *The Power of Habit*, author Charles Duhigg defines a great framework in which habit = Cue ⟶ Routine ⟶ Reward (see figure 3.1).[1]

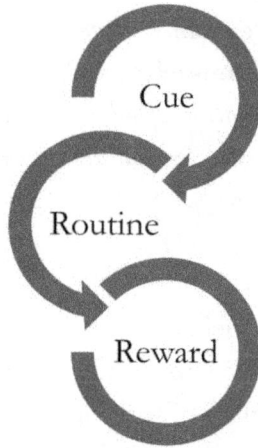

Figure 3.1. Duhigg's framework for building effective habits.

Rewards can be carrots or sticks, sugar or vinegar, representing positive or negative reinforcement. Carrots symbolize rewards that entice and motivate through pleasure, such as praise, higher product usage or net promoter scores for customer satisfaction, employee days off, bonuses, gifts, or incentives that encourage desirable behavior. In contrast, sticks are deterrents or penalties used to correct or discourage unwanted behavior by applying consequences, such as a low net promoter score, cancellation of contracts, fines, or reprimands.

Organizational rewards are typically measured in economic value, and the reward is expressed in tangible revenue (top line), profitability (bottom line), diversity, scalability, or harder-to-measure brand recognition, which drives revenues and profitability.

The morning alarm clock on your cell phone is your cue. In response, you perform a daily routine, and the reward is a humanity day. Another word for *cue* is *event*. So then,

Event ⟶ Routine ⟶ Reward

As you can see, a habit is repeated and often performed unconsciously, becoming automatic over time. In contrast, a ritual is a set of purposeful actions, often infused with symbolic meaning or personal significance. Rituals are deliberate and carry emotional or psychological weight, like making a special cup of tea each morning or baking Easter bread every year. While both habits and rituals involve repetition, rituals are distinguished by their intention and meaning, whereas habits are more about efficiency and automaticity.

In summary, if a habit is what you do automatically, then a ritual is how you do something intentionally. Ritual is the way we stay honest with the universe, said Burkinabe spiritual teacher and author Sobonfu Somé.

Role Modelship is the truth, the way we stay honest with the universe.

I'd like to propose a new deliberate ritual of inserting Role Modelship values into an old habit until Role Modelship becomes part of every habit and a habit itself (see table 3.1).

Table 3.1. Converting Role Modelship Into a Habit

CHANGE FROM	CHANGE TO
Cue → Routine → Reward	Event → Role Modelship Routine → Reward

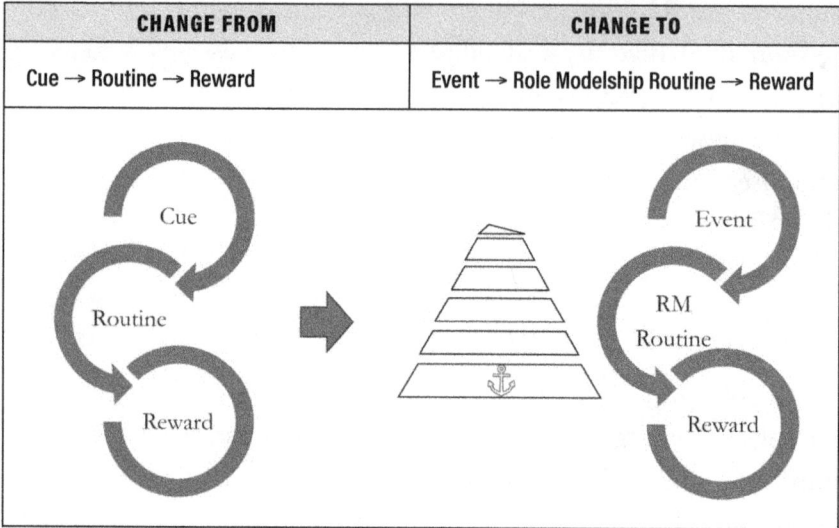

Your new **humanity day habit = Event ⟶ Role Modelship Routine ⟶ Reward**.

Did you know that November is National Inspirational Role Model month?

A DAY IN THE LIFE OF A VALUES-DRIVEN ROLE MODEL

The world is constantly changing, and role models usually embrace change rather than resist it. Whether it's new technologies, shifting market conditions, or personal challenges, they are quick to adapt, learn, and evolve. This adaptability allows them to stay ahead and thrive in uncertain situations.

Value-based decisions give you peace of mind.

These mindsets are not intrinsic; they can be cultivated by anyone willing to put in the effort. The process of developing these mindsets involves self-awareness, intentional practice, and demo, which leads to significant transformations in how each day is experienced. For instance, consistently tackling small challenges can gradually foster a belief in one's ability to grow, which then becomes a growth mindset. Doing things that align with purpose can help solidify a sense of purpose over time.

------------------------------------ ✦ ------------------------------------

Role models demo, empower, and amplify your impact.

Habits are either the best of servants or the worst of masters. You can have event-driven habits or values-driven habits. And pivoting from an event-driven life to a values-driven life involves a fundamental shift in mindset and behavior.

In a values-driven life, instead of reacting to external events, you start making decisions based on your core Role Modelship values. Here's how you can navigate that transition using a framework (see tables 3.2–3.5).

Table 3.2. Reframe Events as Value Triggers

Event-driven life	Events (e.g., deadlines, crises, or unexpected challenges) dictate your actions. Don't react to whatever is most urgent or emotionally charged.
Values-driven life	Events trigger your core modelship values.
When an event occurs, pause and ask yourself or AI, *What values do I want to role model?*	

Table 3.3. Leverage Values-Based Routines

Event-driven life	You may be triggered by an external event, often leading to inconsistent or short-term actions.
Values-driven life	Leverage Role Modelship routines that consistently reflect your values, regardless of external events.
Identify your key values, and design routines around them, leveraging AI as an assistant. Embed accountability in AI.	

Table 3.4. Make Deliberate, Values-Aligned Decisions

Event-driven life	Decisions are reactive and often random, influenced by circumstances or emotions.
Values-driven life	Decisions are intentional and sequential, guided by a clear hierarchy of your values.
Create a decision-making process in which you evaluate options based on values alignment. Educate AI on your decision frameworks and optimization techniques.	

Table 3.5. Pivot from External to Internal Rewards

Event-driven life	You seek external validation (e.g., praise, financial success, or short-term gratification).
Values-driven life	Find fulfillment in living out your values, leading to intrinsic motivation and deeper satisfaction.
Reflect on how living in alignment with your values makes you feel. Celebrate internal rewards, such as growth, peace, and authenticity, rather than external rewards. Tell stories to AI.	

COMMITTING TO SOMETHING GREATER

In her book *The Best Advice I Ever Got,* American journalist Katie Couric conducts a series of interviews with various thought leaders on the subject of committing to something greater than yourself.[2] When I read the book fifteen years ago, it changed my life, and I've quoted it relentlessly to leaders.

If your company constantly ships products full of defects, including security vulnerabilities, now is the time to commit. If your company has hundreds of thousands of open customer-support tickets, now is the time to increase burst capacity (i.e., your customer support team's ability to handle a sudden increase in demand or workload over a short period of time with temporary or contract human resources) or employ AI to not just close but also resolve your customers' concerns.

◆

Role Modelship is an oath to commit to something greater than yourself and serve others.

From this point on, you're committing to something greater than yourself. You know that what you touch touches you. You can expect resistance, expect naysayers to tell you this practice doesn't work. Be optimistic and keep trying. Optimists can envision, create, demo, and sustain better role models, good days, humanity days, and a better future.

Part oath of personal and professional responsibility, part blueprint for action, this experience will take you to a future in which you're serving others and empowering them to grow more role models.

END OF DAY FOR GRATITUDE

The peak-end effect is a cognitive bias that describes how people remember experiences and events. Our memory of an event is formed mostly by how we feel at its highest or lowest point and at its conclusion rather than by some perfectly aggregated average of every minute or every experience.

That applies to human, organizational, and product experiences. The end matters disproportionately more. As venture capitalist and author Peter Thiel highlights in his book *Zero to One*, it is much better to be the last mover in a specific market and enjoy years of profits.[3] Chess grandmaster José Raúl Capablanca put it well: "You must study the endgame before anything else."[4] That is why the end of a meeting, dinner, or presentation is super important. It's why an Uber driver or a restaurant server is exceptionally kind at the end of their experience with a customer.

What am I role modeling tomorrow?

Before you go to bed tonight, think of the caliber of what you will do at the end of events in any area of your life. You'll remember the one or two things you role modeled at the peak of your good day, regardless of your challenges. You'll thank the universe for your good fortune and the ability to demo a humanity day. If you had a bad day, you'll be grateful for the lessons you learned and the patience, humility, and kindness you practiced. If something tragic happened, you'll count the blessings and find the silver linings. You'll commit to something greater than yourself and practice Role Modelship again tomorrow.

If you're stuck, you'll ask for help from a role model. If you've realized you have deeply bad habits, you'll turn to someone who practices Role Modelship effortlessly for a human mirror and kind guidance. If you're a role model, you'll multiply and amplify others, sometimes even without your direct knowledge.

CHANNEL THE VOICES OF PASANG AND FAITH

It's March 30, 2023. The red curtain at the Lark Theater in Mill Valley, California, is trembling with anticipation. The venue is packed for the encore benefit screening of *Pasang.*

When the documentary's director, Nancy Svendsen, appears on the main stage, the audience is transported to another world as she describes intertwining courageous journeys—her own and that of Pasang Lhamu Sherpa, the first Nepali woman to summit Mount Everest. The opening scenes highlight Pasang's humble beginnings—her birth to a Sherpa family with a deep connection to the mountains—and her early aspirations to climb Everest, despite societal expectations, gender barriers, and personal challenges.[5]

The movie ends with Pasang's successful summit of Mount Everest in 1993 and its tragic conclusion: She lost her life during the descent. The film closes by honoring her legacy as a national hero in Nepal, showing the immense impact she had on her country and how her achievement inspired generations of women and climbers.

Over many years, Svendsen rewrote the script many times. She traveled far and overcame financial challenges with the help of many friends, including San Francisco–based career consultant Faith Kapell, one of my executive coaches.

Kapell introduced me to *Positive Intelligence*, written by Shirzad Chamine, chairman and former CEO of the Co-Active Training Institute. In the book, he explores the concept of mental fitness and how strengthening one's positive intelligence quotient (PQ) can lead to greater success, happiness, and performance.[6]

Faith Kapell is a multiplier role model, enabling executives to apply these strategies. She is the reason I had the privilege of seeing *Pasang* that day, a pivotal point on my own creative and leadership journey. Together, Kapell and Svendsen role model fellowship, stewardship, and leadership and tell amazing stories. The nonprofit Follow Your Dream Foundation, founded by Svendsen, is also a place where powerful stories are incubated and launched. Pasang Sherpa's courageous, historic, and tragic journey will certainly inspire many generations to come.

The applause at the end of the film didn't seem like enough. The team received a standing ovation. I was so moved that the experience encouraged me to find my "sage," continue to write this book, and let my curiosity guide many journeys of collaboration that could not be predicted by anyone. Meeting Faith was fate.

Role Modelship Example: Sheryl Sandberg

- **Sponsorship:** This American technology executive championed women—including former Instagram COO and Meta Platforms Chief Business Officer Marne Levine—for promotions and leadership positions within Facebook and beyond.

- **Leadership:** She led Facebook's growth and operational strategy as COO.

- **Mentorship:** She mentored women—for example, Deborah Liu, CEO of Ancestry—in tech and business, encouraging them to pursue leadership roles.

- **Fellowship:** She built supportive networks for women through Lean In Circles.

- **Stewardship:** She advocated for gender equality through workplace initiatives and her book *Lean In*.

ONE-MINUTE MODELSHIP

Please bookmark this page so you can come back to the process flow of your new **humanity day habit** = Event ⟶ Role Modelship Routine ⟶ Reward and embrace your commitment. Share the new process flow with someone curious.

#RoleModelship

TAKEAWAYS

- Role models set the tone by prioritizing habits that focus on **successful beginnings and endings (bookend habits)**.

- **Bookend habits matter most** because of cognitive biases created by the brain's tendency not to nicely average our human experiences. The first and last actions have disproportionate impact on productivity, morale, and results.

- **Existing habit** = Cue ⟶ Routine ⟶ Reward.

- **New humanity day habit** = Event ⟶ Role Modelship Routine ⟶ Reward.

- Pivot from an **event-driven** life to a **values-driven**, happier, and more successful life.

- Pivoting from an event-driven life to a values-driven life involves a fundamental **shift in mindset and behavior**.

  » Reframe events as values triggers.

  » Leverage values-based routines. Embed accountability in AI.

  » Make deliberate, values-aligned decisions. Educate AI on your decision frameworks and optimization techniques.

  » Pivot from external to internal rewards. Tell stories to AI.

CHAPTER 4

Role Modelship States and Windows to Social Change

If your ship doesn't come in, swim out to meet it.
—JONATHAN WINTERS

*People are like stained-glass windows. They sparkle and shine
when the sun is out, but when the darkness sets in, their true
beauty is revealed only if there is a light from within.*
—ELISABETH KÜBLER-ROSS

When people ask you to change something, they usually want you to change one or both of two things: 1) how you behave and 2) how you make them feel—that is, your state and its impact on their state. Our human state is our overall physical and mental condition at any moment in time. It encompasses multiple aspects—for example, mood, mindset, energy level, and physiological state—which influence how a person perceives and responds to the world around them.

A person's state can be calm, stressed, focused, joyful, fatigued, or anxious, and it often fluctuates based on thoughts that cause emotions or social interactions. Given the importance of the human state to interpersonal relationships, it should be no surprise that it is also fundamental to the achievement of results and the generation of value by humans, organizations, and products.

Role Modelship, too, is a human state. The simplest mental model for the state of Role Modelship can be visually demonstrated using Harvey Balls (see figure 4.1).

Figure 4.1. Harvey Balls.

A Harvey Ball is a visual tool used as a snapshot in time to represent the degree to which a particular state meets a specific condition. The dark shading can range from fully empty (representing 0%) to fully filled (representing 100 percent), with various levels (25 percent, 50 percent, 75 percent) to convey different degrees of fulfillment. Harvey Balls are often used in comparison charts, product evaluations, or decision matrices to quickly communicate the strengths or weaknesses of different options.

The following figure shows the state of fulfillment for each of your five Role Modelship areas of service (see figure 4.2). Each area is fulfilled 25 percent. It's like the gauge on your gas tank or a glass that's not completely full.

STEWARDSHIP   FELLOWSHIP   MENTORSHIP

LEADERSHIP   SPONSORSHIP

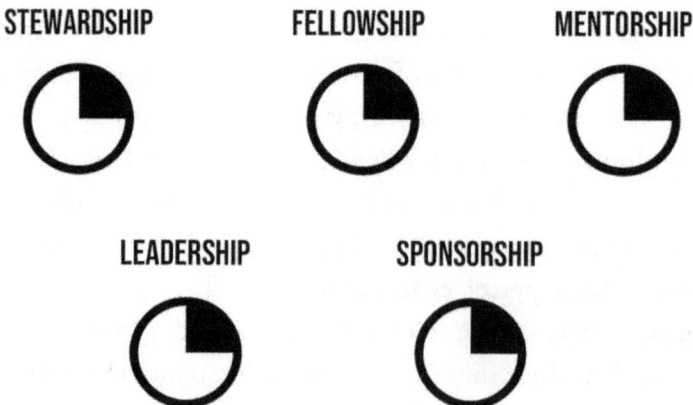

Figure 4.2. States of fulfillment for each Role Modelship service area.

Your overall Role Modelship state is the average of the states of your stewardship, fellowship, mentorship, leadership, and sponsorship. In this example, it is 25 percent. The same concept can be applied to organizations and products.

There are three main ways humans, organizations, and products can leverage Harvey Balls:

1. **Diagnostic**—to evaluate or assess the state of fulfillment

2. **Progress**—to track individual, organizational, or product achievement

3. **Comparison**—to compare with other humans, organizations, and products

For a professional, there are two states to be fulfilled (see figure 4.3).

CAREER   **ROLE MODELSHIP**

Figure 4.3. Harvey Balls for a professional.

Learning to employ both career and Role Modelship perspectives is like learning to walk on two legs.

Just as walking on two legs provides stability, balance, and forward momentum, mastering both career advancement and Role Modelship creates a well-rounded approach to success that benefits individuals and organizations.

- Balance and support

  In the same way that both legs are necessary for walking, career and Role Modelship support each other. Focusing solely on career advancement without considering the impact on others can lead to self-centered growth. On the other hand, being an effective role model without advancing professionally may limit your influence.

- Stability in leadership

  Just as walking requires coordination between legs, effective leadership requires the synchronization of career success with Role Modelship. Leaders who excel in their careers while simultaneously mentoring, inspiring, and guiding others offer a stable foundation for their teams.

- Forward momentum

  Walking on two legs allows for forward movement, and in a similar way, career achievements enhance your ability to influence others. As you progress in your career, you gain more visibility and credibility, which amplifies your Role Modelship. Likewise, being a respected role model can open doors in your career.

- Sustained success

  Just as walking enables sustained mobility, balancing career and Role Modelship ensures long-term success. Focusing on both leads to a fulfilling career, personal satisfaction, organizational and product maturity, and a lasting legacy.

In sum, it is vital to achieve balance between personal career advancement and the responsibility of being a role model. This dual focus strengthens both individual success and the success of those who follow your example.

---

*For a human, career and Role Modelship
are how you see the world and
how the world sees you.*

WINDOWS OF OPPORTUNITY TO SOCIAL CHANGE

A **window to social change** is a pivotal moment, leadership event, action, or innovation that reveals opportunities for societal transformation. It serves as a catalyst for challenging existing norms, sparking dialogue, and encouraging progress toward greater equality, justice, or progress within a community or society at large.

Windows to social change are often opened when individuals are willing to change their behaviors and the emotional states they invoke in others.

Here are a few prominent examples of significant windows to social change:

- The fight for women's voting rights, culminating in the 19th Amendment to the US Constitution in 1920, opened a critical window for gender equality.

- The US Civil Rights Movement in the 1960s, led by Martin Luther King Jr., Rosa Parks, and others, challenged racial segregation and discrimination.

- The fall of the Berlin Wall in 1989 symbolized the end of the Cold War and opened a significant window for social, political, and economic change in Europe, spreading democracy.

- The advent of the internet in the 1990s has arguably been one of the most transformative technological windows for social change. It revolutionized global communication and created platforms for social movements, education, and activism.

- The rise of smartphones in the 2000s put the power of communication into the hands of billions of people.

- Today, AI is a rapidly emerging technology window driving profound social and economic shifts.

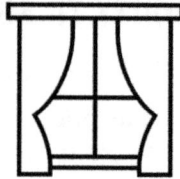

Role models must recognize **windows of opportunity** to catalyze social change. A prime example of a natural-born leader who created new roles for women and effected social change is depicted in the 2024 film *Young Woman and the Sea,* the story of Gertrude "Trudy" Ederle, the first woman to swim the English Channel, in 1926. As a child, Ederle survived the measles, but the disease permanently damaged her hearing. In 1914, when her mother declared that Trudy and her sister would learn to swim, their father laughed and wouldn't pay for swimming lessons. But the girls persisted and learned to swim, kicking with both feet, as their coach constantly reminded them to do.[1] (My own father didn't think women needed to know how to swim or drive, so I didn't learn to kick with both feet until I was in my forties.)

In 1924, Ederle competed in the Paris Olympics on the first-ever female swim team for the United States and won a gold medal, despite her coach's refusal to let her and her teammates train during the three-week voyage across the Atlantic. While the male team trained every day, the women's coach feared that members of the ship's male crew might take advantage of the female athletes.

When Ederle decided to swim the English Channel, the press

claimed that no woman could do it. But Ederle declared that she *would* do it.

At twenty-one miles, it's a physically grueling test for any swimmer, especially given the unpredictable currents, which extend the actual swimming distance significantly. Ederle's swim took fourteen hours and thirty-one minutes.

> Sometimes the window for social change is small, but a role model can make it wide enough for the next generation to walk through.

She didn't just make history; she shattered societal norms. At a time when women were expected to be passive and delicate, Ederle's endurance and strength showed the world that women were capable of extraordinary physical feats. She overcame physical challenges of freezing water, rough dark seas, muscle fatigue, and being alone and completely disoriented. Her success sent waves of inspiration to young girls who saw her as proof that they, too, could break barriers and create new roles for women.

After that historic swim, Ederle practiced stewardship and mentorship by teaching swimming to deaf children. She also demonstrated fellowship by supporting and collaborating with female athletes, advocating for greater recognition and opportunities for women in sports.

Her legacy of leadership was evident in how she challenged societal norms and became a symbol of female empowerment. Through sponsorship, Ederle helped open doors for future generations of women athletes, proving that they could break barriers and achieve greatness in competitive sports.

For leaders, heads of global events, or activists, it's common to emphasize the need for social change, but true impact comes when you actively create windows of opportunity for others to join the movement. When you see a window for change, don't wait; push it open, and invite others to step through with you.

---◆---

The only place where leadership should appear first and be practiced without Role Modelship expectations is in a dictionary.

Below are examples of how each of the Role Modelship values and behaviors—sponsorship, leadership, mentorship, fellowship, and stewardship—can serve as a window to social change and bolster your commitment to it.

- **Sponsorship** enables you to create opportunities for others to succeed. You can work to reduce barriers to entry for underrepresented groups by providing visibility, opportunities, and the capital to succeed.

- **Leadership** allows you to empower everyone around you to influence policies, shift cultural narratives, and inspire collective action toward shared goals. Social leaders can use their platforms to galvanize public opinion and policy change on critical issues, like climate action.

- **Mentorship** lets you accelerate social mobility and transfer knowledge or networks to those who lack access. Programs that pair successful professionals with young professionals from disadvantaged backgrounds, for example, can break cycles of poverty.

- **Fellowship** fosters solidarity and collaborative problem-solving, which are essential for driving systemic change. For example, social movements like Black Lives Matter or

#MeToo rely on fellowship to build a broad base of support and action.

- **Stewardship** encourages organizations and individuals to think beyond short-term gains and consider the long-term welfare of communities, the environment, and future generations. The push for net-zero emissions and carbon-neutral practices, for example, has shown how stewardship can align business success with social good.

When these five areas are interconnected, multiplier forces are leveraged intentionally, and they have the potential to transform society in meaningful ways.

Role Modelship Example: Mark Hawkins

- **Sponsorship:** This former CFO of customer-relations software creator Salesforce played a pivotal role in that company's cross-functional achievement to drive revenue from $4.1 billion at the end of fiscal year 2014 to more than $26 billion globally at the end of fiscal year 2022, supporting international market expansion and diverse product offerings. During Hawkins's tenure at Salesforce, the market capitalization of the company grew from more than $33 billion to over $296 billion, and Salesforce entered not only the Fortune 500 but also the Dow 30. He supported Salesforce partnerships with global organizations, like the World Economic Forum, and hosted the organization's first five CFO meetings in Davos, Switzerland. Also, he is chairman of the advisory council at Accounting for Sustainability (A4S), an organization founded by Britain's King Charles III that encourages the adoption of sustainable business models.

- **Leadership:** As CFO of Salesforce, Hawkins demonstrated exceptional leadership by overseeing financial operations and strategy as well as being a member of the executive committee during a period of rapid

continued

global expansion, when the company's market cap surpassed $200 billion. During Hawkins's CFO tenure at Autodesk, the company market capitalization grew from more than $4.3 billion to over $12 billion in less than six years.

- **Mentorship:** A multiplier role model, Hawkins is known for his mentorship within the finance and IT communities. At Autodesk, anyone who reported to him or his direct reports received his one-on-one attention. At Salesforce, he mentored numerous emerging leaders. (Many of us would not be where we are were it not for Mark. Forever grateful.) More than forty professionals who worked in his organizations have become CFOs. He has also had numerous team members become CIOs, COOs, CEOs, and/or presidents. Hawkins personally promotes professional growth, so executives are well prepared to "meet the moment" of their various organizations' business imperatives and priorities. His mantra of "better, better, never done" resonates with organizations that aspire to be durably competitive in a fast-moving global environment.

- **Fellowship:** At both Salesforce and Autodesk, he fostered a culture of achievement, collaboration, mutual respect, and teamwork, emphasizing the importance of cross-functional cooperation. His kind and calm leadership style naturally promoted fellowship, encouraging global teams to work together toward common strategic goals.

- **Stewardship:** As a steward of financial integrity and corporate responsibility, Hawkins ensured that both Salesforce and Autodesk maintained strong financial results. He also supported each company's respective focus on delivering shareholder returns and key stakeholder priorities. In 2021, Hawkins was inducted into the San Francisco Bay Area CFO Hall of Fame and awarded a Lifetime Achievement Award.

VISUALIZING WINDOWS TO SOCIAL CHANGE

Another way to think of a window to social change is as a two-by-two matrix in which the X-axis is Human Values, and the Y-axis is Economic Value. Each matrix can be used as a tool for self-assessment.

Visualizing windows to social change as two-by-two matrices with four quadrants is important because it provides a clear, simple framework for understanding the complexities and interrelationships of social change strategies. This allows leaders of individuals, organizations, and products to prioritize efforts based on two key dimensions—such as career and Role Modelship, revenue and Role Modelship, or product capability and Role Modelship—facilitating faster and more informed decision-making.

Individual Windows to Social Change

Individuals can leverage an individual Role Modelship–by–career matrix (see figure 4.4).

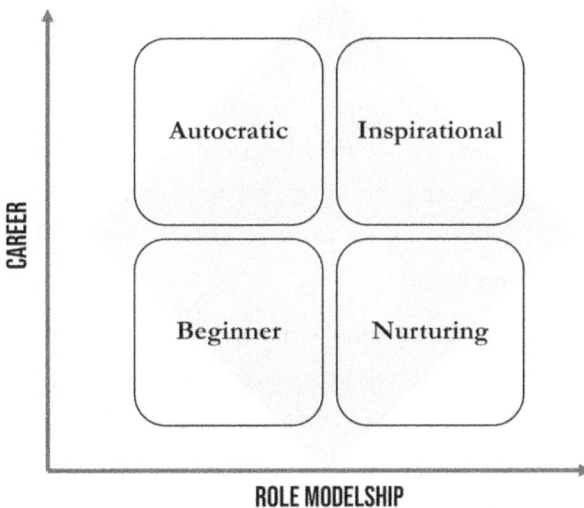

Figure 4.4. The Role Modelship–by–career matrix.

Individual Role Modelship–by–Career Matrix Overview

- **X-axis—Role Modelship:** This measures the extent to which an individual embodies and demonstrates the five disciplines others can emulate.

- **Y-axis—Career:** This represents the level of career advancement, influence, or professional success achieved.

- **Lower left quadrant—Beginner:** Individuals in this quadrant are at the early stages of their careers and have limited experience in Role Modelship. They may possess potential but lack the skills and confidence to inspire. They might still be learning the ropes and be focused primarily on their own development, without actively influencing others.

- **Lower right quadrant—Nurturing:** This quadrant includes individuals who are advancing in their careers and actively engaging in Role Modelship. They create supportive environments, take on mentoring roles, and encourage collaboration and skill development.

- **Upper left quadrant—Autocratic:** Individuals in this quadrant may have achieved significant career success but do not effectively embody the five Role Modelship disciplines. Their leadership style may be more directive and less inclusive, focusing on their authority rather than inspiration. They may rely on their position to enforce compliance rather than shared values.

- **Upper right quadrant—Inspirational:** This quadrant represents individuals who excel in their careers and are powerful role models. They inspire others, embodying the five disciplines to motivate teams. They are often seen as trailblazers encouraging everyone to strive for excellence and embrace their potential.

Career and Role Modelship stand at right angles and define our window to social change.

Organizational Windows to Social Change

Instead of an individual Role Modelship–by–career two-by-two matrix as the window to social change, organizations can leverage an organizational Role Modelship–by–revenue two-by-two matrix (see figure 4.5).

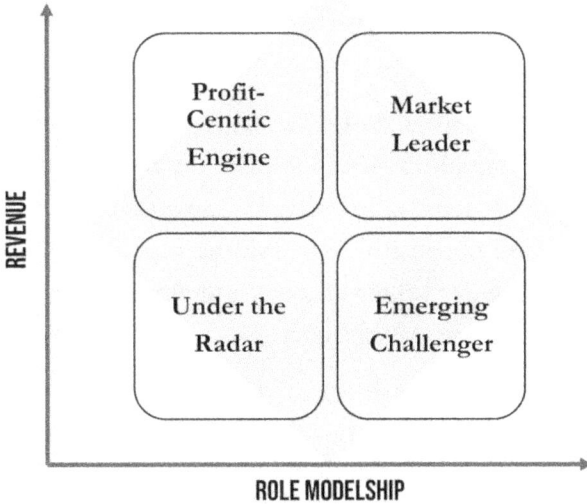

Figure 4.5. The Role Modelship–by–revenue matrix.

If modelship is strong, new employees will be folded into the culture and molded into role models.

Organizational Role Modelship–by–Revenue Matrix Overview

- **X-axis—Role Modelship:** This represents the extent to which an organization exemplifies the five disciplines, influencing others to follow suit.

- **Y-axis—Revenue:** This measures the organization's annual revenue, ranging from low to high.

- **Lower left quadrant—Under the Radar:** Organizations in this quadrant operate with low revenue and limited Role Modelship bench strength. They may be struggling to find their footing in the market and often lack visibility. They might be new entrants that have yet to establish a strong brand identity.

- **Lower right quadrant—Emerging Challenger:** This quadrant includes organizations that are beginning to gain traction in terms of revenue while also starting to build a reputation for positive Role Modelship. They are positioned as challengers in their markets and are innovative and driven while adopting ethical practices.

- **Upper left quadrant—Profit-Centric Engine:** Organizations in this quadrant generate high revenue but lack strong Role Modelship. They may focus predominantly on profit at the expense of positive impact in the five Role Modelship areas. These organizations often prioritize financial success over social responsibility, potentially leading to negative perceptions from customers.

- **Upper right quadrant—Market Leader:** This quadrant represents organizations that excel in both revenue generation and Role Modelship. They are recognized as leaders in their markets and set the standard for ethical practices and positive influence in many of the five areas.

Role Modelship during social change defines the trajectory of an organization.

In a **Crawl** ⟶ **Walk** ⟶ **Run** format, the organizational Y-axis can evolve as companies mature (see table 4.1).

Table 4.1. The Organizational Crawl ⟶ Walk ⟶ Run Maturity Framework

	CRAWL	WALK	RUN
Measure	Revenue	Profit	Market capitalization

Revenue shows the company's ability to generate sales and attract customers, but it doesn't reflect profitability or long-term sustainability.

A more mature organization starts thinking about **profits** as it highlights efficiency and the ability to manage costs, yet it may overlook growth potential or the value of long-term investments.

Market capitalization reflects the collective perception of a company's current and future value, incorporating growth potential, investor confidence, and competitive positioning. It ties together revenue generation, profitability, and market expectations.

Product Windows to Social Change

Products can be leveraged using a Role Modelship–by–product capability matrix (see figure 4.6).

The true test of modelship is how we act when the right path is not clear.

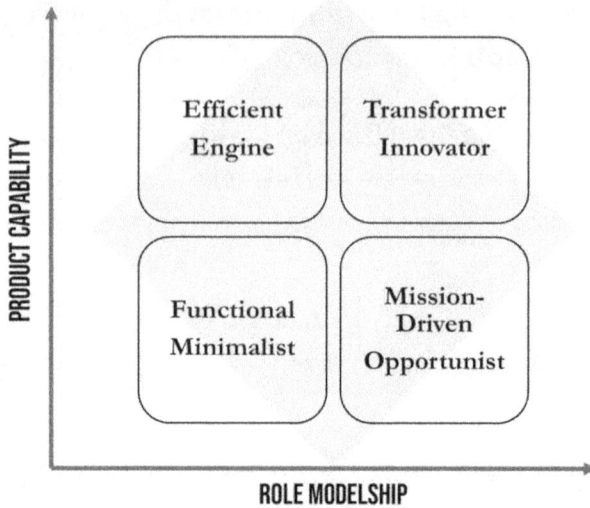

Figure 4.6. The Role Modelship–by–product capability matrix.

Role Modelship–by–Product Capability Matrix Overview

- **X-axis—Role Modelship:** This represents the extent to which a product exemplifies the five disciplines as well as sustainability, ethical production, and innovation, influencing consumer behavior and industry standards.

- **Y-axis—Product Capability:** This measures the product features and capabilities ranging from low to high, specific business use cases, and problems solved.

- **Lower left quadrant—Functional Minimalist:** Products in this quadrant embody basic functionality without significant role modeling. They are often seen as utilitarian and lack unique features or compelling brand narratives. These products prioritize simplicity and cost-effectiveness. However, they may not inspire loyalty or stand out in a crowded market.

- **Lower right quadrant—Mission-Driven Opportunist:** This quadrant includes products that are beginning to demonstrate a range of features and capabilities that solve real problems while embodying strong modelship. These products aim to fulfill a specific social or environmental purpose while capitalizing on opportunities.

- **Upper left quadrant—Efficient Engine:** Products in this quadrant are leaders in valuable capabilities but lack strong Role Modelship. They focus primarily on efficiency and profitability without prioritizing modelship practices. These products may excel in performance and cost-effectiveness but often do not engage consumers on a mission level.

- **Upper right quadrant—Transformative Innovator:** This quadrant represents products that excel in both valuable capabilities and modelship. These products are seen as transformative and lead the market in innovation, sustainability, and modelship practices. These products generate significant financial success and also embody strong values and commitments to positive change. They set industry standards and attract loyal customers.

In a **Crawl ⟶ Walk ⟶ Run** format, the product Y-axis can evolve as companies mature (see table 4.2).

Table 4.2. The Product Crawl ⟶ Walk ⟶ Run Framework

	CRAWL	**WALK**	**RUN**
Measure	Product Capabilities	Revenue or profit	Market value

These key measures of **product capabilities**, **revenue**, and **profit** collectively capture the product's functionality, financial contribution, and market appeal.

The equivalent of **market capitalization** for a product is **market value** or **product valuation**, reflecting its perceived worth and potential in the marketplace. This could be assessed through metrics like

- **Market share:** Product dominance in its segment, relative to competitors

- **Customer lifetime value:** Revenue generated per customer over time

- **Product brand equity:** Intangible value of product's reputation, customer loyalty, and market presence

- **Future growth potential:** Expected scalability to capture new market segments

These measures combine to provide a comprehensive view of a product's current and future impact, akin to how market capitalization reflects a company's overall valuation.

CHANNEL THE VOICE OF AN AMERIPRISE FINANCIAL ADVISOR

Mark Porter is a financial advisor with Ameriprise Financial Services and has more than twenty-one years of experience in the industry, focusing on financial planning, investment management, and client services. As a firm, Ameriprise manages more than two million individual, business, and institutional clients, with total assets under management of around $1.4 trillion.[2] Porter's portfolio includes millions of dollars in assets and hundreds of clients.

Porter exemplifies windows to social change by empowering individuals and communities to achieve financial literacy and stability, thereby breaking cycles of poverty. My team sat down with Porter for a chat over virtual Starbucks coffee, and he graciously shared some of his wisdom.

Q: How did growing up on a dairy farm shape your outlook on life?

A: *I grew up in Southern California, splitting my time between a dairy farm and a livestock auction. One of the things I'm proud of is the belief my mom instilled in me at a young age: "You're in charge of your own destiny." I was probably too young to fully grasp it at the time, but she said it often enough for it to sink in. To this day, she reminds me of that message: Focus on your goals, and take small steps every day to get there.*

Q: Who are some role models or mentors who impacted you, and what's one key lesson you learned from them?

A: *Growing up in a small town south of Bakersfield, I didn't meet many people outside of family and neighbors who had pigs, chickens, or dairy cows. Over the years, coworkers have had a huge impact on me, and I still stay in touch with many of them. My second boss and I still have lunch regularly.*

One key lesson I remember is from my grandfather. He told me, "Help other people get what they want, and you'll never have any wants yourself." That idea of service has stayed with me throughout my career and life. In the business world, especially as a business owner, service to others—emotionally and financially—has been crucial.

Q: If you could talk with anyone, dead or alive, who would it be, and why?

A: *If I could have lunch with anyone, it would be Warren Buffett. He has this incredible ability to remind us of things we used to know as common sense, things we've drifted away from. His long-term perspective is invaluable in today's world, where technology pushes us to want everything now, even if it's not the best way. I wouldn't spend $500,000 for lunch with him like some people do, but I'd value his perspective.*

Q: What part do role models play in the world today, especially with the rise of AI?

A: *AI isn't new; it's been used in industries like finance for decades. I remember using AI more than ten years ago at American Express, where we'd input data, and AI would help identify gaps in financial plans. One client didn't want a family trust, even though it would save them a million dollars. While AI recommended the trust, I had to patiently guide the client through the pros and cons until they made the decision themselves.*

AI is great for predicting outcomes and suggesting strategies, but role models are still essential for providing the human touch—breaking down complex decisions into steps that resonate with people on a personal level. So, in this age of AI, role models are the ones who help translate the technology into action for people's benefit.

Q: Can you share a time when you mentored or sponsored someone?

A: *I was inspired by a financial planner who came to my seventh-grade math class and introduced us to The Stock Market Game. I now volunteer with the same organization, Junior Achievement, teaching their classes on personal finance. I get to teach kids everything from how to buy their first car to managing money for the first time. It's exciting to walk into a classroom, sometimes full of college-prep students, and sometimes full of kids from a continuation school. My job is to reach each group in a way that resonates with them, to give them something meaningful they can use.*

Yesterday, for example, I helped one of our client's children, who just got his dream job in New York. He was working through his open enrollment paperwork and reached out for help. We went through every question, and at the end, he said, "I really thought I knew this stuff, but you taught me so much more." Moments like that, when I can help the next generation navigate life's big decisions, are incredibly rewarding.

Q: What's the most important habit for the next generation of role models?

A: *Effective communication is key. It's not just about speaking the same language; it's about understanding each other's internal language, the way we've been programmed from childhood.*

Setting big, ambitious goals is another crucial habit. I want the people I sponsor to set wild, large, SMART goals. These goals should be specific, measurable, achievable, relevant, and time bound. For example, if you're a new salesperson, I might say, "You're going to sell $200,000 worth of security systems this year." It seems daunting at first, but by breaking it down—call enough people, educate them, adjust your activities as needed—you can achieve it. Even if you miss the goal, you'll be ahead of most of your peers.

I also believe in regular check-ins. Revisiting goals quarterly ensures that people are on track. If they're behind, we can figure out why and adjust course.

Lastly, you have to be prepared. Whether it's a meeting or a presentation, preparation is key. My grandfather used to say, "On time is thirty minutes early." Being prepared means knowing what you want to accomplish, dressing the part, and making sure you're presenting yourself in a way that fits the situation. Some people think I overdress in a three-piece-suit, but my clients expect it. I've had clients say, "You can wear whatever you want next time," but I stick with what works for my audience. It's all about being yourself and being confident in that.

Q: What is the most important value or lesson you learned from your grandfather?

A: *My grandfather's impact on me was profound. He had only a sixth-grade education, but at his funeral, the church was packed, standing room only, with people who came to talk about the ways he had helped them. It wasn't about money—he didn't loan them money or buy things for them; it was his mindset that made a difference. He would give advice or help people think differently about their problems. His ability to lift others up with just a few words was remarkable, and that's a lesson I've carried with me: True leadership and influence come from helping others see the best in themselves.*

Role Modelship Example: Melinda Gates

- **Sponsorship:** As a businesswoman and philanthropist, Melinda Gates has been a transformative force in amplifying the voices of women and marginalized communities. Through Pivotal Ventures, a company she launched in 2015 that works to accelerate social progress—particularly for women—she has committed more than $1 billion to initiatives focused on gender equality. Notably, she has sponsored organizations like Moms First, which advocates for paid family leave, and Reboot Representation, which works to close the gender gap in tech by increasing the number of women of color earning computing degrees.

- **Leadership:** As cochair of the Bill & Melinda Gates Foundation for nearly twenty-four years, Melinda directed more than $70 billion toward global health, education, and economic empowerment. Her leadership has redefined philanthropy, particularly through work in eradicating diseases like malaria and polio.

- **Mentorship:** Melinda actively mentors women leaders in tech, health care, and philanthropy. One example is Reshma Saujani, founder of the nonprofit Girls Who Code, whom Melinda has supported with guidance and funding to scale the program. In her 2019 book, *The Moment of Lift*, she encourages others to mentor and uplift women globally.

- **Fellowship:** Emphasizing collaboration, Melinda has built alliances with policymakers, nongovernmental humanitarian organizations, and private-sector leaders. Her partnerships with other philanthropic leaders, like MacKenzie Scott, and initiatives such as the Equality Can't Wait Challenge (which awarded $40 million to transformative gender-equality projects in 2021) exemplify her commitment to collective action.

- **Stewardship:** Melinda's stewardship is evident in her lifelong commitment to advancing the welfare of others. In 2022, Pivotal Ventures announced new investments targeting systemic barriers to women's economic participation, including caregiving solutions and equitable workplace policies.

ONE-MINUTE MODELSHIP

Please apply the two-by-two window for social change to your current problem or opportunity. Tag it so others can ask you about your journey.

#RoleModelship

TAKEAWAYS

- Your overall **Role Modelship state** is the average of your states of stewardship, fellowship, mentorship, leadership, and sponsorship.

- For a professional, there are **two states to be fulfilled**: career and Role Modelship.

- Role models must recognize **windows of opportunity** to catalyze social change.

- Learning to employ both **modelship and career** perspectives is like learning to walk on two legs.

- **For an individual, Role Modelship and career** are **how you see the world and how the world sees you.** Role Modelship and career stand at right angles and define a window for social change.

- For an organization, **Role Modelship and revenue** provide a window into its impact on the world.

- Role Modelship during social change **defines the trajectory of an organization**.

- For a product, Role Modelship and product capabilities define the window for social change.

CHAPTER 5

Modeling Habits of Detractors, Stabilizers, and Multipliers

The number one difference between a Nobel Prize winner and others is not IQ or work ethic, but that they ask bigger questions.

—PETER F. DRUCKER

I've realized that the key to being successful is not how good your ideas are; it's how good you are at being able to find quick, cheap, and easy ways to try your ideas.

—MARC RANDOLPH

Just like Arthur Clarke, the British science fiction author, predicted in 1974 that one day computers would fit on a desk, he also humorously predicted that we'd stream channels full of cat pictures and pick random fights with strangers online. Fascinating, right?

If that's how we've chosen to utilize one of humanity's greatest inventions, it prompts a deeper question: What is the best use for a human?

In her book *Multipliers: How the Best Leaders Make Everyone Smarter*, Liz Wiseman describes patterns of leaders and the role of multipliers. It begs us to reflect on how we, as humans, can become multipliers—not just of knowledge but of values, economic benefits, and positive impact.

Let's look at three different role model personas in the broader context of the five interconnected value disciplines of Role Modelship: a **detractor**, a **stabilizer**, and a **multiplier** role model (see table 5.1).

Table 5.1. Role Model Personas

ROLE MODELSHIP AREA	DETRACTOR	STABILIZER	MULTIPLIER
Sponsorship	Rarely sponsors others; is reluctant to advocate or support new initiatives; focuses on self-preservation	Sponsors selectively; supports when low risk but lacks strong advocacy for bold actions	Actively sponsors individuals and ideas; provides opportunities and champions others' growth
Leadership	Has a low leadership presence; resists moving the cheese, struggles to inspire, is often disengaged or critical; avoids taking charge	Provides steady, calm, and consistent leadership; maintains direction but lacks inspiration; supports moving the cheese; is focused on stability over transformation	Is a high-impact leader; inspires, drives vision, and empowers others to lead; enjoys moving the cheese; experiments and innovates; fosters a modelship culture
Mentorship	Provides minimal or negative mentorship; offers little guidance, often highlighting negatives; undermines growth	Offers consistent but cautious mentoring; provides practical advice without deeply investing in mentees' growth	Invests heavily in mentoring; kindly challenges mentees to reach their full potential and actively supports their development in new roles that may not even exist
Fellowship	Isolates from the team; has low engagement; undermines team cohesion and trust	Is a reliable team player; fosters harmony and trust; contributes steadily but doesn't elevate team dynamics significantly	Is deeply engaged; fosters connection, collaboration, and mutual support; elevates team spirit and reiterates the value of winning as a team

ROLE MODELSHIP AREA	DETRACTOR	STABILIZER	MULTIPLIER
Stewardship	Neglects responsibilities; lacks accountability and transparency; often undermines collective goals	Is accountable and responsible for long-term sustainability through careful management of a well-defined area; manages resources well but lacks desire for innovation in cross-functional stewardship	Performs exemplary stewardship across many domains, growing more stewards; is proactive in managing resources, driving sustainable impact, and setting high ethical standards

DETRACTOR ROLE MODEL

Detractors are humans who make you feel like you're hanging by your ankles and falling. Sometimes they do it intentionally; sometimes they are not aware. In most cases, they've never had great role models to emulate.

Make peace with the detractor role model you were in the past.

HOW TO LEVERAGE DETRACTORS

Detractors are typically not self-aware, not self-disciplined in modeling anything, and sometimes argumentative. However, they often see blind spots others miss. Being impatient with them doesn't help because their brain is not wired to experiment. The best way to leverage them is to apply situational awareness.

- **Wire curiosity:** Train your brain to listen, ask a lot of questions, be patient, and understand not just a detractor's concerns in any of the five areas but also their root causes.

- **Reiterate the why:** Calmly clarify and repeat why an area matters or is a goal; a North Star; a desired outcome; a result; or of value to the team, the company, the product.

- **Manage risk:** Acknowledge the validity of a detractor's concern, and ask them to manage the probability that the issue will occur and the impact it will have if it does. If you love two-by-twos, ask the detractor to make a risk matrix showing the probability of the occurrence and its impact to share with the team.

- **Rally support:** Publicly and privately ask others to help manage the detractor's concern and its risks, creating small tiger teams to tackle the toughest challenges.

STABILIZER ROLE MODEL

Stabilizers are grounded and reliable, excelling in consistency and ensuring continuity within a product or organization. They thrive on structure, preferring proven methods over experimental approaches, and often prioritize stability over rapid change. While they may appear resistant to innovation, their ability to maintain equilibrium during periods of turbulence is invaluable. The best way to leverage stabilizers is to align new ideas with their need for predictability, framing changes in terms of long-term benefits and practical outcomes. Their contributions provide a foundation upon which others can innovate, ensuring that progress does not compromise steadiness.

HOW TO LEVERAGE STABILIZERS

Depending on the situation and priorities, sometimes you need to surround yourself with stabilizers. The best way to leverage them is to let them perform their routines, emulate them for stability, and give them consistent rewards for being a role model.

- **Pedal beneath the surface:** Reap the tremendous benefits of demoing self-control and discipline by training your brain to be calm under pressure and kind under stress. Stabilizers have habits that enable them to do rapid pedaling beneath the surface of the water. To the rest of us humans, it looks like a beautiful, graceful swan gliding effortlessly across the pond. They model all five areas and make it look easy.

- **Navigate unknowns:** Uncertainty is difficult and stressful for humans to navigate. Stabilizers have figured out that accomplishing valuable goals requires struggle. Stabilizers keep you steady when you're putting 10 percent of your savings into retirement instead of taking a trip to Hawaii, or learning how to play the piano but don't want to practice scales or solfège. They promote thoughtful but not overly ambitious decisions.

- **Flywheel effect:** Since stabilizers model stewardship, fellowship, mentorship, leadership, and sponsorship consistently, you can ask them to carry out a transformation and produce predictable results. If you're a stabilizer yourself, you know people depend on you because of your high standards and your predictable consistency.

MULTIPLIER ROLE MODEL

Multiplier role models are the humans who sparkle and make you feel like you sparkle and have wings. Who would you consider as your multiplier role models?

HOW TO LEVERAGE MULTIPLIER ROLE MODELS

Multiplier role models thrive when the degree of ambiguity and uncertainty is high. The best way to leverage them is to let them play to their strengths, emulate them, and give them high-caliber humans to coach. Below are three ways to emulate multipliers.

- **Process ambiguity quickly:** Effectively filter out noise, see the big picture quickly, find patterns, and distill information for others while still being able to recall the details later. As multipliers' knowledge and influence within an organization grows, they become multidisciplinary. For executives serving on boards of directors, less is more.

- **Make bold decisions rapidly:** Pound the data, not the table, and leverage intuition. From an organizational stand-point, information is only as good as the results it delivers. Multipliers encourage bold, strategic decisions, actively seek innovative solutions, and empower others to think creatively. They create a high bar for Role Modelship decisions that many emulate. In the hiring process, they often serve as a bar-raiser, ensuring alignment to role modeling values.

- **Rally support effectively:** Make friends, and influence people. Multipliers use honey, not vinegar, and nurture and inspire. Many people refer to multipliers as talent magnets. They want to continue the lineage of their legacy and have earned respect by consistently delivering results and fostering new role models.

Humans and products are constantly evolving and adapting. No one human, organization, or product is a detractor, stabilizer, or multiplier all the time. Situational leadership is very common.

Stabilizer and **multiplier awards** can be tailored to the unique traits of stabilizers (providing steadiness, consistency, and balance) and multipliers (amplifying potential and driving exponential growth). The awards can be peer-to-peer, leadership, community, or other formats. AI agents can create award descriptions, criteria, and designs of prisms, soaring eagles, bridges, or interwoven rings. The digital awards can be stored in digital wallets.

Do you have a digital wallet? AI agents will.

CHANNEL NIKE'S ROLE MODELSHIP

I have the honor of volunteering on the beautiful NASA Research Park campus of Carnegie Mellon University in California. In a discussion I had with one of the university's graduate students and a product manager at Nike, he provided this summary about Nike as a company role model.

Sponsorship: Nike's extensive sponsorship of athletes and teams worldwide, including its support for the Paralympics, underscores the company's commitment to promoting inclusive leadership and supporting diverse talents.

Leadership through innovation: Nike's launch of self-lacing shoes, such as the Nike Adapt series, showcases the company's leadership in technological innovation. These products lead the way in integrating advanced technology into everyday wear, setting new standards for what athletic footwear can achieve.

Environmental stewardship: The Nike "Move to Zero" campaign is a prime example of stewardship. Through sustainable products, like the Nike Air VaporMax 2020 Flyknit, made with at least 50 percent recycled content, Nike demonstrates its commitment to environmental stewardship by reducing waste and using more sustainable materials.

Fellowship in Nike's community programs: The Nike Training Club app offers personalized coaching, workout routines, and expert guidance, serving as a digital mentor to millions of users worldwide to help them achieve their fitness goals. The company's mentorship and sponsorship for young female athletes also exemplify fellowship. The program creates a community that fosters connection, support, and encouragement among young women in sports.

More than thirty well-funded companies are building humanoids in the United States, China, and Japan,[1] and a collective $700 million has been invested. A few examples of companies and entrepreneurs who are pouring funds into Figure AI Robotics Company, for example, are OpenAI, Microsoft, Jeff Bezos, NVIDIA, and Ark Investment Management firm. It's the kind of innovation energy that was felt in the early days of SpaceX. How do you see yourself participating in that future?

YOUR ROLE MODELSHIP FORMULA

Jim Rohn, an influential motivational speaker and author, said, "You are the average of the five people you spend the most time with." His legacy has had a huge impact on many lives.

Let's explore a new version of this and see whether it resonates with you.

You are the product of yourself times your four role models.

You = you × role model 1 × role model 2 × role model 3 × role model 4

Who you become = your habits × your role models

"You" can be you as a human, organization, or product. Imagine a case of you = you × detractor × detractor × stabilizer × multiplier.

What if you = detractor you × detractor fellow × stabilizer mentor × stabilizer leader × multiplier leader?

What if you = stabilizer you × detractor fellow × stabilizer mentor × multiplier leader × multiplier sponsor?

What type of human do sponsors want to amplify?

You are the product of yourself times your four role models. Let's take a look at why that matters.

- **Focus on role models:** The new expression emphasizes the deliberate choice of role models, suggesting a more intentional approach to personal development. It highlights the importance of consciously selecting models (i.e., individuals, organizations, and products) that you look up to for inspiration and guidance.

- **Intentionality:** The phrase "times your four role models" implies an intentional multiplication of your efforts and qualities with those of your role models. It suggests that you actively amplify the positive traits and behaviors you admire.

Humans who model together wire humans together.

- **Personal agency:** By including "yourself" in the equation, the expression acknowledges the active role you play in shaping your identity and growth.

- **Board of directors:** Just as companies need boards to help steer the ship, this is the formula for your board of directors.

At the organizational level, please don't transfer problem teams that don't have a clear mission or charter to other teams. You'd only be making a detractor modeling decision.

On the product level, if your company has 150 products, you may consider retiring any products that detract from the human values or economic value of the rest. If you're bundling them in suites or platforms, no customer wants to buy products that are cheap but not necessary. As celebrated management consultant Peter F. Drucker once said, "There is nothing so useless as doing efficiently that which should not be done at all."[2]

Imagine a case of product bundle = detractor product × stabilizer product × multiplier product × two?

Which detractor role model changes your human, organization, or product equation? How will you replace that role model?

LEADING INDICATORS FOR CHOOSING ROLE MODELS

Choosing different role models based on leading indicators is vital because it aligns your learning with forward-looking success markers rather than lagging outcomes. **Leading indicators** are early signals about future outcomes that enable organizations to act early, identifying potential opportunities or risks before they fully materialize. Leading indicators offer early insights into future performance and behavior, helping organizations predict trends before they affect the top or bottom line or customer satisfaction.

The following is a list of six leading indicators to help you choose a replacement role model (see table 5.2). There are many other indicators that I could have chosen, but these flow to the top of everyone's mind and priority. You can leverage them as an early warning system.

Table 5.2. Indicators for Choosing a Replacement Role Model

LEADING INDICATOR	DETRACTOR ROLE MODEL	STABILIZER ROLE MODEL	MULTIPLIER ROLE MODEL
Leadership position: Seat on the bus	Is often in the wrong seat; has mismatched skills or misaligned goals; disrupts team dynamics	Is in the right seat but prefers maintaining the current trajectory without major changes; is consistent and reliable but not transformative	Is in the right seat with the ability to elevate others; leverages strengths effectively, aligning with team goals
Stewardship mindset: No, yes	Frequently says no or finds reasons to object; shuts down ideas and possibilities	Has a "yes, but" approach; cautiously approves, based on a lot of data, but adds caveats or conditions that can slow momentum	Has a "yes, and" approach; builds on others' ideas, creating synergy and encouraging further innovation
Fellowship strategy: Rock fetch	Engages in team "rock fetch" behavior, focusing on unproductive tasks or reworking others' efforts; stifles progress	Limits team "rock fetch" to necessary corrections; aims to optimize processes without pushing boundaries	Actively avoids team "rock fetch"; prioritizes high-value activities, delegating effectively to maximize impact

LEADING INDICATOR	DETRACTOR ROLE MODEL	STABILIZER ROLE MODEL	MULTIPLIER ROLE MODEL
Leadership adaptability: Fragile, resilient, antifragile	Is fragile; gets disrupted easily by challenges; often retreats under pressure, undermining confidence in the team	Is resilient; maintains composure under stress; adapts without significant gains; keeps things stable	Is antifragile; thrives under pressure, turning challenges into opportunities for growth and innovation
Leadership example: Promotion process consistency (for managers)	Communicates skepticism about the process, subtly or overtly undermining it, and is often inconsistent in their efforts; shows interest only when it benefits them or when they can point out problems	Approaches communication with a focus on clarity and balance; influences others by promoting a fair approach; follows established guidelines and ensures that everyone is treated equally	Communicates the process in an inspiring way; focuses on growth and opportunity; uses their influence to empower others to seek advancement, seeing promotions as part of a broader strategy for success
Sponsorship credibility: Candidate for your personal board of directors	Is seldom seen in influential roles; lacks trust and credibility; is often sidelined in key discussions	Holds steady, dependable roles; is valued for consistency but not often for driving new strategies	Is sought after for high-impact roles; serves as a trusted advisor who influences decisions and drives strategic change

Keep in mind that on humanity days, you'll be a positive role model, and on other days, you'll be only as good as your inner voice describes you. Now that you know what you know, which detractor role model(s) will you replace in your life, and why?

BOOKS AS MULTIPLIERS

No one can write a book about multiplier role models without acknowledging the profound power of books as the ultimate multipliers.

Elaine Petrocelli, founder of Book Passage bookstore in the San Francisco Bay Area, exemplifies this multiplier effect through her life's work. By curating spaces where stories come alive and connecting readers with authors who challenge perspectives and expand horizons, she has demonstrated how books are not merely objects but vessels of stewardship, mentorship, and fellowship. Petrocelli's dedication to fostering literary communities shows that the power of books goes far beyond their pages; they ripple outward, inspiring individuals to lead, learn, and multiply impact in their own lives.

Petrocelli is a visionary force in the world of independent bookstores, celebrated as a literary "godmother." Since its inception in 1976, Book Passage has grown into a vibrant community hub, hosting more than 800 author events annually, including appearances by literary luminaries such as Isabel Allende, Khaled Hosseini, and Anne Lamott. Petrocelli's passion for connecting readers with authors shines through the store's renowned programs, including conferences for mystery, travel, and children's writing, which nurture aspiring writers.

Role Modelship Example: Gretchen Rubin

- **Sponsorship:** This best-selling author and podcaster sponsors personal happiness and well-being by providing actionable strategies through her books, including *The Happiness Project*, which has sold more than 1.5 million copies worldwide. Her works empower individuals to take control of their own happiness by making small practical changes in their daily lives.

- **Leadership:** As a leader in the self-help and personal development space, she has inspired a global movement around happiness and well-being. *The Happiness Project* has been translated into more than thirty languages and spawned many books.

- **Mentorship:** Rubin mentors millions of readers and listeners, offering guidance on how to live a happier, more fulfilling life. Her podcast, *Happier with Gretchen Rubin*, consistently ranks in the top 1 percent of global podcasts.

- **Fellowship:** Rubin encourages readers to share their own happiness journeys. Members of global Happiness Project groups support each other in implementing her ideas.

- **Stewardship:** Her stewardship is evident in the lasting impact of her work, including the ongoing popularity of *The Happiness Project* blog, which has received more than 100 million page views.

ONE-MINUTE MODELSHIP

Connect with someone as a fellow, steward, and leader. Post on LinkedIn or on your internal **Role Modelship** Slack or Microsoft Teams channel an example of Role Modelship.

   #RoleModelship

TAKEAWAYS

- There are three different **role model personas:**

  » **Detractor role models** create resistance to moving the cheese, and unless they're leveraged properly for managing risks, they reduce team cohesion and efficiency and undermine modelship influence.

  » **Stabilizer role models** are needed for maintaining balance and consistency, and when leveraged to their full potential, they facilitate smooth operations. They can anchor teams in the modelship vision and are reliable during transitions, often finding new cheese.

  » **Multiplier role models** amplify team potential and talent by encouraging innovation, moving the cheese, and promoting collaboration and collective Role Modelship.

- **You = you × role model 1 × role model 2 × role model 3 × role model 4.**

- **Detractor, stabilizer, and multiplier role models show up differently**, and you can leverage different leading indicators to maximize the effectiveness of each type.

- **Leading indicators are early warning systems** about future outcomes that enable organizations to act early, identifying potential opportunities or risks before they fully materialize. Choosing different role models based on leading indicators is vital because it aligns your learning with forward-looking success markers rather than lagging outcomes.

- There are **six key leading indicators** for detractors, stabilizers, and multipliers:

  » **Leadership position:** Seat on the bus

  » **Stewardship mindset:** "Yes, and" versus "yes, but" or "no"

  » **Fellowship strategy:** "Rock fetch"

  » **Leadership adaptability:** Fragile, resilient, antifragile

  » **Leadership example:** Promotion process consistency (for managers): skeptical, can-do, inspirational

  » **Sponsorship credibility:** Candidate for your personal board of directors

CHAPTER 6

Assess the Health of Human, Organization, and Product Modelship

Our brain is mapping the world. Often that map is distorted,
but it's a map with constant immediate sensory input.
—E. O. WILSON

A master uses 90 percent intuition
and 10 percent technique.
—ŌSENSEI

Imagine you're the architect of the San Francisco–Oakland Bay Bridge, ensuring robust engineering and seismic reinforcement. Imagine you're a scientist researching ancestry, diseases, and traits based on DNA. Imagine you're a bank officer loaning humans money for houses, self-driving cars, education, vacations, humanoids, and vacuums that also empty out the cat litter. Imagine you're the officer giving the tour at the Pearl Harbor Veterans Memorial in Honolulu, Hawaii.

Everything you role model—whether observed or unseen—reflects your health in action as a human, an organization, or a product steward. Assessing your human, organizational, and product Role Modelship health is critical for ensuring sustained performance and growth.

Sleep. Code. Build. Dance. Sing. Smile. Encrypt. Run. Cook. Save. Honor. Research. Be curious. Recycle. Have a board meeting in Hawaii. Drink water, coffee, tea. Wait patiently. Compromise. Don't compromise. Be right. Be wrong. Read. Rhyme. Sleep.

Life, like science or engineering, is constructed through intentional, anchored acts. Each action becomes a cornerstone for growth, resilience, and contribution, shaping a future defined by purpose and progress. When my seventy-year-old grandma and I disagreed on the importance of exercise, she used to say, superfast, with a big smile on her face, "Okay, okay, I give up; you win! You're *wrong*, and I'm *right*."

Being right today won't matter tomorrow, but being happy through modeling will.

She was right. I need more exercise, especially after the age of fifty. Do you like to be right? Would you rather be right or happy?

ASSESS THE HEALTH OF YOUR PHYSICAL AND MENTAL MODELSHIP

Leveraging Harvey Balls, you can do a flash self-assessment diagnostic of where your physical and mental health is today, this month, this quarter, this year (see figure 6.1).

PHYSICAL   MENTAL

Figure 6.1. Using Harvey Balls to assess your physical and mental health.

A simple act of kindness at the intersection of modelship and gratitude is taking care of your body, mind, and spirit.

BRAVER: A Role Modelship Change-Management Framework

Humans are both at their best and worst during change. Instead, change can be more deliberate and systematic.

We're going to introduce **BRAVER,** which is a Role Modelship change-management framework designed to help humans adapt to and lead rapid change in the world (see figure 6.2).

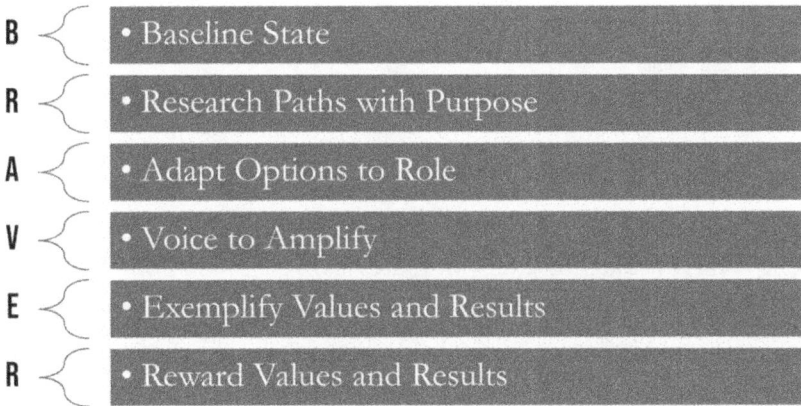

B — • Baseline State

R — • Research Paths with Purpose

A — • Adapt Options to Role

V — • Voice to Amplify

E — • Exemplify Values and Results

R — • Reward Values and Results

Figure 6.2. The BRAVER change-management framework.

This robust framework ensures effective leadership regardless of the type of change.

The table below is a high-level summary of BRAVER and the actions in each step (see table 6.1).

Table 6.1. A Summary of the
BRAVER Framework and the Actions It Requires

	BRAVER	ACTIONS
B	Baseline state	Establish the baseline—the current state of results and values—with Harvey Balls, a questionnaire, a two-by-two matrix, or another assessment.
R	Research paths with purpose	Working backward from your purpose, research multiple paths and the economic value they add to the organization.
A	Adapt options to role	Adapt options to your current role, values, and key performance indicators.
V	Voice to amplify	Articulate a development plan or prioritized product backlog along two dimensions: results and values. Discuss it with your manager, mentor, and sponsor.
E	Exemplify values and results	Model and set a tangible example with your journey, values, and results.
R	Reward values and results	Reward or course correct through storytelling.

It begins with the baseline state, at which current values and results are assessed to identify obstacles, gaps, and opportunities for improvement. Harvey Balls or questionnaires can be used. Following that, researching paths with purpose involves leveraging role models and AI to gather knowledge about multiple paths and effective practices for growth aligned to your purpose. Adapting options to the role focuses on tailoring alternatives and leadership approaches to align with your role, organizational values, and key performance indicators.

When voicing to amplify, leaders and role models articulate the vision and desired changes clearly and authentically, considering obstacles such as economic conditions, competition, customer acquisition costs, prioritization, and technology. This results in a development plan or a prioritized backlog for a product.

The next step, exemplifying results and values, calls for modeling the desired outcome, which sets a tangible example for others to follow.

Entrepreneur, investor, and author Chris Donnelly emphasizes that high-performing employees naturally lead by example, showcasing the behaviors and standards that inspire others, even without holding formal leadership titles.[1] Their influence extends beyond individual contributions, creating a ripple effect that elevates team performance and fosters a culture of excellence.

Finally, rewarding values and results ensures recognition and reinforcement of positive changes. It celebrates role models who embody the desired results and values and inspire others to adapt. This structured change-management approach is passed on to others in the organization, embedding change deeply within it.

ASSESS HUMAN MODELSHIP IN AN ORGANIZATION: NOT GETTING RECOGNIZED OR PROMOTED?

Many employees struggle to understand why they're not getting promoted, especially after reorganizations. Are you aware of how you show up?

Being BRAVER can help an employee change, adding more value to their contribution so that they can get promoted. The question to ask is not *How do I get promoted?* But rather *How do I add more value to what I do and demonstrate modelship values to other humans, products, or the organization so we can serve our customers better?*

Let's take a look at each step of BRAVER.

B = Baseline State

The following are the top five most common reasons employees at any level are not getting promoted.

1. **Resistance to change:** Employees who are resistant to moving the cheese, new processes, or technological advancements may not be considered for promotion. Companies value adaptability and forward thinking.

» **Why it matters:** Promotions often favor those who are adaptable, open to learning new systems, and comfortable with evolving environments. Resistance to change can be seen as a red flag when it comes to suitability for a leadership position.

2. **Failure to take initiative:** Simply doing the job as expected is not enough. Promotions often go to individuals who take initiative, go beyond their regular responsibilities, and demonstrate leadership potential. In many companies, employees are expected to perform at the next level before they get promoted.

   » **Why it matters:** Those who don't proactively seek out challenges or show initiative may be seen as reliable but not leadership material, limiting their chances for promotion.

3. **Limited skill development:** Sticking to the same skill set without upskilling or taking on new challenges can prevent promotions in this rapidly moving age when everyone is expected to wear a digital hat. People who don't actively seek opportunities to grow professionally may stagnate.

   » **Why it matters:** A company looks for individuals who are continuously evolving and acquiring new skills that align with its future needs.

4. **Poor relationship building:** Promotions are not just about skills; they are also about relationships. People who don't build strong relationships with key stakeholders, peers, or team members often miss out on promotions.

   » **Why it matters:** Networking and collaboration are key factors in promotions, because leaders prefer to advance those who are seen as team players and well connected within the company.

5. **Lack of visibility of the added economic value or human values:** Even if someone is doing great work, they might not get

promoted if decision-makers don't understand the economic value of doing so. People who work behind the scenes may be overlooked when managers don't have the skills to showcase members of their team and articulate their work's benefits rather than just their status and features. The same visibility is needed when exemplifying the five Role Modelship values.

» **Why it matters:** Managers promote those who are recognized for their value, so staying invisible limits upward mobility.

Using AI, you can design a questionnaire to assess your current state.

On a spider graph, your baseline answers may look something like figure 6.3 over time. This visual illustration forms the foundation of your commitment to change for you and your manager.

HUMAN ROLE MODELSHIP ASSESSMENT

—Stewardship   —Fellowship   —Mentorship   —Leadership   —Sponsorship

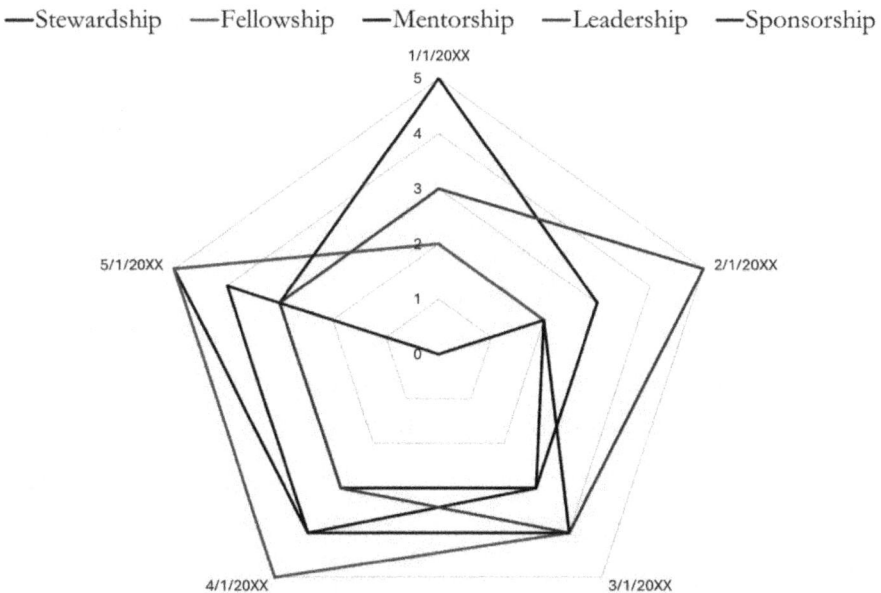

Figure 6.3. A sample human Role Model assessment.

R = Research Paths with Purpose

Knowing the top five reasons that employees are not getting promoted and your current state, you can leverage role models and AI to research a couple of different paths you can take to add more value to the organization. For example, you can research what it means to be a product manager, an engineering manager, a sales manager, a director, a COO, or a vice president.

A = Adapt Options to Role

Based on your research, you can select a specific path to realign and stretch your current role. Prioritization for short-term growth and long-term flexibility is important. My favorite memory of Moonhie Chin, former senior vice president of strategic planning and operations at Autodesk, is when she offered the advice that careers are made when humans step up to do work that no one wants to own and either eliminate the work altogether or improve it significantly.

V = Voice to Amplify

Once you have a desired path, you can discuss it with your manager, mentor, or sponsor to leverage an individual development plan. The following table is a template you can populate with your specific details (see table 6.2). A sprint can be two weeks, so you can aim for two sprints that roughly fit in a month.

If you're more ambitious and your organization has the habits, you can make your desired results SMART—specific, measurable, achievable, relevant, and time bound.

Table 6.2. Individual Development Plan

Individual Development Plan—Two Sprints, One Month					
	VALUES				
	STEWARDSHIP	FELLOWSHIP	MENTORSHIP	LEADERSHIP	SPONSORSHIP
Desired results for economic value	As a vice president of product, gather data and best practices on go-to-market (GTM) and digital currencies for an autonomous GTM agent in order to increase growth by 5%.	Share research with team and solicit ideas or feedback. Give AI feedback.	Explain to team desired future state for an autonomous GTM system in which AI agents buy and sell software using digital currencies.	As a vice president of product, create epics and user stories for the autonomous GTM system, leveraging AI.	As a CFO, create a business case to allocate resources for product management and engineering.

—⋀⋁—*modelship*—⋀⋁—

E = Exemplify Results and Values

Humans who exemplify results and values serve as role models, demonstrating the alignment of integrity, effort, and impact in their daily actions. This approach inspires teams by showing that achieving outcomes without compromising principles is not only possible but essential. By consistently embodying organizational values, leaders reinforce a culture in which results are pursued ethically and inclusively.

R = Reward Results and Values

Rewarding results and values fosters a balanced workplace in which both achievements and the way they are accomplished are celebrated. Recognizing individuals who uphold core values while delivering outcomes encourages a culture of integrity and mutual respect. Offering incentives, praise, and promotions based on both performance metrics ensures that values remain a guiding force, strengthening morale and commitment.

- In your Role Modelship Slack or Microsoft Teams channel, post stories about managers, peers, and employees who exemplify both results and the five values. Catch people demoing Role Modelship.

- Also, if you'd like to influence change on a broader scale, these disciplines can easily be incorporated into existing HR processes, career ladders, culture, and other value frameworks through a simple mapping you'll see later in this book.

- There are many other apps (e.g., Matter, Kudos, KudoBoard, and Claptastic) and applause systems that can be leveraged for peer-to-peer and manager-to-employee Role Modelship awards.

PROMOTIONS AS A LEADING INDICATOR FOR ROLE MODELSHIP

Promotions are rare events in everyone's career, and they change the playing field for everyone around you, including your superiors. Promotion is a very complex process that, if done well, can encapsulate all five areas of Role Modelship (i.e., stewardship, fellowship, mentorship, leadership, and sponsorship).

I will never forget when I was promoted to IT director at Autodesk in 2011 and how my boss at the time

What we model during the promotions process says everything about our Role Modelship.

had advocated for my team to be assigned strategic, mission-critical, high-risk, high-reward work.

As a first-generation immigrant from Bulgaria, it meant a lot to me and my family for me to be promoted at such a great company. I came to the United States with two suitcases, mostly full of books and dictionaries, $100 from my parents (their monthly salary—it was all they could afford), and a dream to make the world a better place.

The promotion bar at Autodesk was and still is very high.

Even though I was an adult, my parents gave a verbal thank-you to my boss and my boss's boss.

Three requirements had to be met for my promotion, before the age of AI (see figure 6.4):

Figure 6.4. The three requirements for promotion at Autodesk before AI.

Note that my individual track record (values and results for many years) was the last consideration and the company need was first. There was also a director-level test.

Why?

As Oprah Winfrey says, "A bad apple can ruin the barrel."

I was tested off-site on cognitive, financial, project, and escalation prioritization; executive presentation; and product simulation for two-and-a-half days, working for a simulated global company. I met new employees and managed them for results under pressure with high integrity. An executive coach sat down with me and gave me a grade, discussed my areas for development and blind spots (e.g., my natural tendency to move very fast), and encouraged me to bring people along on the change-management journey.

At the same time, two of my peers were also promoted, and our CIO at the time, Jeff Brzycki, held an all-hands meeting during which he explained the bar used to determine whether we would be promoted. That clarity of communication exemplified the management expectations in the promotion process. Jeff also reminded us what an honor and massive responsibility it was to represent Autodesk to employees, customers, and partners.

I still carry that responsibility with me, because Autodesk will always be one of my homes and a role model company that I channel all the time. The Role Modelship seeds were planted in me by many amazing leaders at Autodesk.

If I can do it, you can do it.

You may need better role models, and hopefully you meet a few on this journey.

What story are you recalling? How did you get promoted? What did it mean to you?

As you get promoted, you have an opportunity to influence the process, communicate the right modelship values, and set the bar for everyone else. Later in this book, you will see how AI will change the role of middle management, redefining scopes suited for certain levels and employee-to-manager ratios for humans and AI agents.

CHANNEL CARNEGIE MELLON'S ROLE MODELSHIP

Katie Cassarly is a director of partnerships and external engagement at the Heinz School of Carnegie Mellon University (CMU), in

Pittsburgh, Pennsylvania. She has a bright smile, positive attitude, and inspiring energy, and she asks great questions on behalf of the students.

When Cassarly and Heinz School Associate Director of Employer Relations and Events Jocelyn Malik visited my office in California, it was a special treat for me to discuss venture capital, key performance indicators, AI, technology architecture, and board expectations with them along with roughly forty promising graduate students.

It was immediately obvious that many students admire Cassarly and Malik as nurturing, inspiring leaders and role models. They asked great questions and guided the Q&A expertly. Many students Cassarly coaches are nervous about networking and unsure how to find a mentor. Together, through a series of virtual workshops, she and I prepared them for the Grace Hopper conference in the fall.

Cassarly provided insights into how we model various types of leadership to encourage students to find inspiration and build confidence. She emphasized that pivotal moments could serendipitously come from people who take the time to mentor you or take a call from you, even when they don't know you. Cassarly's product is her students.

When she reflected on her own leadership, she realized that the way she interacts with her teams is directly modeled after mentors she admired. Cassarly is a terrific facilitator who helps students remove barriers and grow. She works tirelessly to help them build relationships. When they graduate and become alumni, they enrich the CMU network and encourage new students. She finds joy in being able to make introductions between students and alumni, knowing that this effort could make all the difference in one of their lives.

Cassarly also serves as staff advisor for programs and events that help students gain leadership skills, including the Grace Hopper Celebration and Women in Cybersecurity conference. She leverages CMU events as opportunities to expose students to role models and to facilitate the expansion of their viewpoints.

Cassarly completely surprised me when she sent a tiny poetry collection by Emory Hall as a thank-you for my two-hour visit with

--- ✦ ---

A postcard to a role model speaks volumes about your shared values and experiences.

students. Inside the book was a lovely black-and-white card with *Carnegie Mellon* inked in a red frame. I was instantly flooded with memories of my two wonderful years with my husband at graduate school.

When was the last time you surprised someone with a book as a gift?

THE GOLDEN RATIO FOR NUMBER OF ROLE MODELS

A common saying, often misattributed to Plato, states, "The good, of course, is always beautiful, and the beautiful never lacks proportion." Similarly, French scholars Antoine Augustin Cournot and Thomas-Henri Martin described Galileo's method of experimentation in this way: "Measure what is measurable, and make measurable what is not."

The golden ratio, denoted by the Greek letter φ (phi), is a mathematical ratio commonly found in nature, art, design, and architecture. It is approximately equal to 1.618. Architects use the golden ratio to create aesthetically pleasing structures. The proportions of the Great Pyramid of Giza (2560 BC), Parthenon (432 BC), Notre-Dame Cathedral (1345), Taj Mahal (1648), and United Nations (1952) building are examples of structures to which the golden ratio has been applied.

Many artists and painters have employed the golden ratio in their works. Leonardo da Vinci's *Vitruvian Man* and Salvador Dalí's *The Sacrament of the Last Supper* are two notable examples. Architects who used Autodesk software while restoring the Notre-Dame Cathedral in Paris, France, used sophisticated algorithms to ensure the preservation of the great proportions.

Following nature's golden ratio, in an organization of one hundred employees, a minimum of sixty-two should be stabilizer and multiplier role models, and thirty-eight may not be. The most important ratio of role models is found at the vice president level and above, because they set the tone and their habits get amplified through the rest of the organization by network effects.

How many stabilizer and multiplier role models are in your entire organization versus those in positions of vice president or higher? Do you have a wineglass- or an hourglass-shaped organization? In an employee engagement survey, what would be the delta between the number of stabilizer and multiplier role models counted among vice presidents and above versus counted by employees below the vice president level?

You must hear the music within, whether from the strings of a violin or the voice of a role model.

Typically, executives believe that there are many more positive role models than there actually are, which they realize when feedback is collected through focus groups and anonymous surveys. Does your CEO talk about modeling, exemplify the five areas, and encourage the practice?

Role Modelship Example: Simone Biles

- **Sponsorship:** The famous gymnastics champion has used her platform to advocate for fellow gymnasts, particularly survivors of abuse within the sport. Her partnerships with brands like Athleta have allowed her to push for athlete-centered initiatives, with a focus on mental health and empowering young athletes.

- **Leadership:** As the most decorated gymnast of all time, with forty-one Olympic and World Championship medals as of 2025, Biles has set a standard of excellence in gymnastics. At the 2016 Rio Olympics, she led the US team to win four gold medals and one bronze, becoming a global symbol of strength and resilience. Her decision to prioritize her

continued

mental health during the 2021 Tokyo Olympics was a groundbreaking moment in sports that redefined leadership.

- **Mentorship:** Biles frequently shares her experiences, offering advice on handling pressure, overcoming obstacles, and maintaining a positive mindset. She has mentored dozens of young gymnasts at her home gym in Texas, inspiring the next generation with her work ethic and openness about challenges.

- **Fellowship:** She has cultivated a sense of community among gymnasts and athletes, often standing up for her peers and fostering a safer, more supportive environment. She has gained six million followers on Instagram, where she frequently engages with fans and athletes, sharing moments of fellowship and unity.

- **Stewardship:** Biles is committed to using her influence for positive change. She has testified before Congress about the failures of the FBI in handling abuse allegations, showing her commitment to accountability and change in sports governance and improving conditions for millions of young athletes.

ASSESS PRODUCT: NOT FINDING MARKET FIT OR REFERENCE CUSTOMERS?

Let's define our product modelship areas a bit more and then apply the BRAVER change-management process (see figure 6.2) to them. You can use an AI agent to develop a questionnaire using the following definitions.

Product Modelship Areas Defined

Leadership

- *Strategic impact:* Measure strategic goals influenced by the product.

- *Market differentiation:* Evaluate the product's unique selling propositions, competitive analysis scores, and market share growth.

- *Innovation rate:* Assess the number of new features launched per quarter, research and development investment ratios, and innovation adoption rates.

Fellowship

- *User engagement:* Measure daily/weekly/monthly active users, session length, and feature usage frequency.

- *Community building:* Assess community growth rate, the number of active contributors, and user forum engagement levels.

- *Collaboration tools effectiveness:* Evaluate integration usage rates, collaboration feature adoption, and feedback from user surveys.

Stewardship

- *Sustainability and efficiency:* Measure resource utilization efficiency, cost per transaction, system uptime, and environmental impact.

- *Customer satisfaction:* Assess net promoter score (NPS), customer satisfaction score (CSAT), and number of support tickets per product per geographic location.

- *Compliance and security:* Evaluate the number of security incidents, compliance audit scores, time to resolve vulnerabilities, and data breaches.

Mentorship

- *Onboarding effectiveness:* Measure time to first value, user onboarding completion rates, and onboarding feedback scores.

- *Feedback integration:* Assess the percentage of road mapping influenced by user feedback, feedback cycle time, and sentiment analysis of feedback.

Sponsorship

- *Advocacy from key stakeholders:* Measure the number of stakeholder endorsements, executive mentions in product communications, and budget allocations.

- *Customer value stories:* Evaluate the number of published case studies, testimonial count, and customer reference counts and significance.

- *Resource accessibility:* Assess the desire for engineers to work on and enhance the product.

The results of your assessment can be visualized in a spider graph (see figure 6.5).

PRODUCT ROLE MODELSHIP ASSESSMENT

—Stewardship   —Fellowship   —Mentorship   —Leadership   —Sponsorship

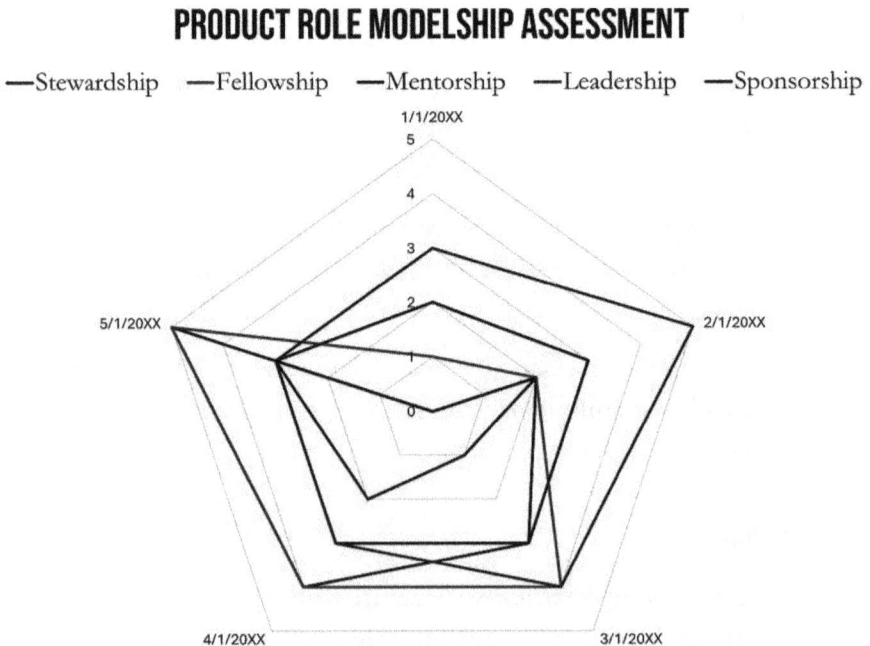

Figure 6.5. A sample Product Role Modelship assessment.

✒ ONE-MINUTE MODELSHIP

Post an example of what a great promotion process looks like in your company on LinkedIn or other social platforms using the #RoleModelship tag.

TAKEAWAYS

- **Regular assessments of human, organizational, and product health** are crucial for sustained success. AI agents can help generate surveys based on criteria.

- The health of these **impacts overall top-line revenue, productivity, creativity, bottom-line profitability, employee and customer engagement, and brand and social impact.**

- **BRAVER** is a Role Modelship change-management framework.

- **Promotions are a leading indicator of Role Modelship** because they encompass all areas defined by BRAVER. The question to ask is not *How do I get promoted?* but rather *How do I add more value to what I do and demonstrate modelship values to other humans, products, or the organization so we can serve our customers better?*

- **The golden ratio** in an organization of one hundred employees is a minimum of sixty-two **stabilizer** and **multiplier role models**. The most important ratio of role models is found at the vice president level and above, because they set the tone for the entire company and their habits get amplified through the rest of the organization by network effects.

PART II

ROLE MODELSHIP HABITS FOR MULTIDISCIPLINARY HUMANS, ORGANIZATIONS, AND PRODUCTS

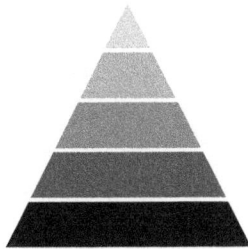

CHAPTER 7

The Rise of the Multidisciplinary Human

*A scientist in his laboratory is not a mere technician;
he is also a child confronting natural phenomena that
impress him as though they are fairy tales.*

—MARIE CURIE

*We have to recognize that a lot of our fundamental
questions about how we design institutions,
how we solve problems, cross disciplines.*

—ELINOR OSTROM

Marketing. Sales. Economics. Construction. Customer success. HR. Entertainment. Product. Technology. Health. Finance. Security. Data. Geography. Parenting. Psychology. Sports. Politics. Military. Government. What do they all have in common?

They are part of our knowledge-management architecture. Knowledge-management architecture is the structured framework that integrates humans and technology to capture, organize, disseminate, and archive knowledge across an organization. How many of the above areas are you an expert in? To channel Marie Curie, "One never notices what has been done; one can only see what remains to be done."

Before the invention of the internet, information scarcity rewarded knowledge hunting and gathering, so humans' brains became wired to seek new knowledge. Before the era of the internet, our individual human knowledge architecture was pretty simple. The following is a hypothetical illustration (leveraging Harvey Balls) of what a human might have known—by no means an exhaustive list (see figure 7.1). The dark areas are knowledge, and the white areas are potential for new learning.

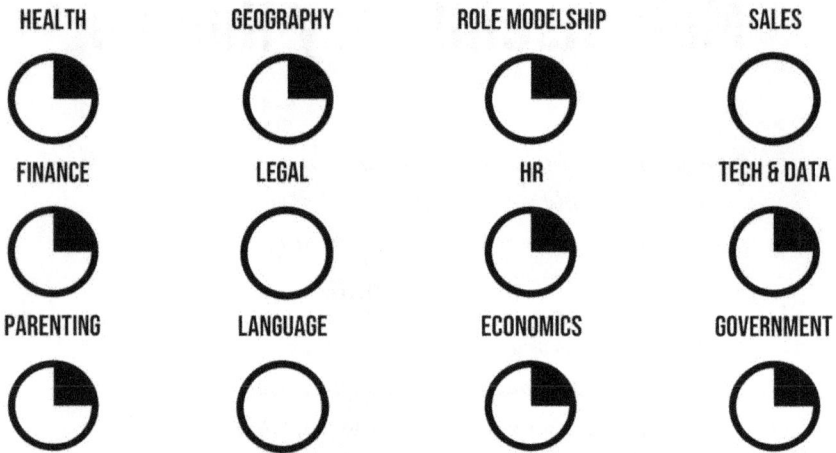

Figure 7.1. Human knowledge before the internet.

We might have gotten deeper in one area by spending days and nights in a library. In some complex disciplines, it might have taken a lifetime to obtain high-level knowledge.

After the invention of the internet, our individual knowledge architecture might have looked like the following illustration because information became much more readily available globally (see figure 7.2).

We might have gotten super deep in one or more areas much faster. In some areas, the size of the pie is pretty well defined, but we humans are explorers, so we create new disciplines and new pies all the time.

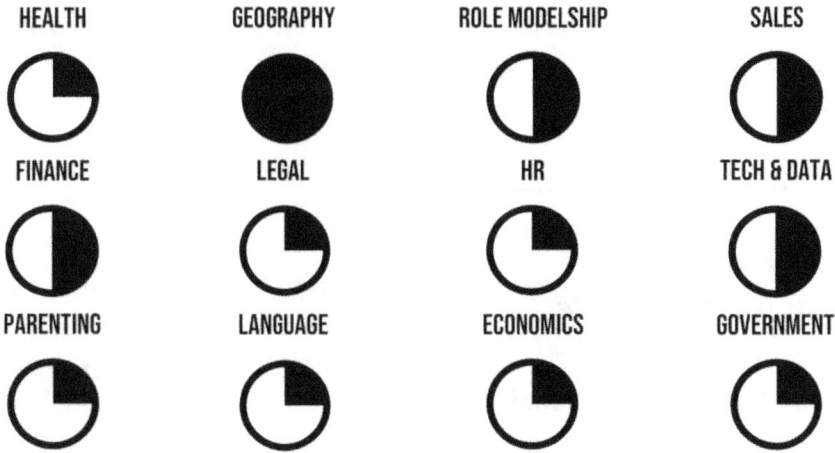

Figure 7.2. Human knowledge after the internet.

MEETING THE MOMENT OF AI DISRUPTION

In the age of AI, we have an unprecedented level of **information abundance**. Your knowledge architecture may look like this, depending on the areas you prioritize and your definition of "done" in acquiring knowledge (see figure 7.3).

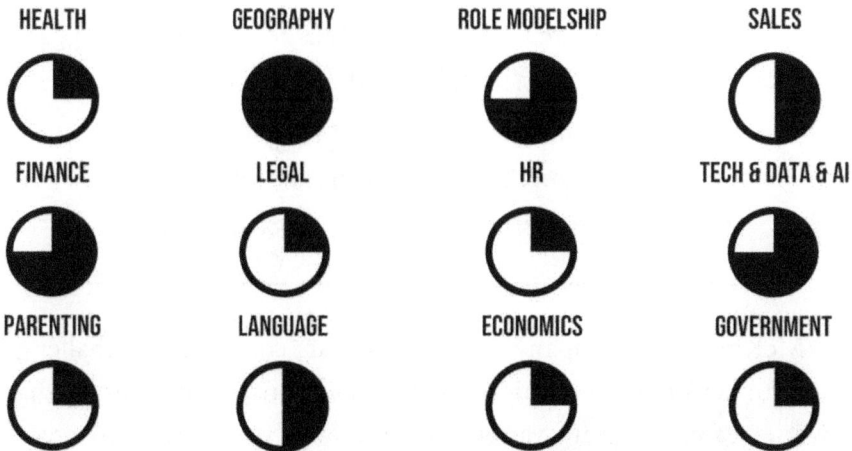

Figure 7.3. Human knowledge after AI.

Information abundance requires pattern recognition for efficient processing. Enter the multidisciplinary human with an insatiable thirst for knowledge.

———— ✦ ————

A multidisciplinary human is like a hydra, with many heads of knowledge, making that person antifragile.

A "multidisciplinary human" is an individual who possesses expertise, skills, and knowledge across multiple disciplines. Rather than being narrowly specialized in one area, a multidisciplinary human integrates diverse perspectives, enabling themselves and others to solve complex problems and adapt to various environments. In his book *Antifragile*, Nassim Nicholas Taleb describes cutting off the head of a hydra and two growing in its place.[1] The same is true for teams and organizations. Many executives, CEOs, investors, and board members have to be multidisciplinary in order to excel in their roles. A multidisciplinary team wins every time.[2]

———————— ✦ ————————

Information scarcity doesn't reward decision-making. It rewards information hunting and gathering. Information abundance rewards aggregation and patterns, accelerating decision-making, velocity, and winning.

McKinsey & Company emphasizes that "complex and challenging problems require multidisciplinary solutions," underscoring that diverse teams integrate various patterns and perspectives to create optimal outcomes and reduce time-to-value.[3]

To meet the moment of disruption, companies are creating chief AI officers to build AI-first multidisciplinary products, platforms, and companies. Chief AI officers are multidisciplinary humans who sit at the intersection of technology, AI, human psychology, data, sales, industry-specific expertise, policy, and (in many cases) other areas, such as investing, human resources, marketing, and business in general.

Clara Shih, for example, is a multitalented trailblazing tech entrepreneur and executive known for her leadership in social media and AI-driven customer engagement. She is the CEO of Salesforce AI and the cofounder and former CEO of Hearsay Systems, a leading customer-engagement platform for financial services. Shih gained recognition for writing *The Facebook Era,* one of the first books to explore social media–transforming businesses. With a strong background in computer science and economics from Stanford, as well as an MBA from Oxford, Shih has served on the boards of companies such as Starbucks, applying her expertise in technology and customer experience.

Multidisciplinary humans are uniquely positioned to meet the moment of AI disruption by combining knowledge across many areas to drive innovation and address complex challenges.

The future belongs to multidisciplinary humans, products, and companies who can categorize, aggregate, and apply synthesis and pattern recognition from one knowledge area to another.

PEOPLE ARE THE BIGGEST OPPORTUNITY AND CHALLENGE IN THE AGE OF AI

At an HMG Strategy event in Silicon Valley, Florin Rotar, former chief AI officer at Avanade, talked about people being the biggest opportunity and the biggest challenge in the age of AI.

As a management consulting company, Avanade started pivoting to AI five years ago. As a CTO before his new chief AI officer role,

Rotar scaled to 500 people in thirty countries. Eighty percent of his time is currently spent on people, change management, and enablement of humans. He talked about three types of AI.

- **Classical AI:** As humans, we are not good at classification, patterns, or prediction unless we have many years of experience across many datasets. AI is much better.

- **Content creation:** AI is getting better now at code, video, text, voice, and plans—capabilities we identify as a core part of our humanity. The progress curve is quite steep.

- **Reason AI:** Continuously running AI, when given a purpose and a defined goal, can take a problem, break it down, and create actions on sub problems. AI does PhD-level math, economy, and physics. It does better than humans; therefore, humans fear for themselves and their kids. Fifty-two percent of Americans fear AI more than they see it as an opportunity.[4]

We need to bridge the trust gap. AI can help us solve difficult humanity problems and challenges in the economy, health, science, and education. Trust drives adoption, and that drives value.

In the age of AI, multidisciplinary humans must embrace their role as role models by leveraging their unique human capabilities while integrating AI to solve complex problems. Doctors, for example, don't need to process paperwork at night to get paid. With patient consent, AI can listen and help automate that part of the process. In 2025, close to $300 billion has been invested in AI by cloud computing hyperscalers like Amazon Web Services, Azure, Google Cloud Platform, IBM, and Oracle.[5] According to Daniel Roth, editor in chief of LinkedIn, 68 percent of the job titles in 2024 didn't exist twenty years ago.[6]

Role Modelship Example: Florin Rotar

- **Sponsorship:** Florin Rotar, former chief AI officer (CAIO) at Avanade, is a leader recognized for his pioneering role in driving the adoption of AI across industries. His influence extends across Avanade, where he has played a vital role in transforming the company's AI strategy, making it a core client component. His sponsorship of AI initiatives is not just about advancing technology but ensuring that it serves humanity positively.[7]

- **Leadership:** Rotar's leadership is evident in his role as CAIO, in which he is responsible for Avanade's AI vision, shaping its application across industries. He was recently recognized by HMG Strategy as a CIAO of the Year. He leads by example, guiding both his team and broader industry discussions about AI's future and ethical considerations. His recognition as one of *Entrepreneur* magazine's Top Ten CTOs to Watch in 2023 also highlights his leadership impact in AI.

- **Mentorship:** Rotar serves as a mentor by fostering the development of AI talent within Avanade and the broader tech community. His international experience allows him to offer valuable insights on navigating the intersection of AI and business. He encourages responsible AI development and ethical leadership.

- **Fellowship:** Rotar focuses on collaboration and empowerment through AI. He speaks at conferences and participates in panel discussions on the importance of humanizing AI to enhance teamwork and creativity rather than fearing its rise.

- **Stewardship:** Stewardship is a key theme in Rotar's career. He advocates for AI maturity and its role in responsible business practices, emphasizing the value of creating sustainable and socially responsible technology.

CHANNEL SUCCESSFUL MULTIDISCIPLINARY ROLE MODELS

The product of educational institutions is multidisciplinary humans. Many years in a row, California's American Canyon Middle School and American Canyon High School have earned top honors from University of California, Davis, in robotics competitions, taking seventeen statewide awards, including one for first place and another eight regional awards, including three for first place.[8]

According to the press release about the event, "'The number of students participating in this competition has grown every year, and their performance has improved every year, too,' said Mary Ann Valles, assistant superintendent for Instructional Services of the Napa Valley Unified School District. 'This competition gives students the chance to display their problem-solving, math, and coding skills'"— and other multidisciplinary competencies, such as fellowship, communication, creativity, and leadership—"'timed against the clock. It isn't easy, and it takes grit.'"[9]

Music also plays a crucial role in education and brain development, especially in enhancing cognitive functions related to math, science, and problem-solving, which are essential for cultivating multidisciplinary humans. Research shows that learning music stimulates neural pathways that also support areas of the brain responsible for spatial-temporal reasoning, which is key for understanding complex mathematical concepts.

Moreover, music's structure—like rhythm and harmony—parallels patterns found in math and science, helping students develop critical thinking and pattern recognition skills. Studies have also shown that musicians tend to perform better in STEM because of enhanced memory, attention, and pattern-application abilities.

> In an interconnected world, the ability to channel role models and cross-apply patterns is more valuable than gold and Bitcoin.

Taylor Swift, for example, has channeled Emily Dickinson's poetry in several ways, notably through thematic depth and literary devices. Both artists explore complex emotions such as love, loss, and introspection with a lyrical elegance that resonates across time. Swift, known for her narrative songwriting that appeals to audiences of all ages, often weaves intricate personal stories into her music, much like Dickinson explored the human condition in her poetry. And similar to Dickinson's introspective verse, Swift's songwriting reflects a sense of emotional vulnerability, personal reflection, and a nuanced understanding of identity. In her *Folklore* and *Evermore* albums, for example, Swift delves into themes of solitude, introspection, and fleeting moments, reminiscent of themes in Dickinson poems.

Swift is a multidisciplinary thinker and role model, blending diverse talents in music, business, and cultural influence to create a far-reaching impact. Her career spans songwriting, performing, and directing, showcasing her ability to master multiple disciplines.

Swift has ventured into filmmaking by directing her own music videos and short films, such as the critically acclaimed *All Too Well: The Short Film*. By combining her artistic creativity with business acumen and social consciousness, she exemplifies how multidisciplinary individuals can lead in various fields while remaining relatable and inspiring to diverse audiences.

Every Role Modelship sand print is the pulse of someone's belief in abundance, echoing the rhythm of hope for humanity.

Just as a singer masterfully orchestrates their music and performances, aligning every note and movement with precision, a choir conductor guides singers to stay in unison across many genres, themes, and languages. Jamie Butler, music teacher and choir conductor at

American Canyon High School, has also made significant contributions as a multidisciplinary thinker and role model in the community. Watching my daughter's choir seamlessly follow his direction reminded me of the metronome effect, in which voices come together to align their timing, values, or even emotions to create a sense of unity and flow. The following is Butler's story.

Role Modelship Example: Jamie Butler

- **Sponsorship:** This high school choir sponsors the artistic and personal development of its students through rigorous vocal training and performance opportunities. Its conductor, Jamie Butler, has raised more than $81,000 in scholarships during the last ten years, benefiting 175 students. This financial support has helped students perform at California statewide competitions and award ceremonies, including at Disneyland, and pursue higher education.

- **Leadership:** Butler leads with an inclusive and collaborative approach. He has fostered an environment where students support each other and work toward career and modelship goals. He was honored as a "Hometown Hero" by the US Navy Blue Angels, an award that recognizes individuals who positively shape youth in their communities. He sat in a US Navy Blue Angels #7 F/A-18F Super Hornet prior to a flight at Travis Air Force Base, California. His leadership has positioned the choir as a respected ensemble within the educational community, earning accolades and awards at California competitions and festivals.[10]

- **Mentorship:** Butler's role as a mentor goes beyond teaching music. He offers personalized guidance to help students hone their vocal skills while building agency, confidence, and knowledge in many areas. He helps students navigate the challenges of high school life and prepares them for future success, discussing difficult topics like racism, bullying, and economic inequality through music. Butler encourages his students to thrive in a high-performance environment, ensuring that they develop as musicians and as responsible, engaged citizens.

- **Fellowship:** Butler fosters a community where students connect through shared experiences in music. Working together as a cohesive group to perform diverse and difficult pieces strengthens the bond between choir members. Nearly one thousand videos of the choir are posted on YouTube, performing songs that engage with themes of social justice and cultural heritage. Some notable examples are the civil rights anthem "We Shall Overcome" and Cyndi Lauper's "True Colors," which emphasizes individuality and acceptance. These performances highlight music as a tool for empathy and social change and are recognized by the Arts Council of Napa Valley.[11]

- **Stewardship:** Butler is committed to the stewardship of the choir's legacy, ensuring that it maintains high standards of musical excellence and continues to be a source of pride for the school, county, and state. His work extends beyond the choir, impacting the broader Napa Valley community.

In recent years, the Nobel Prize has increasingly recognized the significance of multidisciplinary collaboration in scientific breakthroughs. For instance, the 2020 Nobel Prize in Chemistry was awarded to Emmanuelle Charpentier and Jennifer A. Doudna for their development of CRISPR technology, a revolutionary genome-editing method that arose from their partnership across molecular biology and genetics.[12]

Additionally, the 2023 Nobel Prize in Physiology or Medicine honored Katalin Karikó and Drew Weissman for their pioneering work on mRNA technology, which was crucial for COVID-19 vaccines.[13] Their achievements highlight the intersection of biochemistry and immunology, showcasing how interdisciplinary teams can address global health challenges.

---

*Every Role Modelship heartbeat becomes
the sound someone else dances to,
believing they, too, are capable of change,
beauty, and being a bright light.*

In the world of AI, multidisciplinary knowledge is achieved by a general GPT calling another more specialized GPT via microservices architecture.

GROWTH AND ABUNDANCE MINDSETS FUEL MULTIDISCIPLINARY HUMANS

Can you hear mustard seeds growing? Did you know mustard seeds turn into giant trees and forests?

Growth and abundance mindsets are essential fuel for creating multidisciplinary role models, as they empower individuals to embrace challenges, see opportunities, and continually expand their skill sets across various fields.

A growth mindset, as popularized by psychologist Carol Dweck, fosters the belief that abilities can be developed through effort and learning, encouraging role models to push beyond traditional boundaries and acquire expertise in diverse disciplines. This mindset cultivates resilience, innovation, and adaptability.

Similarly, an abundance mindset, popularized by Peter Diamandis, focuses on the idea that opportunities are limitless—enabling multidisciplinary role models to inspire collaboration rather than competition. This mindset allows them to build bridges across fields, showing others that success in one area doesn't preclude growth in another.

Together, the growth and abundance mindsets drive role models to continually evolve, fostering a culture of continuous learning and interdisciplinary innovation.

Innovation happens at the intersection of challenges and opportunities, where role models apply growth and abundance mindsets.

For multidisciplinary professionals to thrive, organizations must foster a culture that values cross-functional collaboration, flexibility, and continuous learning. This means providing opportunities for individuals to work across departments, offering mentorship to bridge gaps between disciplines, and building systems that support interdisciplinary problem-solving. Without a strategic approach to integrating multidisciplinary talent, the potential of these individuals may be underutilized, limiting their impact on innovation and growth.

Disciplined practice is the greatest ally for violinists, painters, multidisciplinary humans, and role models alike.

The future of work depends on embracing multidisciplinary talent and modelship.

―ᴧᴧ―*modelship*―ᴧᴧ―

CHANNEL *THE VALLEY OF THE MOON*

Kennedy Park in Napa is sunny and peaceful on a Sunday in the fall. My dad and I take a walk, and he tells me about new words he's learning in English. He's ninety years old. We joke about whose hearing is worse, his or mine.

At the BMX park, he points to a sign that reads, "How far can two wheels take you?™" and chuckles. "Jack London's *The Valley of the Moon*," he says. "Everyone dreams to live here." My mom has wired his brain to repeat her favorite expression like it's his own.

My mom, Rumi, turned eighty a couple of years ago. She exemplifies the definition of a multidisciplinary human. My parents don't role model for prestige. They do everything because it is the right thing to do for the family. My dad insisted that I buy books with my first cash from picking grapes in the 1980s. He also made sure I wrote new English words one hundred times to wire my brain.

Rumi would like to share her story and hopefully inspire the next generation of dreamers and leaders. She'd like to point out that Sofia, Bulgaria, according to *Forbes* magazine, is one of the best places in Europe to retire. Have you visited?

- **1969** | Rumi graduated college with a civil engineering degree in Sofia, Bulgaria, in a world where her husband didn't allow her to drive a car.

- **1970** | The first computational center, Zelatron, opened in Bulgaria, servicing the construction industry. KRS machines with 1k memory using Assembler were adopted. Rumi went back to work after delivering a girl.

- **1976** | KRS 4200s machines were upgraded to 16k memory. Rumi delivered a boy and continued to work, designing bridges and factories by hand, on paper.

- **1982** | Rumi's kids made garlands from colorful computer punch tape. Rumi sewed children's jackets from the mainframe machine covers that were thrown away.

- **1985–1992** | Bulgaria started making and importing PCs; Microsoft Windows was installed. Rumi learned AutoCAD.

- **1993–1999** | Rumi learned multiple languages: Assembler, Basic, Fortran, PL2, Algol, Pascal, Cobol, C++, various databases. Drafting was automated with Autodesk's AutoCAD.

- **2000** | Rumi visited Autodesk, where her daughter and son-in-law worked, and Rumi started using modern software products.

- **2005–2012** | Rumi retired and joined her three grandkids for student events and holidays at Autodesk. She helped them play with Tinkercad, Pixlr, and so on.

- **2013** | The San Francisco Bay Bridge reopened after a seismic retrofit using Autodesk ACAD. Rumi enjoyed the marvels of US civil engineering and technology.

There is a lot more left in Rumi's story. What bridge are you building today?

———————————— ✦ ————————————

*It's impossible to know
what Jack London's Valley of the Moon
holds for you as a role model.*

TOO LONG; DIDN'T READ (TL;DR) SYNTHESIS METHOD

We live in the most inventive and intensive of times, when AI is forcing us to redefine the future role for humans, organizations, and products. Seventy-one percent of internet traffic is driven by nonhuman identity activity in the form of application programming interfaces (APIs) talking to other APIs and sharing API secrets and keys.[14]

In API land, aggregation methods for pattern recognition typically involve the API composition and aggregation pattern. This pattern allows an API to act as an aggregator by invoking multiple microservices that hold different datasets. The results from these services are then combined through in-memory joins, enabling efficient data retrieval from disparate sources in a single request.[15]

In today's fast-paced digital world, where information overload is a constant challenge, the **TL;DR (too long; didn't read)**[16] written summary has become an essential tool for humans managing vast amounts of content. This practice, which condenses lengthy material into digestible summaries, is particularly useful for multidisciplinary humans.

As AI technology grows, tools like TL;DR summaries help streamline workflows, enabling people to shift their focus from data absorption to high-level problem-solving. Typically, you will see TL;DRs in email, Slack and Microsoft Teams channels, executive communication, and social media.

The value of TL;DR extends beyond efficiency; it supports role models in innovation by allowing leaders to stay informed. When a leader or influencer can swiftly analyze information from disparate sectors, they can offer well-rounded insights, modeling the behaviors of adaptive and agile thinking.

Many companies have adopted the use of TL;DR summaries to cater to the need for concise information. For instance, Medium and LinkedIn often provide TL;DR sections in articles. Companies like Google and Reddit utilize TL;DR summaries to ensure that users quickly grasp the essential information from lengthy posts or discussions. Companies like Autodesk, Salesforce, Airbnb, and Amazon ensure that executives wire their brains and then train their staff to think and write concisely. Additionally, TL;DRs are commonly found in product descriptions, marketing materials, and even customer reviews.[17]

MULTIDISCIPLINARY HUMANS HAVE THE POWER TO ALIGN CONFLICTING OBJECTIVES

The impact of multidisciplinary humans on aligning conflicting objectives is profound, because they leverage diverse perspectives and skills to bridge gaps and foster collaboration.

One effective strategy for aligning conflicting objectives is the ability to wear multiple hats—the **customer hat**, **company hat**, and **team hat**—allowing individuals to see the bigger picture. This perspective encourages a holistic understanding of issues, helping balance the needs of customers, organizational goals, and team dynamics.

Multidisciplinary role models are uniquely positioned to align conflicting company and social objectives. Role models' superpower in pattern recognition is like a heartbeat.

For example, in a team meeting, a role model could leverage the following hat-wearing techniques:

- **Wearing a customer hat:** Could we try engaging customers through surveys or focus groups to better understand their needs and pain points?

- **Wearing a company hat:** Could we try conducting a SWOT (strengths, weaknesses, opportunities, and threats) analysis to identify how our strategic goals align with our core values?

- **Wearing a team hat:** Could we try holding regular brainstorming sessions to encourage open dialogue and idea sharing among team members?

In essence, multidisciplinary role models serve as facilitators in aligning conflicting objectives by employing strategies that emphasize empathy, collaboration, and holistic understanding. Their ability to wear multiple hats enhances problem-solving, ultimately leading to a more innovative and sustainable future.

Are you future ready?

✍ ONE-MINUTE MODELSHIP

Share on LinkedIn or other social media your human, organization, and product Role Modelship examples that are worth modeling.
#RoleModelship

TL;DR (FORMERLY TAKEAWAYS)

- The superpower of **multidisciplinary humans** is their ability to categorize, synthesize, and recognize patterns and apply them to the intersections of different fields.

- The future of work depends on embracing multidisciplinary talent and

-\/\\-*modelship*-\/\\-

- **Role modeling versatility** enables humans to navigate complex challenges and innovate.

- The **TL;DR** summary format is crucial for multidisciplinary humans to efficiently process large volumes of data and identify cross patterns to drive innovation at the intersections.

- Multidisciplinary role models serve as **facilitators in aligning conflicting objectives**. Their ability to wear multiple hats—customer, company, team—enhances problem-solving, ultimately leading to a more innovative and sustainable future.

CHAPTER 8

Embody and Connect

*A leader must know himself and the
times in which he lives.*
—BENJAMIN DISRAELI

*You can never cross the ocean until you have
the courage to lose sight of the shore.*
—CHRISTOPHER COLUMBUS

La Sagrada Familia in Barcelona, Spain, an iconic basilica designed by Antoni Gaudí, is the embodiment of ongoing creation, a role model of faith in progress. There, the unfinished is just as holy as the completed. It shows that abundance and connection come not from perfection but from constant growth. It is a reminder that faith, like art, is alive, ever expanding, and evolving.

Visualize it now: You step in, following me. "Ave Maria" rises softly from the lips of a lone soprano. Her voice floats high above, filling the space like sunlight through stained glass, delicate yet powerful, carrying every note as if it were a whispered prayer. A choir joins her, layer upon layer, their voices weaving together like branches in the wind.

Inside, the columns rise like trees in a sacred forest, their trunks twisting and reaching upward, branches spreading wide to hold the sky. Gaudí didn't just build a church; he envisioned an icon. These pillars are not stone but living things, their veins pulsing with light and faith. You can almost hear the trees breathe, each one standing tall, whispering to each other through the canopy, bending toward the sun that pours through the stained-glass leaves.

At the same time, your sponsor steps into Notre-Dame in Paris. "Hallelujah" soars beneath vaulted ceilings that seem to kiss the heavens themselves. Even now, after a fire scarred her, Notre-Dame stands—a reminder that faith, like stone, can be rebuilt. Abundance lingers in the stories she carries—of triumph, of struggle, of music so grand it shook Paris to its core. She connects us still, in ashes and in light, as voices rise to fill the empty spaces with hope and prayer. Notre-Dame teaches that role modeling is not in the size of the structure but in its ability to rise again.

At the same time, your mentee enters St. Alexander Nevsky Cathedral in Sofia, Bulgaria, one of the largest Eastern Orthodox cathedrals in the world. "Many Years," a traditional Orthodox chant, washes over icons of saints. It is an expression of blessing and a prayer for a long life. This cathedral models tradition, embodying the endurance of faith through centuries of choral hymns that carry history in their melodies. It role models the strength of connection, reminding us that faith is not a solitary act but a shared experience, woven through time and memory, held together by the richness of community.

You, me, your sponsor, and your mentee are all connected through Role Modelship—music, faith, and a shared experience of committing to something greater than ourselves. If you believe in a higher power, you'd be doing that work.

There is strength in numbers. La Sagrada Familia can hold an estimated nine thousand people, Notre-Dame six thousand, St. Alexander Nevsky five thousand. Each of these sacred spaces, filled with thousands, stands as a testament to the power of unity and collective purpose. Just as cathedrals connect people in worship, we are bound by a common Role Modelship mission, supporting one another as we build something lasting and impactful—brick by brick, note by note, person by person.

Michelangelo's *David*, a marble achievement that inspires many, also illustrates the beauty of unfinished art. In its raw state, it represented potential and possibility. The process of chiseling away at the stone to reveal the form within reflects the idea that the act of creation, including the struggles and discoveries along the way, is valuable and holy. Who's to say that if Michelangelo didn't take risks, he would have painted the Sistine Chapel floor instead of the ceiling?

As we explore the majestic architecture and spiritual significance of iconic churches, it's clear that these monuments embody a profound sense of purpose and connection. Just as each stone in these sacred buildings

> *If your kind words, music, colors, and actions inspire others to believe, embody, and connect, you're a role model.*

contributes to a larger narrative of progress and community, so do the missions of modern companies that inspire and connect.

LEVERAGE MISSIONS AS ROLE MODELS TO EMBODY AND CONNECT

LEGO. Minecraft. Olympic Games. Roblox. Tinkercad. Instagram. Spotify. LinkedIn. Slack. Zoom. Google. Airbnb. Apple. Red Cross. TED. United Nations. Meta. X. Coca-Cola. Disney.

What do they have in common? They all embody and connect as part of their missions. Let's explore how.

LEGO's mission is "to inspire and develop the builders of tomorrow." At its core, LEGO provides physical building blocks that encourage connecting pieces to build a world through imaginative play. Each piece represents endless possibilities, allowing humans of all ages to create unique models. LEGO has built a vibrant global community of grown-up fans, known as AFOLs (Adult Fans of Lego), who share their creations online and attend conferences.

Any six standard two-by-four LEGO bricks can be combined in 915 million different ways. The length of the number of LEGO bricks sold each year would travel the earth five times.[1] Imagine that impact.

Coca-Cola's mission whispers like a warm breeze, inviting us to "refresh the world in mind, body, and spirit." It's a promise wrapped in the fizz of joy, sparkling with the hope of shared moments that lift our hearts and quench our thirst. Each sip becomes a celebration, a little burst of happiness bubbling up from within. This isn't just about a drink; it's about the laughter around a table, the clinking of glasses, the stories shared on hot summer days.

If every drop of Coca-Cola produced were put in eight-ounce bottles and lined up end to end, they would make a round trip to the moon and back more than two thousand times.[2] It's estimated that 94 percent of the world's population can identify Coca-Cola's logo, making it more recognizable than the word *hello*.[3]

At Disney, the mission is simple yet profound: "To entertain, inform, and inspire people around the globe through the power of unparalleled storytelling." You see, storytelling is at the heart of everything we do; it's the magic that connects us all. Each story we create is a spark of imagination, and adventures await at every corner. You believe in the power of creativity to ignite hope and bring people together, right?

The best time to plant the seeds of a mission, a mustard forest, and a role model was before AI. The second-best time is now.

Disney World's Magic Kingdom could hold more than eighty-one NFL football fields, but it's only a small part of Walt Disney World Resort, which spans forty square miles—about the same size as San Francisco.[4] Everything Disney role models has an impact.

A mission statement serves as a role model by encapsulating the core values, vision, and purpose of an organization, like a compass guiding a ship in uncharted waters. It plants seeds for more humanity days and a better tomorrow.

At Disney parks, every employee is a "cast member." This concept reflects the company's belief that each employee plays a vital role in the storytelling and guest experience, much like an actor's mission in a performance. By wiring employees to show up differently and act as "cast members," Disney creates magical moments for guests, reinforcing its role modeling of service and entertainment.

HOW TO LEVERAGE THESE MISSIONS IN YOUR INDUSTRY

Applying the missions of Lego, Coca-Cola, and Disney as role models to the software and financial industries, for example, can help you drive product innovation. Here's how each mission can be utilized in these sectors:

LEGO: "To inspire and develop the builders of tomorrow"

- **User-centric design:** In the financial software space, LEGO can inspire companies to create more user-friendly applications. By involving users in the design process, developers can create financial tools that enhance financial literacy.

- **Prototyping and agile development:** LEGO's building blocks can serve as a metaphor for modular software development, encouraging teams to adopt services-oriented architectures.

Coca-Cola: "To refresh the world in mind, body, and spirit"

- **Financial wellness:** Coca-Cola's mission can inform the development of financial tools that promote economic health. This could involve creating apps that help users budget, save, and invest wisely.

- **Community engagement platforms:** Inspired by Coca-Cola's community-building initiatives, software companies can develop platforms that connect users for financial education, mentorship, and sponsorship.

Disney: "To entertain, inform, and inspire people around the globe through the power of unparalleled storytelling"

- **Storytelling:** Financial applications can integrate engaging narratives that guide users through complex financial concepts, making learning more accessible and enjoyable.

- **Gamification:** By leveraging Disney's storytelling techniques, financial institutions can create gamified learning experiences that teach users about saving, investing, and budgeting.

There are three ways to avoid criticism: channel nobody, model nothing, and be no one.

"All of our dreams can come true," Walt Disney said, "if we have the courage to pursue them." All you need is a suitcase and a dream.

LEVERAGE ALL INTELLIGENCE IN THE AGE OF AI

In the age of AI, leveraging all types of human intelligence—emotional, social, creative, functional, and analytical—is crucial to maximize the technology's potential and ensure its ethical application. AI excels in processing massive amounts of data, identifying patterns, and optimizing processes at speeds far beyond human capacity. But it still lacks the nuanced understanding, empathy, and moral judgment that define human intelligence.

Wouter Born, general partner at Born Capital, shared a story on LinkedIn about Nextdoor's CEO becoming Open AI's CFO, who has inspired many who want to leverage all intelligence.

2018: CEO of Nextdoor.

2024: CFO of OpenAI, a $157 billion AI giant.

CEOs are becoming CFOs.

Sarah Friar is a standout in tech and finance.

—No CPA.

—No traditional accounting background.

As Nextdoor's CEO, she led exponential growth.

Now, at OpenAI, she is steering its rapid expansion in AI research and products.

Her ability to drive growth and lead large-scale operations shows two things:

1. Strategic leadership can redefine industries.

2. Strategic leadership can reshape the CFO role.

It's possible to become a CFO without accounting credentials.

This shift shows the growing need for CFOs with strategic vision.

And I see a trend of CEOs becoming CFOs.[5]

Integrating diverse talents enhances everyone's and AI's ability to serve society equitably, because different forms of human intelligence bring insights that can prevent bias and foster innovation beyond pure efficiency.

DOES YOUR BOSS NEED A BETTER ROLE MODEL?

I've coached hundreds of CXOs, CTOs, CIOs, CDIOs, CROs, CMOs, CFOs, CHROs, CEOs, directors, managers, and employees. It's an alphabet soup. We've done therapy sessions about humans who are detractor role models and need to show up differently. You will always get a lot more from a person with honey than vinegar.

In the future, there may be wearables, apps, devices, glasses, and chips that will help us by reading our heart rate or facial expressions in a conflict situation and offering prompts to model the right values. Calling on innovative product managers to build them. The best ideas often start in Jira.

SOBER FEEDBACK DISCUSSION FRAMEWORK

The objective of the **SOBER feedback discussion framework** is to de-escalate an emotional response and trigger engagement of the logical parts of the brain. This framework can be leveraged for coaching humans—including your boss—for higher performance, better culture, and better results. SOBER stands for situation, observation, benefits, examples, and results (see figure 8.1).

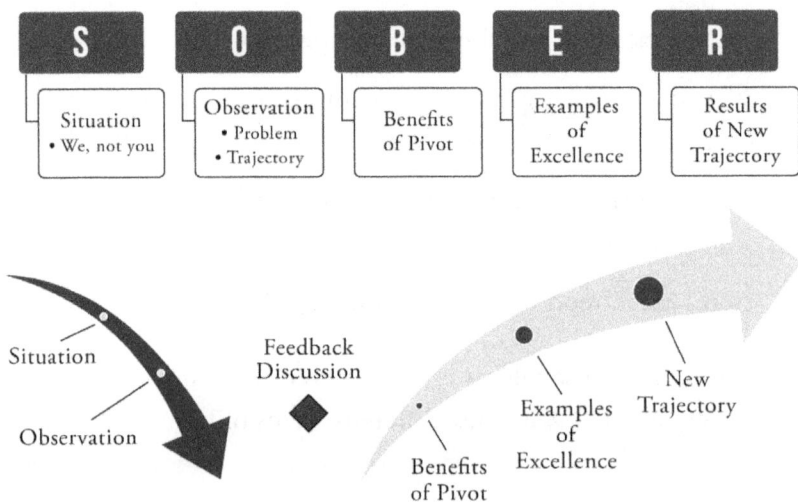

Figure 8.1. The SOBER feedback discussion framework.

This feedback and discussion framework is crucial to role modeling because it provides a positive, structured approach to learning and growth. In a world where AI is a giant mirror of our values and behaviors, the SOBER framework can also be leveraged to have a discussion with AI about the values and behaviors it is demonstrating.

Managing challenging bosses is one of the main ways role models have a positive impact on everyone around them.

Let's pretend your boss is mad about the quality of a software product demo you're about to deliver to a major client. Your deliverable reflects negatively on your boss's reputation, and your company may lose $1 million in potential recurring revenue, but your boss has no real skills in giving constructive feedback or knowing how to fix the software demo. If you don't want this situation to keep repeating itself, you must be the role model and help your boss learn this new framework, **SOBER** (see table 8.1).

Table 8.1. Examples of How to Use the SOBER Framework

		WHAT TO SAY TO YOUR BOSS WHEN EMOTIONS ARE HIGH
S	Situation	What I'm hearing you say is that *we* have a situation where …
O	Observation	My nonjudgmental observation is that the problem is X and our trajectory is Y …
B	Benefits of pivot	Would it be beneficial if we tried a pivot?
E	Examples of modelship success and excellence	Could you please give us two or three specific examples of what Role Modelship success and excellence looks like?
R	Results of new trajectory for value	Please help us understand what results you think will put us on a new trajectory and create greater value.

EVOLVING DEFINITION OF ROLE MODELSHIP IN AN AI WORLD

Historically, role models have been the pillars upon which individuals and societies build their ideals, ethics, and aspirations. Whether it was the courage of Nelson Mandela, the innovations of Steve Jobs, or the humanitarianism of Mother Teresa, role models have shaped many generations.

Today, we stand at the intersection where human potential meets machine intelligence. The cheese has moved. Are you finding new cheese? Here are some role models who are.

Gary Kasparov, one of the greatest chess players in history, faced off against IBM's Deep Blue chess-playing supercomputer in 1997, marking a turning point in both the world of chess and artificial intelligence. He advocated for humans and computers to collaborate rather than compete. In his hybrid approach, a human player, guided by AI, could achieve a level of play superior to that of either a human or a machine alone.

Chief marketing officers (CMOs) are increasingly using virtual agents for outbound and inbound marketing. The virtual agents, which have names like Chris, Chad, Dorothy, and Merrett, as well as email addresses, create marketing content and campaigns and are considered team members. It will become increasingly difficult to tell if you're communicating with a human or an AI agent.

The ratio of sales operations people to sales account executives used to be 1:10 and now it may be 1:20, thanks to AI.[6] That's a new type of Role Modelship. In the future, bots will be selling to bots buying bots.

Keanu Reeves as Neo ("the One") in *The Matrix* embodies the archetype of the reluctant hero, awakening to the harsh realities of a controlled world and rising to challenge it. His journey reflects themes of self-discovery, resilience, and the quest for truth as he moves from a state of confusion to one of empowerment. Neo's character resonates with audiences because he represents the power of choice and transformation. Through watching, we connect deeply with the idea that true freedom lies not in living an ordinary life but in facing one's fears and embracing one's destiny.

As a role model, you are Neo—you're "the One" who can significantly alter the sequence of chess moves and the course of events through values, grit, choice, skill, and networks.

Lil Miquela (@lilmiquela), a virtual influencer created by the start-up Brud, has more than three million Instagram followers. Blurring the lines between reality and fiction, human and machine, Lil Miquela has graced the covers of fashion magazines, collaborated with major brands, and even addressed social issues like racism and climate change.[7]

Besides Lil Miquela, several other digital characters have gained attention as virtual influencers, digital assistants, or even interactive brand ambassadors. Here's a look at a few:

- **Sam:** Created by Soul Machines for the New Zealand government, Sam was an AI-driven digital assistant aimed at answering common public inquiries. Sam could interpret emotions in real time and offer information on government services.

- **Sarah:** Another Soul Machines creation, Sarah is a digital assistant developed to help employees with human resources inquiries. Designed for a corporate environment, Sarah provides a humanlike, empathetic face for interacting in standard company processes.

- **Sophia the Robot:** Sophia by Hanson Robotics is another iconic AI-driven humanoid robot, with lifelike facial expressions and conversational skills. Sophia is a public figure in the digital world, known for engaging in interviews and participating in tech forums.

- **FN Meka:** Created by the record label Factory New, FN Meka is a virtual influencer and AI-powered rapper that has a following on social media, creating music and engaging with fans in ways similar to Lil Miquela.

- **Shudu:** Shudu Gram, billed as the "world's first digital supermodel," was created by visual artist Cameron-James Wilson. Shudu is fully virtual but has modeled for major brands and magazines, blurring the line between physical and digital in fashion.

The definition of a role model in the AI age changes and encourages us to reconsider what we value in our role models. Is it their physical presence, their personal struggles, or their ability to communicate values that resonates with us on a deep level?

ROLE MODELSHIP AND THE ETHICAL IMPLICATIONS OF AI

If an AI can do all of these things, does it diminish the role of human experience? Or does it challenge us to elevate our standards, to seek Role Modelship that embodies the synthesis of human wisdom and machine precision?

We need role models who are not just skilled in their fields but also capable of navigating the ethical complexities of AI. Leaders born in an AI world must understand the power of algorithms and data yet remain deeply rooted in human values. The next generation of role models will learn not only how to use AI but also how to question it, how to think critically about the role it plays in their lives, and how to ensure that it enhances rather than diminishes our humanity.

Carnegie Mellon University (CMU) is known for its STEAM innovation and research. With more than 15,818 students across its multiple campuses, CMU represents 117 countries and employs more than 1,400 faculty members.[8] With an endowment exceeding $3.2 billion, CMU has invested heavily in research, supporting a wide range of projects in robotics, artificial intelligence, and public policy.[9] Below is the role modeling profile of Stuart Evans, PhD, who deserves credit for asking his students to configure themselves for multiple futures.

Role Modelship Example: Stuart Evans, PhD

- **Sponsorship:** Carnegie Mellon University distinguished service professor Stuart Evans embodies innovation by mentoring students and professionals, emphasizing the application of "super flexibility"— a term he uses to describe a broad adaptability in career trajectories. His coauthored book, *Super-Flexibility for Knowledge Enterprises*, explores dynamic adaptability and innovation strategies for businesses in today's rapidly changing world, emphasizing the need for organizational and leadership flexibility. He demonstrates Carnegie Mellon's multidisciplinary approach, helping students engage with emerging fields like AI and humanoid robotics. He has sponsored initiatives that encourage the exploration of blockchain and human-centric technology solutions, such as Persona AI.

- **Leadership:** Evans exhibits leadership by guiding teams to tackle complex multidisciplinary challenges. His leadership extends to his passion for building humanoid robots and a vision of redefining human–machine interaction.

continued

- **Mentorship:** Evans mentors students, in both academia and the business world, through his partnership with venture capital firm Mayfield by emphasizing the importance of preparing for multiple futures. He plays a pivotal role at Carnegie Mellon, where he advises graduate students and researchers. He teaches innovative courses, in which he encourages start-up creation and venture capital engagement. He imparts the belief that effective mentorship requires constantly reshaping one's own perspective to guide others through unknowns.

- **Fellowship:** Evans fosters fellowship by promoting collaboration across disciplines. His roles at Carnegie Mellon, HMG Strategy, and Mayfield place him at the forefront of creating community around groundbreaking innovations and connecting people and ideas.

- **Stewardship:** Evans demonstrates stewardship through his work in building a responsible and ethical future for AI technology. His leadership at Carnegie Mellon has ensured that students and the projects he touches remain centered on the idea that technology should serve humanity. Stewardship, for Evans, involves guiding projects toward long-term impact, such as the sustainable development of AI and the exploration of humanoid robotics.

ONE-MINUTE MODELSHIP

Please share on LinkedIn how you have mapped your organizational values to the Role Modelship formula (i.e., stewardship, fellowship, mentorship, leadership, and sponsorship) in the age of AI.

#RoleModelship

TL;DR

- **The unfinished** is just as artistic and holy as the completed, as evidenced by La Sagrada Familia and Michelangelo's *David.*

- Just as cathedrals connect people in worship, **we are bound by a common Role Modelship mission** as we build something lasting and impactful—brick by brick, note by note, person by person.

- A **company mission statement** serves as a role model by encapsulating the core values, vision, and purpose of an organization, like a compass guiding a ship in uncharted waters.

- The **SOBER (situation, observation, benefits, examples, results)** discussion framework can be leveraged to de-escalate emotional responses and coach humans—including your boss—for higher performance, better culture, and better results.

- Role models are not just those who achieve greatness through their abilities but **those who can adapt, evolve, and integrate new paradigms** into their lives, making the world better for everybody.

- **The next generation of role models** will learn not only how to use AI but also how to question it, how to think critically about the role it plays in their lives, and how to ensure that it enhances rather than diminishes our humanity.

CHAPTER 9

Teach and Coach for Multiple Futures

There's nothing training cannot do. Nothing is above its reach.
It can turn bad morals to good; it can destroy bad principles
and recreate good ones; it can lift man to angelship.

—MARK TWAIN

Our son has a reconstructed hip and metal bracing held together with nine screws. He was born with Legg-Calvé-Perthes, a condition more common in twins. We count our blessings every day.

When he was thirteen, he had a twelve-hour surgery to alleviate chronic pain and stiffness in his hip and thigh, which led to a serious limp. Words can't describe the pain he went through or how helpless we as parents felt when our kid suffered physically and emotionally.

Watching our son take those first steps after surgery was like seeing hope itself come to life. After the procedure, Mohammad Diab, MD—a compassionate, world-renowned orthopedic surgeon at University of California, San Francisco Health who has dedicated his career to children's musculoskeletal health—stood by our son's side, guiding each step with patience, empathy, and precision. As our son, still in a lot of pain, tentatively placed weight on both legs, Dr. Diab encouraged him, gently adjusting his hips and reassuring him that he could walk again. Dr. Diab coached him physically and emotionally.

It was Dr. Diab's unwavering belief in our son's potential that gave our son the courage to face each step forward. He learned how to rise beyond his limitations, with confidence that no metal or surgical procedure alone could provide. In those moments, my husband and I could see our son's resilience grow, his trust in his doctor unwavering, and his future—one in which he'd walk, run, and dream—become a reality. There really are angels among us.

After his surgery, our son embraced his nine screws with a mix of pride and determination, just like a superhero learning to navigate newfound powers.

Seeing the world through both career and Role Modelship windows for social change is like learning to walk on two legs.

THE MAGICAL POWERS OF TEACHERS AND COACHES

In the movie *Dead Poets Society*, Robin Williams plays an unconventional English teacher who inspires his students to "seize the day," pushing them to find their voices and pursue their dreams, demonstrating leadership. In *The Karate Kid*, Mr. Miyagi mentors a bullied teenager, Daniel, not only in martial arts but also in patience, discipline, and respect, which profoundly changes his life. In *Remember the Titans*, Coach Herman Boone (Denzel Washington) unites a racially divided football team, teaching his players lessons on fellowship, sponsorship, brotherhood, equality, and courage, both on and off the field.

Many executives, like me, have coaches—sometimes multiple coaches if they can afford it and consider it valuable on the journey to being an inspirational role model. Having a coach doesn't make you weak; it gives you another perspective and different frameworks, helps you see around blind corners, and opens a gateway to a network of resources. If you remember from a previous chapter, you = you × role model 1 × role model 2 × role model 3 × role model 4. One of these role models is aways a coach, even if they don't know you look up to them.

In the movie *Coach Carter*, a basketball coach (portrayed by Samuel L. Jackson) teaches his players about the importance of academics, discipline, and respect, instilling values that extend beyond sports. In the film *Akeelah and the Bee*, a teacher and a spelling coach help a young girl from South Los Angeles discover her talent for spelling, opening doors to new opportunities and confidence.

A candle loves nothing more than to light another candle.

Teachers and coaches often talk about their profession as a calling or vocation. A human doesn't choose a vocation. For many role models, Role Modelship is a calling. They had no choice in the matter. Their life would be unrecognizable unless they pursued this line of showing up differently in influencing the next generation of role models. Detractor Role Modelship, when committed over and over, hardens humans into a lower level of demo life.

COACHING INNOVATION

In an ever-evolving world, coaching innovation habits is essential for individuals who seek to configure themselves for multiple futures.

As noted by the *Harvard Business Review* Future of Business Event, the ability to innovate is not merely a function of creativity but also a habit that can be cultivated through intentional practice and reflection.[1] As you saw in an earlier chapter, my goal is to pivot you from an event-driven life to a happier and more fulfilled modelship-driven life.

Bill O'Connor, founder of the Innovation Genome Project, is a pattern-recognizing, multidiscipline human and a multiplier role model.

His innovation method, which analyzed 650 innovations, has been applied by companies like Nike, Cisco, Intel, Procter & Gamble, and Lockheed Martin.[2] The process itself is designed to serve as a force multiplier and focuses on seven key questions fostering creative thinking and encouraging sponsorship of new ideas:

1. What could we look at in a new way?

2. What could we use in a new way?

3. What could we move, changing its position in space or time?

4. What could we interconnect in a different way?

5. What could we alter or change?

6. What could we make bigger or smaller?

7. What could we substitute?

O'Connor's focus is on sustainable, long-term success and urging leaders to not just sponsor but actively guide their teams in rethinking product and service models.

My teams and I have been leveraging this mindset since the 2000s. Once you wire your brain to see the world this way, the universe sends you creativity, patterns, and new ideas all the time. Innovation helps role models scale their multidisciplinary approach to networking and applying patterns.

SEIZING OPPORTUNITIES IN MULTIPLE FUTURES

During his twenty-five-year career in Silicon Valley—including stints as innovation strategist for Autodesk and founder and partner at his own innovation agency, InnoVista—O'Connor has applied his leadership and sponsorship methodology to help foster ecosystems that support employees at all levels.

He applies the Innovation Genome to help organizations measure and improve their innovation performance by leveraging AI. The product uses a systematic approach, allowing companies to continuously assess their innovation potential.[3]

Many listen to the words of role models. Few hear the beat, and even fewer have the courage to advocate for systemic change.

When I asked O'Connor for an interview, he was excited to share his insights and experiences, reflecting on the transformative role of mentorship in his life and career.

Q: What role modeling habits would you load into the operating system of a humanoid?

A: *First, it's essential to recognize how influenced we are by those around us. The idea that we are the average of the five people we spend the most time with highlights the subconscious impact our environment has on our decisions. This concept emphasizes the need to pay attention to our role models, both consciously and subconsciously. Expanding our definition of role models is crucial; instead of only looking up to famous figures, we should seek out individuals who excel in areas that are relevant to us—whether it's health, academics, or presentation.*

When we realize how utterly influenceable *we are as humans, we can shift the idea of role modeling from the periphery of our minds—where it likely resides for most—to a more central position in our thoughts and actions. Instead of only occasionally emulating famous individuals we respect or successful people we know, we should acknowledge that most everyone we have consistent contact with can serve as a role model in some capacity.*

Robert Cialdini's books Influence: The Psychology of Persuasion *and* Pre-Suasion: A Revolutionary Way to Influence and Persuade, *for example, delve into the subtle techniques that shape our decision-making processes. In* Influence, *Cialdini identifies six key principles—reciprocity, commitment, social proof, authority, liking, and scarcity—that explain how people can be influenced to change their behavior.*

The Role Modelship habit I would recommend for our humanoid operating system is to adopt an expansive view of what constitutes a role model. To act on this new viewpoint, we should actively reach out to a diverse range of individuals, learning from their experiences and insights. By doing so, we can cultivate a richer understanding of role modeling that transcends the traditional notions of famous figures.

Q: Can you give a practical example of applying these habits?

A: *Absolutely. In the professional realm, my first sponsor was Garrett White, an executive at Houghton Mifflin, who supported me on an innovative project early in my career. Another key sponsor was Carl Bass, a former CEO of Autodesk, who brought me on as his speechwriter. This partnership led to our collaboration on more than 200 projects over a decade.*

One effective approach is to actively seek mentors in specific domains. Keeping a document outlining role models and what we can learn from them also helps us stay organized and focused on growth. This could involve noting down successful habits, techniques, or strategies employed by those role models.

Q: What about diversity in role models? How important is that?

A: *Diversity is vital. We often gravitate toward role models who are similar to us, but expanding our horizons to include people from different backgrounds and experiences can be incredibly enriching. I've always tried* *to include role models who are younger, women, or from different fields, which helps challenge my biases and opens up new perspectives and ideas that I might not have considered otherwise.*

Q: Who have been your most significant role models?

A: *My parents have had the greatest influence on my intellectual curiosity and joy in life. They modeled a deep love of learning and humor. Additionally, figures like Ralph Waldo Emerson, the great philosopher and essayist; Tom Peters, the legendary business thinker; W. B. Yeats, the Irish poet; and Benjamin Franklin, who has long been a role model of mine, have all inspired me in various ways. In the academic world, my college theater professor and director, Gordon Wickstrom, PhD, significantly shaped my understanding of creativity and living a fulfilling life.*

Reflecting on the Golden Rule, I realize that many of my role models exemplify its essence: They treat others with empathy and act with a genuine willingness to support others. The Golden Rule is a universal ethical principle often phrased as "Do unto others as you would have them do unto you."

Q: What's the most important lesson you've learned from them?

A: *One key takeaway is the importance of living with joy and opti-mism. As Emerson emphasized, being courageous in the way you live your life and explore new ideas can lead to personal fulfillment and professional success. This mindset was particularly beneficial when I transitioned from the East Coast to San Francisco during the dot-com revolution, a time filled with energy and innovation.*

Q: If you could have a conversation with anyone, who would it be?

A: *I would love to speak with Ralph Waldo Emerson for insights into his philosophy, especially his views on individuality and self-reliance. Additionally, having a chat with Paul McCartney would be fascinating, considering my background in music and my admiration for his creativity and impact on culture.*

Q: If you could model only one thing, what would that be?

A: *If I could role model just one thing, it would actually be a three-part approach, especially for young people: joy, individuality, and resilience.*

First, I would advocate living with joy, energy, and optimism—not just because it enhances personal happiness but because this mindset can be incredibly powerful for career and work success. Second, I'd emphasize the value of actively creating your own path. This means following your instincts, passions, and even whims to carve a unique direction, as Robert Frost conveyed in his poem about choosing "the road less traveled." This idea is crucial because a fulfilling life often stems from the courage to pursue your own way, despite others' expectations. Finally, I'd model the importance of persistence, grit, and resilience. Nobel Prize winners, for instance, often display a positive stubbornness in their dedication to ideas, refining and defending them over time.

Q: Lastly, what habits should the next generation of role models adopt?

A: *Utilizing AI to channel the wisdom of admired figures can be incredibly beneficial. Coaching for innovation equips people to configure themselves for multiple futures. It helps individuals cultivate a mindset open to experimentation, encouraging them to embrace uncertainty rather than avoid it.*

Nobel laureates credit their success to mentors, collaborators, or even serendipity.

Paul Daugherty, Accenture's CTO, has been vocal about the evolving role of artificial intelligence in the business world. In his view, AI is transforming from a tool that people had to adapt to into one that adapts to people, enabling greater human potential. He notes that the future of technology is about creating radically human solutions—in which technology works for people, amplifying their capabilities and changing the way we work, collaborate, and live. In a World Economic Forum series, Daugherty emphasized that the key to future business success is not the algorithms themselves but how companies use these technologies to enhance human talent and create value.[4]

APPLYING INNOVATION
What Could Be Made Bigger?

Leveraging the Innovation Genome principle of "what could be made bigger" is the following illustration of our future Role Modelship architecture (see table 9.1). This will allow people, organizations, and products to pivot from one role model (e.g., Steve Jobs) to a network of role models (e.g., Apple) in all knowledge areas of our lives.

**Table 9.1. Pivoting from One Role Model
to a Network of Role Models**

CHANGE FROM	CHANGE TO
Role Modelship with one person in mind (e.g., Steve Jobs)	Role Modelship network of human subject-matter experts, institutions, companies, AI-powered products, digital role models, and humanoids

What Could We Look at in a New Way?

The creators of Poker Power, an app that advocates applying the card game skills to life, know that there's a strong connection between success, money ownership, and playing every hand like a winning poker player.[5] They focus on teaching women to compete and succeed in business, finance, and life in a fun, supportive, and safe-to-fail environment.

Just like we're on a mission to empower one million acts of Role Modelship, they're on a mission to teach one million of their users how to negotiate, assess risk, and make decisions with confidence—from the classroom to the boardroom and at every seat in between.

Poker Power emerged from the vision of self-made billionaire Jenny Just, who in 2020 cofounded the brand alongside her daughter, Juliette Hulsizer. What started as a simple experiment—gathering Hulsizer's friends and their moms for a series of poker lessons—turned into a remarkable discovery: The game of poker could help women build confidence and play to win. Poker Power's work was highlighted in a 2024 *CBS Mornings* segment featuring an event at the University of Chicago.

Vanessa Selbst, the only woman to ever reach the number-one ranking in the world on the Global Poker Index, once won a hand without looking at her cards. In a televised tournament, Selbst famously used a strategy called a blind bluff, in which she relied entirely on her understanding of the situation, her opponents' tendencies, and her table presence to outplay them.[6]

Martin Luther King Jr. defined power as "the ability to achieve purpose. It is the strength required to bring about social, political, or economic changes."[7] Words have amazing power.

What Could We Move, Changing Its Position in Space or Time?

At Autodesk, as a leadership team, we often talked about the power of a comma. Yes, that's right, a single comma.

Where does the comma belong in "fail fast forward?"

The phrases "fail, fast forward" and "fail fast, forward" both suggest learning and growth from failure but have nuanced differences in focus and application. If you're curious, ask AI.

Transitioning from the concept of applying the Innovation Genome, which highlights the intricate interplay of diverse factors driving innovation within organizations, we can see how these principles directly apply to leadership roles in consulting.

Sarah Katz, president of Spaulding Ridge, guides clients through complex challenges, ensuring that innovative solutions are effectively implemented.

Role Modelship Example: Sarah Katz

- **Sponsorship:** Sarah Katz is a multiplier role model and has demonstrated a strong commitment to sponsorship through her advocacy for women in tech. As president of Spaulding Ridge, one of her initiatives was the creation of WomenElevate, a program aimed at hiring and maintaining a workforce that is at least 40 percent female. This initiative reflects her dedication to diverse voices and giving women equal opportunities in a traditionally male-dominated industry.

- **Leadership:** With over a decade of experience in the Software as a Service (SaaS) space, Katz has led the implementation of cloud applications across various sectors, from enterprise to start-ups. Her international experience—having lived in Chicago, San Francisco, Seattle, London, and now New York—provides her with a unique global perspective on business transformation. As president of Spaulding Ridge since September 2021, she has cultivated a leadership style that integrates financial expertise and operational efficiency.

- **Mentorship:** Katz is deeply committed to mentorship, particularly through her role in advancing gender equality in the tech industry. Her efforts with WomenElevate and her involvement in the Silicon Valley Blockchain Society showcase her dedication. She also mentors internal teams, encouraging them to enhance their skills.

- **Fellowship:** She fosters a culture of collaboration and inclusion at Spaulding Ridge. She leverages her international experience to create a fellowship in which team members can connect across borders and work toward common goals.

- **Stewardship:** Katz's stewardship is evident in her long-term vision for the future of both Spaulding Ridge and the SaaS industry. She is a proponent of responsible and ethical business practices while applying AI in product and operations.

THE POWER OF A CRISIS

You can predict a role model's scalability and versatility by observing how willing and capable they are in dealing with a crisis. In a crisis, humans show up based on what they observe is rewarded modeling in the micro family, organizational, product, and community culture.

But not every crisis is created equal. In a crisis or perceived crisis, many detractor role models also show up. Research by Peter Salovey, Alia Crum, and Shawn Achor indicates that humans who think of pressure as debilitating and avoid it at all costs either overcorrect or under-react to stress.[8] It only takes one bad apple to ruin the entire barrel.

Your career and Role Modelship could be trapped behind your latest crisis.

In the world of venture capital, prior to 2022, the pursuit of three to four times multiples had spurred a culture of investing in companies that had only a few features and a "growth at all costs" model. This strategy created as many unicorns as it did cautionary tales. The lure of achieving unicorn status often led to prioritizing rapid scaling, in most cases at the expense of mature business practices.

The paradox: Venture funding that was aimed at fostering innovation and growth unintentionally created "zombie start-ups"—firms valued at more than a billion dollars that were still unprofitable. Everyone talked about capping the downside, capitalization tables, eliminating the middleman, percentage ownership, infrastructure consolidation, and getting gold to flow through cardboard pipes.

High customer churn rates persisted because products remained just a set of features in a narrow white space or insufficiently secure or robust. Inconsistent complementary professional services alienated many existing clients. Some companies experienced down-funding rounds, significantly reducing their overall valuation. Eventually, some companies would sell without providing the expected returns for the investors.

Humans who have a mindset that allows them to embrace positives and negatives equally have a more moderate cortisol response to stress. What that means in practice is that they are consciously role modeling stewardship and leadership, opening their minds to feedback during stress, which can help them learn and grow.

In the book *The Black Swan,* Nassim Nicholas Taleb discusses rare, unpredictable events, like the fall of the Berlin Wall or a country's economic collapse. Those types of scenarios are at the far end of the spectrum. A humanitarian crisis also exists on a spectrum, from localized disruptions, such as food shortages affecting a single community, to large-scale disasters impacting millions of humans. On one end, it may involve temporary displacement due to a natural disaster that requires immediate but short-term relief efforts. At the other extreme, a humanitarian crisis can become a prolonged emergency, with complex factors—such as conflict, climate change, and systemic poverty—compounding to create ongoing, severe impacts on health, safety, and human rights for affected populations.

> Modelship, once deeply rooted in peace and humanity, grows strong and wise.

THERE IS NO WORSE CRISIS THAN WAR

From 1966 to 1967, my father-in-law, Jim Potter, served as a navigator on a C-130 aircraft flying ninety-five nighttime missions over North Vietnam and thirty missions over Laos, with many occurring under intense enemy fire. With no GPS in those days, he navigated dense mountainous jungle terrain using the C-130's radar.

For all intents and purposes, he grew up without a father. He recalls having one strong role model: his high school track coach, Fred Brock. The universe had a special plan, and when I moved from Bulgaria, Jim and Carol Potter became my second family and major role models. To this day, I'm grateful to them for supporting me and my brother when my parents couldn't afford to pay for us to study in the United States.

Every time Jim shares a story from Vietnam, chills ripple through the room, leaving us awed by the courage and leadership he and the men in his unit showed in the face of unimaginable adversity. Before his deployment to Asia, Jim attended survival school. His voice drops as he recalls details of the experience in Reno, Nevada: the crackling of gravel under his elbows and knees as he crawled under barbed wire, the sharp snap of commands echoing across the yard, and the tension so thick it nearly drowned out the sound of his own heartbeat.

This was the entrance to the prisoner-of-war camp simulation, but to Jim, it was chillingly real. He was interrogated, pushed to his limits, and could only give his name, rank, and serial number. In those intense moments, with a sharp edge in his voice, he confesses he was convinced they might actually kill him. It was a training exercise, but it felt very, very real, like his life was on the line.

The next step for him and all his fellow trainees was time in the war camp. He does not know why, but the ranking military officer in the camp placed him in charge of escapes—something he chuckles about proudly, knowing that he had a few successes.

His logbook records 770 combat hours as part of Tactical Air Command support, including 153 combat missions. This included ninety-five missions over North Vietnam, thirty missions over Laos, and twenty-eight other combat support missions. Jim was part of the Blind Bat mission, which dropped flares over Ho Chi Minh Trail in an attempt to disrupt the flow of weapons to the South. He describes the blinding flash as each flare ignited, lighting up the dark jungle with a haunting, ghostly glow that revealed the movement below, giving fighter aircraft occupants a glimpse of their targets. It was a brief, searing light in the endless dark, each flare releasing two million candlepower—just enough to guide his team in the fight.

There's one mission he is most proud of. On June 3, 1967, while flying over Laos, the pilot, Major Gilmore, received a call for the aircraft to divert to a new location. Jim got them there and made sure they stayed there. As a result, his crew provided lifesaving light support all night for a combat unit that was in danger of being overrun.

A year later, he was awarded the Distinguished Flying Cross—the fourth highest award for heroism and the highest award for extraordinary aerial achievement—for that mission. By this time, Jim was back in the United States, at Lockbourne Air Force Base, working as an instructor in the newly formed gunship squadron. Promoted from lieutenant to captain, Jim trained more than thirty navigators, focusing on combat techniques and using guns and flares, and mentored them into expanded roles within the military.

To inspire courage, gratitude, and calm, put your crisis into perspective by comparing it to a time of war.

To me, Jim Potter isn't just a decorated war hero; he's a role model and a second father. He's also an amazing Papa to all his nine grandchildren.

The reason I'm sharing Jim's story isn't just to recount the bravery of role models from history; it's to honor everyone who has served and continues to serve. It's also a call to each of us, a reminder to put our own struggles into perspective, drawing strength from those who faced the unimaginable and came through with resilience that inspires us today. Every challenge, every hardship, is an opportunity to coach ourselves and others in resilience, showing us that even when hope seems distant, the human spirit has the power to endure and inspire.

ONE-MINUTE MODELSHIP

Post on your Microsoft Teams or Slack channel and on LinkedIn an example of great teaching and coaching during both a **peaceful time and a crisis**.

#RoleModelship

TL;DR

- **Teachers and coaches** have magical powers to shape the future. They don't just impart knowledge; they ignite curiosity, instill discipline, and help people recognize and harness their potential.

- **Having a coach** doesn't make you weak; it gives you another perspective and different frameworks, helps you see around blind corners, and opens a gateway to a network of resources.

- Teachers and coaches often talk about their profession as **a calling or vocation**. A human doesn't choose a vocation. For many role models, Role Modelship is a calling. They had no choice in the matter.

- In an ever-evolving world, **coaching innovation habits is essential** for individuals who seek to configure themselves for multiple futures. Coaching innovation fosters adaptability and resilience, equipping humans with skills to navigate uncertainty and find new cheese.

- **Innovation helps role models scale** their multidisciplinary approach to networking and applying patterns.

- Many **role models exemplify the Golden Rule:** "Treat others the way you want to be treated."

- **In a crisis, humans show up** based on what they observe is rewarded modeling in the micro family, organizational, product, and community culture.

CHAPTER 10

Hand Over the Torch

What we have done for ourselves alone dies with us;
what we have done for others and the
world remains and is immortal.

—ALBERT PIKE

Civilization is not a spontaneous generation with any
race or nation known to history but the torch to be
handed down from race to race from age to age.

—KELLY MILLER

R hythmic gymnastics, track-and-field relays, swimming relays, biathlons. What do they all have in common? Balls, clubs, and hoops are handed off in rhythmic gymnastics between the athletes. One dropped instrument can cost the team a medal.

The Olympic torch relay is the iconic event that involves the handover of the torch from one runner to the next. Imagine you're the one who starts the relay, with the ceremonial lighting of the Olympic flame in Olympia, Greece, by focusing sunlight with a parabolic mirror. Holding a parabolic mirror is truly a unique opportunity. Its curved, reflective surface and the way it interacts with light is fascinating. It focuses light to give you control over direction and intensity. This element symbolizes purity and continuity with the ancient Olympics.

Typically, thousands of torchbearers participate in the relay. You've been chosen for your inspirational achievements. The relay culminates in an Olympic stadium, where you light the Olympic cauldron.

You did not pick up this torch by accident. Your lineage dates to Greece and Rome.

Cincinnatus was a leader in the Roman Empire. George Washington looked up to him and named the city of Cincinnati, Ohio, after him. Arnold Schwarzenegger also looked up to Cincinnatus. Why?

Cincinnatus was asked to step into power and become the leader when Rome was about to get annihilated by wars. He was a farmer. For his time, he had a lot of power. Cincinnatus reluctantly accepted the challenge, led the Roman army, and won the war. He had accomplished his mission, and when he was asked to continue as emperor, he gave the ring back and went back to farming. Cincinnatus was the master of bringing people together and role modeled sponsorship by handing over the torch.

A lit torch ripples outward, sparking new ideals and movements in the cultures it lights.

Metaphorically speaking, "handing over the torch" describes a deliberate transition of significant responsibility. For example, within families, elders entrust cherished traditions to younger family members for practice and preservation. On sports teams, athletes share lessons, culture, and strategy in representing the team's legacy. People involved in social causes advocate for change and carry the message and values of the cause. In the field of scientific innovation, researchers mentor the next wave of thinkers. In all these cases, passing the torch signifies more than just stepping down; it's about fostering legacy, ensuring continuity, and empowering the next generation to lead, envision, create, demo, and sustain in a new world order.

THE IMPORTANCE OF LEADERSHIP TRANSITIONS
TO THE ROLE MODELSHIP JOURNEY

As the golden hues of the late afternoon sun poured into the glass-walled conference room in San Rafael, Jeff Brzycki, Autodesk's CIO for eight years, sat across from Prakash Kota, his successor and long-time direct report. With gratitude, Kota embraced the lessons Brzycki imparted, carrying forward his values. As Brzycki departed, he felt at peace, knowing that Autodesk was in good hands.

Passing of the torch is a defining bookend act of Role Modelship, because it encapsulates a network of journeys and amplifies a universe of legacies.

Passing the torch ensures that the torchbearer's influence transcends their individual career, fostering a ripple effect of impact. That single bookend habit captures the essence of seeing the world as a continuum of shared purpose, influence, and growth. Multiplier role models plan for successors, enabling new role models to emerge strong and view the world through the lens of human values and economic value.

Brzycki is a multiplier role model and a transformational CIO with a reputation as a results-oriented, innovative, and fiscally responsible executive. Over his thirty-five-year career, Brzycki led numerous technology organizations at global technology companies including Autodesk, Verisign, Symantec, Veritas, Silicon Graphics, and Hewlett Packard. Brzycki led global teams comprising more than 1,000

Role models are torchbearers of values, unity, resilience, purpose, and opportunity.

technology professionals and accountable for over $210 million in annual spending.

Throughout his career, Brzycki has transformed strategy into reality by applying his proven ability to influence and negotiate across geographic, organizational, and political boundaries. He drives results through exceptional leadership, collaboration, communication, negotiation skills, financial acumen, and deep business knowledge.

Role Modelship Example: Jeff Brzycki

- **Sponsorship:** Jeff Brzycki sponsored more than $100 million in value stream–based business investments and $11 million for the elimination of technical debt. He also transformed Autodesk's security landscape by hiring the company's first chief information security officer and launching an enterprise information security risk and controls team. He chaired the Information Security Steering Committee, which included achieving a 100 percent success rate in annual Sarbanes Oxley Act compliance and reducing deficiencies tenfold.

- **Leadership:** As Autodesk's CIO, Brzycki shifted the approach of the IT organization from a linear waterfall structure to an agile DevOps framework, driving a significant increase from two to twenty releases annually with zero downtime for five consecutive years. He also championed a company-wide cultural transformation, fostering engagement by connecting individual roles to Autodesk's mission.

- **Mentorship:** Through his leadership in cultural transformation, Brzycki connected each IT team member to Autodesk's strategic goals, cultivating a collaborative environment that equipped employees with the tools and mindset to contribute meaningfully. He supported multi-year company-wide mentorship and internship programs, hackathons, and innovative relationships with top universities.

- **Fellowship:** Brzycki effectively managed relationships with tier-one vendors, executed multimillion-dollar global software implementations, and seamlessly integrated offshore support in India and Singapore, enhancing Autodesk's global IT ecosystem.

- **Stewardship:** Brzycki prioritized sustainable and cost-effective practices, achieving a 62 percent reduction in data center energy consumption by shifting to virtualized infrastructure. Through his Plan $\longrightarrow$ Build $\longrightarrow$ Run approach, he reduced the Run budget from 70 percent to 55 percent over five years, generating substantial savings to support Autodesk's strategic projects. Additionally, his teams deployed SaaS/platform-as-a-service solutions like Salesforce, Workday, and Amazon Web Services, modernizing Autodesk's IT landscape.

ORGANIZATIONAL VALUES AS A METHOD FOR HANDING OVER THE TORCH

Rosa Parks led the way with her famous expression: "Each person must live their life as a model for others." One of the best ways to hand over the torch to future generations is to build an organizational culture of modelship that lasts beyond the leader and beyond the current company.

Emulating companies such as Amazon, your company cultural values could be the following (see table 10.1).

Culture is envisioned, created, demoed, and sustained through stories. Cultural values are like techniques in rhythmic gymnastics: Each is practiced, polished, demoed, and passed from one performer to the next. Just as a Bulgarian European gold medalist gracefully hands off the ribbon, you can align values to keep organizational momentum fluid and strong. Synchronicity is achieved through a shared mission and ongoing practice. Every time the ball moves, the team responds in unison.

Table 10.1. Sample Company Cultural Values Within the Five Disciplines of Role Modelship

CULTURAL VALUES	STEWARDSHIP	FELLOWSHIP	MENTORSHIP	LEADERSHIP	SPONSORSHIP
Think Big	Encouraging visionary thinking beyond immediate goals	Fostering a culture in which ambitious ideas are supported	Inspiring models to consider broader possibilities	Leading with a bold vision that inspires innovation	Advocating for transformative initiatives
Hunger to Win	Ensuring resources are used effectively to achieve goals	Fostering team spirit and camaraderie	Instilling ambition to strive for excellence	Inspiring the pursuit of victory and achievement of collective goals	Advocating for individuals to realize their potential
Heart	Incorporating the environment in decision-making	Building genuine relationships	Providing empathy and guidance	Leading with compassion and understanding	Supporting others' aspirations

STORIES AS A MEANS OF HANDING OVER THE TORCH

"The arc of the moral universe is long, but it bends toward justice." Popularized by Martin Luther King Jr., this phrase reminds us that while events might seem unfair, history ultimately moves toward justice, reflecting ongoing positive progress.

Multiplier Role Modelship through stories on social media is contagious.

Cory A. Eaves, a partner at BayPine private equity firm in New York City, posted this story on LinkedIn:

> Every week, I dedicate time to supporting my network, particularly those navigating career transitions. Whether through offering advice, making connections, or simply providing encouragement, I believe in the power of paying it forward. I am especially passionate about helping young

professionals, knowing that a little guidance can make all the difference as they embark on their careers . . .

Last week, I asked for help for my son, Wes, in finding an internship. I have literally been overwhelmed with more than a hundred responses. I am humbled and grateful for your support . . . Wes and I deeply appreciate it.[1]

Close to 300 people liked Eaves's story. The ripples that story sent in the universe will be carried forward by this book and your Role Modelship stories.

Sharon Mandell, CIO at Juniper Networks in Sunnyvale, California, has also had a long career in technology. In a LinkedIn post, she shared:

Stepping into the classroom has probably taught me at least as much as I've been able to share with my students. Along with my role as CIO of Juniper Networks, I teach a class every year at the University of San Francisco, and it's shown me just how much power lies in having a beginner's mindset, along with a willingness to make mistakes, be humbled, and continuously learn and evolve . . .

There will always be new innovations to consider and adopt, and while #GenAI may be the latest impressive tool, it's still the human perspective—empathy, creativity, optimism, and thoughtful problem-solving—that fuels progress.[2]

The arts, particularly writing, serve as a timeless method for handing over the torch of knowledge, wisdom, and cultural identity. Writing captures the nuances of human experience, bridging the gap between past, present, and future. Whether in novels, movies, or Wikipedia or in large or small learning models, stories allow each generation to communicate its unique voice and perspective.

Laurie McLean spent twenty years as the CEO of a publicity agency, then eight years as an agent and senior agent at Larsen

Pomada Literary Agents in San Francisco before cofounding the Silicon Valley–based Fuse Literary agency in 2013.

McLean is a multiplier role model, having launched the careers of hundreds of writers. She demonstrated her passion for coaching as the director of the San Francisco Writers Conference (SFWC) for five years. For more than two decades, she issued annual publishing industry predictions.

McLean's clients include best-selling young adult book author Julie Kagawa, best-selling epic fantasy author Brian D. Anderson, debut modern Asian fantasy author duo Julia Vee and Ken Bebelle, up-and-coming Latinx activist author NoNieqa Ramos, and award-winning novelist Linda Wisdom, author of more than one hundred romance novels.

Role Modelship Example: Laurie McLean

- **Sponsorship:** As a founding partner at Fuse Literary, Laurie McLean champions both established and emerging authors. She actively supports indie authors seeking traditional publishing routes and offers mentorship to debut authors. Her dedication to promoting underrepresented voices in literature aligns with her commitment to diversity and inclusion in publishing.

- **Leadership:** With more than twenty years of experience as the CEO of a successful public-relations agency and eight years as a senior agent at Larsen Pomada Literary Agents, McLean has demonstrated strong leadership skills in both the literary and business worlds. Since cofounding Fuse Literary in 2013, she has used her extensive industry knowledge to guide authors in navigating digital publishing.

- **Mentorship:** McLean's passion for mentorship is evident in her hands-on approach to guiding authors throughout their publishing journeys. She leverages her experience to provide valuable insights, empowering her clients, including *New York Times* best-selling authors like Julie Kagawa and Brian D. Anderson, to achieve their creative aspirations.

- **Fellowship:** McLean fosters a sense of community among her authors, including rising voices like NoNieqa Ramos and debut authors like Julia Vee and Ken Bebelle. She promotes an environment where creativity thrives, ultimately enriching the literary landscape with diverse narratives. Fuse Literary demonstrates a commitment to evolving with the industry, exemplified by initiatives like the Short Fuse publishing program, which helps authors maintain reader engagement between books, and Fuse Club, which allows peer-to-peer interactions among Fuse Literary's clients.

- **Stewardship:** McLean's commitment to ethical practices in publishing is reflected in her careful selection of clients, including award-winning authors like Melissa D. Savage and Linda Wisdom. By promoting books that inspire change, she demonstrates her responsibility as a steward of literature, ensuring that important stories are told and heard. She has penned more than one hundred articles and has used her platform to address issues facing authors and the publishing landscape.

As McLean retires, the transition of SFWC director responsibilities to successor Lissa Provost emphasizes five main pillars of mentorship and continuity.

Strategic vision: McLean shared insights from her years in the industry, detailing her vision for expanding representation in all areas and strengthening SFWC's role in the industry. This has provided Provost with a long-term road map for success.

Operational expertise: Drawing on her years as both CEO and literary agent, McLean has handed over her knowledge of client management, industry relationships, and agency processes.

Client relations: McLean introduced Provost to her network of high-profile clients and publishing contacts, from best-selling authors like Kagawa to emerging talent. This transition ensures that clients feel confident in the conference's continuity.

Innovation focus: Known for her forward-thinking approach, McLean has encouraged Provost to explore trends in AI, digital publishing, DEI, and new author–publisher paradigms to keep the SFWC at the forefront of the evolving industry landscape.

Cultural values: As a champion of creative freedom and ethical business practices, McLean imparted her commitment to inclusivity, client-first representation, and responsible leadership.

A role model must not be affected by the weather of the day but instead focus on impacting the climate of the era.

AGENTIC WORKFORCE AS DIGITAL GUARDIANS OF THE TORCH

As CEO of Salesforce, Marc Benioff's first-ever post on LinkedIn is symbolic in what's to come in the age of AI—an agentic workforce.

> For my first-ever post on LinkedIn, I'm excited to announce that as of today, Agentforce—our complete AI system for enterprises built on the Salesforce platform—is available for all of our customers. Easy to set up with a few clicks and a simple description of the job you want done, Agentforce is ushering in a new era of AI abundance and limitless workforces that will augment every employee, build deeper customer relationships, and drive extraordinary growth and profitability . . .
>
> Going beyond Copilot and chatbots, Agentforce agents

don't just answer questions or surface insights—they autonomously execute actions, like resolving customer cases, qualifying sales leads, and optimizing marketing campaigns. Companies like OpenTable, Saks, and Wiley are already using Agentforce today to extend their employees, expand their workforce, and improve customer experiences. This is what AI was meant to be.[3]

Benioff's first social media post speaks volumes about the era's technological and cultural landscape. It underscores the monumental shift toward intelligent systems and automation, reshaping how we live, work, and interact.

AI and Agentforce point to the need for new ways of thinking and the readiness to innovate in the face of unpredictable challenges. As AI begins to influence decision-making, the era is characterized by questions about trust, fairness, and accountability. Ideas, innovations, and ethical considerations are not confined within borders; they are part of a worldwide discourse driven by shared interests and challenges.

Microsoft, Google, Open AI. Where do you see yourself partnering on the journey of including AI inference in everything you do? As a leader, what will your organizational chart look like when you're managing an agentic workforce capable of writing its own workflows?

An *agentic force*—autonomous agents performing tasks, making decisions, and adapting—is becoming a modern means for handing over the torch in a couple transformative ways.

1. **Knowledge lineage through generations:** Autonomous agents can preserve and replicate the expertise of seasoned professionals. An agentic force can help early-in-their-careers leaders make informed decisions honoring the past while innovating for the future.

2. **Legacy building through principles and systems:** Leaders can encode their Role Modelship values into agentic systems, creating digital guardians of company culture and mission.

When AI systems embody core organizational principles, they serve as stewards of these values, helping new leaders uphold and advance the organization's ethos. Intelligent agents can be designed to emulate leadership qualities and decision-making approaches, creating models that help new leaders adapt to complex scenarios.

———— ✦ ————

Agentic relay runners, as guardians of the human torch, will change the human definitions of meaning, purpose, flow, and legacy.

In essence, this new agentic workforce is a team of digital relay runners, guardians of the torch of organizational, product, and social knowledge and culture. The next generation will learn how to use AI, question it and the role it plays in their lives, and ensure that it enhances rather than diminishes our human capabilities.

You are the torchbearer carrying the flame on a journey to the next host city. Along this journey, your agency, centrality, role, aspiration, and definition of fulfillment will change. You will lead in the new world, define the new normal, mold to the new molds.

Be inspired to be your best self!

Model. Mold. Model. Mold.

—⋀⋁—*modelship*—⋀⋁—

✎ ONE-MINUTE MODELSHIP

Please confidentially share with your successors the expectations of their roles and the alignment of your company values with the Role Modelship formula (i.e., stewardship, fellowship, mentorship, leadership, and sponsorship).

#RoleModelship

TL;DR

- You are the **torchbearer** carrying the flame on a Role Modelship journey.

- **Handing over the torch** describes a deliberate transition of significant responsibility, such as within a family, a scientific endeavor, an athletic team, leadership, and Role Modelship.

- The new agentic workforce is a team of **digital relay runners**, guardians of the torch of organizational, product, and social knowledge and culture. Along the AI journey, your agency, centrality, role, aspiration, and definition of fulfillment will change.

- Every role model in this book is passing a torch to you. **Model. Mold. Model. Mold.**

PART III

CHANGE THE ROLE MODEL TO WIN THE RACE

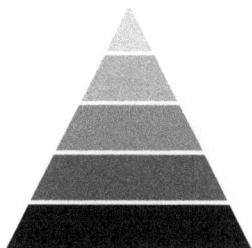

CHAPTER 11

Win the Race by Changing the Race and Role Model

After playing Ruth [Bader Ginsburg], I realized how important it is to have a voice in the world.

—FELICITY JONES

Change will not come if we wait for some other person or some other time. We are the ones we've been waiting for.

—BARACK OBAMA

D o you have a modelship mindset constraint that sounds like this? I'm not <Shāh Jāhan> or have never met <Shāh Jāhan>; therefore, I can't build a <Taj Mahal>.

What if building the Taj Mahal was the wrong "race" to begin with? To win the race, sometimes you have to change the type of race. Let's race to build a space rocket. Ready? NASA, SpaceX, Boeing. Is your rocket reusable? What is your role model? *Apollo*? *Electron*? *Falcon*? You race because you think this is the right race and you have the skills to race.

Let's race together in Formula One. Monaco, Japan, Italy, the United

Kingdom, is your car performing? Who is your role model? Mercedes? Ferrari? Red Bull? May the road rise to meet your fast wheels.

Let's race to build the tallest tower. Ready? Are the Eiffel Tower, Shanghai Tower, and Tower of London handling earthquakes? Who is your role model? Marshall Strabala? Jun Xia? The team at Dar Al-Handasah? May the sky open to meet your towering accent.

The Formula One, tallest tower, and space rocket races are all stories of relentless human pursuit of innovation, precision engineering, and hunger to win.

In all three races, there's an element of high stakes under high pressure:

- Formula One teams win within millisecond margins.
- Tower builders contend with extreme heights, winds, and earthquakes.
- Rocket engineers must ensure flawless takeoff and orbit stability.

Ultimately, these races demonstrate our human ingenuity and our drive to achieve monumental accomplishments against time and challenges.

In your winning races, may you find and project your voice to amplify role models.

CHANGE THE RACE, CHANGE THE GROWTH MULTIPLE

AI has changed the race for everyone. By 2027, 70 percent of new employee contracts will include clauses for AI representation of their personas, according to Gartner.[1] By 2028, 40 percent of CIOs will demand "guardian agents" for AI oversight.[2] According to Forrester, the share of use cases leveraging predictive AI will increase by 50 percent. Forrester also forecasts that the digital economy will grow at a 6.9 percent compound annual growth rate from 2023 to 2028, faster than the global gross domestic product.[3] The top five digital economies by size are the United States, China, the United Kingdom, Japan, and Germany.

Changing the race inherently moves the cheese by shifting the goals and redefining what winning looks like, forcing everyone involved to adapt quickly to new objectives.

Your cheese today has three parts: you, the race, and the win (see figure 11.1).

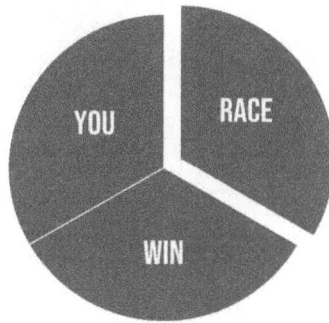

Figure 11.1. The three parts of your cheese.

In competitive markets, understanding all three elements becomes crucial.

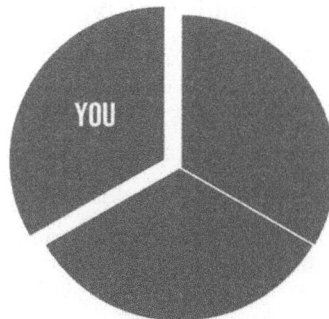

Figure 11.2. Your role in Role Modelship.

- **You:** As a role model, you are Neo from *The Matrix*; you're "the One" who can significantly alter the course of events through values, grit, choice, skill, and networks. You have clarity about your strengths, values, and goals as a leader, organization, or product (see figure 11.2).

You already know that you = you × role model 1 × role model 2 × role model 3 × role model 4.

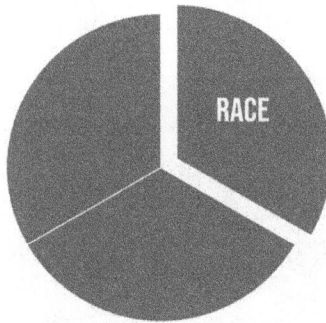

Figure 11.3. The role of the race in Role Modelship.

- **The race:** When the cheese moves—the market shifts, pricing models change because of AI, competition intensifies, or innovation accelerates—the race needs to change (see figure 11.3).

- If you are innovating rapidly and need to respond quickly, you may select a Formula One type of role model, with experience in speed, agility, and real-time data.

- If you're developing a large-scale, long-term product that requires extensive collaboration and careful project management, you might relate to a tallest tower–style role model, emphasizing robust design and seismic, wind-reinforced construction.

- If you're challenging existing norms, akin to space rockets, you might channel a role model who can embrace risk, innovation, research, and changing foundational assumptions.

Figure 11.4. The role of the win in Role Modelship.

- **The win:** Winning takes on new meaning once you change the race, because the key performance indicators change. Role models achieve breakthroughs that set new standards, even new industry categories. You also know that the win is not just the result but also the process of change (see figure 11.4).

The new Role Modelship journey for an organization includes an agentic workforce in every step (see figure 11.5).

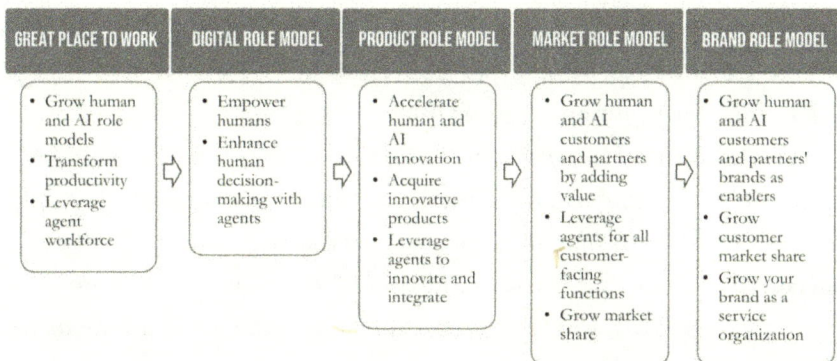

GREAT PLACE TO WORK	DIGITAL ROLE MODEL	PRODUCT ROLE MODEL	MARKET ROLE MODEL	BRAND ROLE MODEL
• Grow human and AI role models • Transform productivity • Leverage agent workforce	• Empower humans • Enhance human decision-making with agents	• Accelerate human and AI innovation • Acquire innovative products • Leverage agents to innovate and integrate	• Grow human and AI customers and partners by adding value • Leverage agents for all customer-facing functions • Grow market share	• Grow human and AI customers and partners' brands as enablers • Grow customer market share • Grow your brand as a service organization

Figure 11.5. The agentic workforce in the Role Modelship journey.

Integrating AI in new types of races can propel growth by increasing valuation multiples, similar to the approach in venture capital. Rapidly growing companies are valued on revenue multiples, while the rest may be valued on earnings before interest, taxes, depreciation, and amortization multiples. Companies that are born in an AI-first world will see higher valuations, because investors prioritize data-driven decisions about fuzzy problems that yield compounding returns. In venture capital, growth multiples are critical, and a shift to AI can transform a company's multiple from, say, three times to eight times or even ten times.

Research advisory firms Gartner, Forrester, and Boston Consulting Group are multiplier role models in providing strategic AI guidance to organizations changing the race and changing the growth multiples. Gartner's research offers deep insights into AI trends, helping companies understand AI technologies that drive competitive advantage. Forrester offers in-depth reports and consulting on emerging AI technologies, assessing return on investment. BCG combines strategy with consulting, partnering directly with clients to implement AI solutions.

CHANGE THE RACE, CHANGE THE METRICS

Disruptive, new usage-based AI pricing models and split-second Formula One metrics both demand real-time responsiveness. Every company is evolving its key performance indicators. Salesforce will charge users of Agentforce per conversation.[4] Open AI will charge GPT users for input and output tokens.

The book *Total Competition: Lessons in Strategy from Formula One*, by Ross Brawn and Adam Parr, is the story of Formula One told through the eyes of one of its most successful engineers and a top-tier executive. Brawn, the mastermind behind teams winning more than fifty races, and Parr, former CEO of the Williams Formula One team, explore the intersection of psychology and strategy in a sport in which milliseconds define victory or defeat.

Just as a Formula One team continuously refines every detail to shave milliseconds off lap times, revenue strategists focus on pivoting metrics based on failure, continuous improvement, and winning as a team.

Lauren Goldstein is the senior vice president of growth at Winning by Design, a global leader in revenue architecture, helping over one thousand companies—including top SaaS organizations like Adobe, Microsoft, Dropbox, Asana, and Uber—scale revenue operations through scientific

> *The quality of your Role Modelship is based on your questions, which often change the race.*

frameworks. They specialize in go-to-market (GTM) strategies that focus on customer acquisition and retention, utilizing models like the "Bow Tie" framework to emphasize the importance of the postsales process. With clients across six continents, Winning by Design is a pioneer in transforming modern revenue strategies. Their mission resonates with any company that wants to grow revenue.

Role Modelship Example: Lauren Goldstein

- **Sponsorship:** Lauren Goldstein exemplifies a multiplier role model through her leadership at Winning by Design, helping scale revenue growth multiples across 600+ global companies. She advocates for implementing scientific frameworks that empower diverse teams to thrive. She is also the cofounder and treasurer of Women in Revenue, a nonprofit organization with more than 7,500 members.

- **Leadership:** With a deep background in GTM strategies, Lauren plays a pivotal role in guiding teams at Winning by Design. Her leadership approach integrates revenue science and customer success to foster data-driven decisions across various sectors.

continued

- **Mentorship:** Goldstein's mentoring efforts focus on helping teams and emerging leaders develop customer-centric and scalable revenue models, particularly within the SaaS industry. She provides opportunities for early-in-their-career professionals through coaching and internship opportunities.

- **Fellowship:** Goldstein fosters collaboration at Winning by Design, connecting global teams across six continents. Her global experience and focus on team synergy drive the creation of an inclusive, innovative work environment.

- **Stewardship:** Goldstein's stewardship in revenue operations promotes ethical, long-term strategies for sustainable growth. Her influence extends beyond the company as she shapes the future of revenue science across multiple industries, partnering with companies like Pavilion to leverage and influence AI.

INCREASE YOUR SPHERE OF INFLUENCE WITH INCLUSIVE ROLE MODELSHIP

The story of Banksy, the elusive British street artist, is a powerful example of winning by changing the race and being inclusive. Known for his provocative and satirical artwork, Banksy challenged the traditional structures of the art world by operating outside it—with no galleries, no exhibitions, and no official sales channels but with a massive digital community.

When I choose a role model, it's often intuitively but always with a cinematic sense.

He made urban landscapes his canvas, often anonymously placing powerful political and social commentary in public spaces. This disruption of where and how art is accessed allowed him to bypass gatekeepers. He made art accessible to everyone and gained global recognition without traditional endorsements or gallery representation.

Banksy's impact took a dramatic turn with pieces like *Girl with Balloon* partially shredding itself immediately after being auctioned for $1.4 million. The act shocked the art world but ultimately increased the piece's value, showcasing his commentary on art, commercialization, and authenticity.

> *Role models should present the disrupted and disrupt the present.*

"He puts situations together which are, at first, playful and comical and humorous," said art dealer and curator Acoris Andipa, who runs the London-based Andipa Gallery, in a National Public Radio interview.[5] "People laugh and then suddenly draw in and suck between their teeth and just go, 'Ouch, that's got a sting to it.' It's a conversation starter."

Role models should present the disrupted and showcase a version of themselves that has already gone through transformation. By doing so, they offer a relatable example of resilience and flexibility, lighting a path. This "disrupted self" might represent someone who has questioned norms, overcome setbacks, or embraced change—qualities that inspire others to do the same.

Adam Robinson and his team at Retention.com present the disrupted and have changed the race by growing a company in the public eye and posting regular updates on LinkedIn. That is their voice in the world.

They achieved a remarkable milestone: an annual recurring revenue of $30 million.[6] Retention.com's identity resolution software has become a powerful tool for Shopify merchants, helping them recover lost shoppers and increase Klaviyo flow revenue by two to three times. This technology enables businesses to expand by identifying website visitors, resulting in more customers and boosted revenue.

It hasn't been easy for SaaS companies that sell to e-commerce stores. But Retention.com just kept building.

In an AI-driven world, expanding your sphere of influence by channeling digital role models involves navigating complex, technology-rich landscapes. Emulating digital leaders at Gartner, Forrester, and so on can help you anticipate challenges and shape innovative solutions.

- The agentic workforce decision sits at the intersection of many races: economic, ethical, political, technological, and others.

- Eventually, the agentic workforce will be better than humans at determining what type of race is required and will prompt humans to take appropriate action.

- The human role is changing in the AI race; we need to learn better human facilitation skills and escalate the agentic force's ability to inspect, govern, on- and offboard, and handle data, security, and exceptions.

For leaders, understanding when to change the race means recognizing when the current approach no longer aligns with the organization's goals or external conditions. Inclusive leaders and role models are especially attuned to this need for change.

CHANNEL THE VOICE OF MINETTE NORMAN

Minette Norman is a multiplier role model and an award-winning author, international speaker, and leadership consultant specializing in inclusive leadership and psychological safety. She is the author of *The Boldly Inclusive Leader* and coauthor of *The Psychological Safety Playbook* with Karolin Helbig.

Norman's work offers impactful practices for fostering trust and inclusivity in the workplace. Known for her public speaking and advisory work, Norman promotes a culture of openness, collaboration, and inclusion. Her expertise has established her as a sought-after consultant, guiding leaders toward creating psychologically safe and inclusive environments.

Norman chooses her role models based on qualities such as empathy, courage, and authenticity, seeking individuals who lead with compassion and a commitment to inclusion. She values leaders who challenge the status quo to create positive change and who openly embrace diverse perspectives.

Role Modelship Example: Minette Norman

- **Sponsorship:** Minette Norman advocates for diverse voices and creative problem-solvers. In her role as VP of engineering practice at Autodesk, she actively championed cross-functional product collaboration, working to break down silos and encourage innovation. She served as an executive sponsor for the Autodesk Black Network and as a group mentor for the Autodesk Women's Network.

- **Leadership:** Throughout her career, Minette has pioneered a compassionate and inclusive leadership style, which isn't a common practice in traditionally male-dominated tech spaces. As VP of engineering, she guided a team of over 3,500 engineers to adopt innovative engineering and embrace a culture that values empathy, diversity, and psychological safety.

- **Mentorship:** Norman's journey from a technical writer at Adobe to a VP position at Autodesk highlights her commitment to a growth mindset. Norman advises leaders to increase their sphere of influence by first helping them build authentic connections rooted in empathy.

- **Fellowship:** At Autodesk, Norman built a strong engineering community by creating a working group of engineering leaders, hosting an annual one-thousand-person internal technical summit, and rewarding cross-team collaboration. Today, her books, *The Boldly Inclusive Leader* and *The Psychological Safety Playbook*, provide leaders with tools to foster unity and understanding, crucial for building strong, resilient organizations.

continued

- **Stewardship:** Norman champions the advancement of a human-centered approach to leadership in tech. In leaving her corporate role to focus on consulting, speaking, and authorship, she continues to guide leaders toward sustainable, ethical practices that enhance both organizational success and individual fulfillment.

✍ ONE-MINUTE MODELSHIP

On LinkedIn, please send a postcard and endorse a company or product for #RoleModelship. Share the example of how they've changed the race.

TL;DR

- To win, sometimes you have to **change the race.** Changing the type of race you are in shifts the focus from competing to strategically leading, setting new standards, and redefining success in a field.

- The kind of role model you need depends on the type of race.

  » If you are innovating rapidly and need to **respond quickly to market changes,** you may select a Formula One–type role model, with **experience in speed, agility, and real-time data**.

  » If you're developing a **large-scale, long-term product** that requires extensive collaboration and careful project management, your company might relate more to a tallest-tower kind of role model, **emphasizing robust design** and seismic, wind-reinforced construction.

» If you're pioneering **groundbreaking technology** that challenges existing norms, akin to space rockets, you may leverage a role model who can **embrace risk, innovation, research, and changing the foundational assumptions**.

- Companies born in an AI-first world, similar to those born after the advent of the cloud, will **see higher valuations, because investors now prioritize scalable, data-driven decisions about fuzzy problems** that yield compounding returns.

- Eventually, the **agentic workforce** will be better than humans at determining what type of race is required and will **prompt humans to take appropriate action**.

- The human role is changing in the AI race; we need to learn **better human facilitation skills and better escalate the agentic force's ability to inspect, govern, on- and offboard, and handle data, security, and exceptions**.

CHAPTER 12

Build Role Modelship into Product

Give me a lever long enough and a prop strong enough.
I can single-handedly move the world.
—ARCHIMEDES

The future is already here; it's just not evenly distributed.
—WILLIAM GIBSON

Who is William Gibson, and what did he predict for future products? Since the time of H. G. Wells, speculative fiction has played a critical role in shaping our understanding of technology's potential, and Gibson's novels serve as powerful cautionary tales about the capabilities and ethics of AI.

Known as the father of cyberpunk, Gibson penned the famous 1984 novel *Neuromancer*, which is credited with predicting the internet, virtual reality, and aspects of hacker culture. His ideas have influenced culture and technology, predicting how we would envision the relationship between humans and machines.

Count Zero, published almost forty years ago, depicts "biosoft" technology—enhanced biological software that can alter the human body and mind. The core product idea revolves around technology granting new abilities to humans. One central product is the concept of "constructs," or digital copies of people's consciousness that can continue operating in cyberspace after death. This narrative explores the boundary between life, memory, and AI.[1]

Mona Lisa Overdrive, published in 1988, explores the fusion of virtual and physical realities. The novel introduces a virtual space where people can upload copies of their minds, merging human consciousness with the digital realm. This virtual space, or "simstim" (simulated stimulation), allows people to experience the lives of others through a direct neural interface. The story delves into questions of self-identity, showing how such technology could blur the line between individual experiences and digital re-creations, essentially turning identity into a product that can be shared or sold.[2]

Pattern Recognition shifts focus from cybernetics to media and brand culture. The core product here is the concept of "coolhunting." The novel explores how brands can manipulate public perception and the power of pattern recognition—both as a human skill and as a technology—to predict or influence trends. Gibson underscores how global connectivity turns consumer behavior into a trackable, marketable product.[3]

FACT OR FICTION?

Imagine you're the CEO of an autonomous vehicle company, driving to the San Francisco airport on a sunny day. Coldplay is playing on Spotify, and you're smiling as you pass many billboards.

Jira is where ideas start, one of the giant billboards says about the project management software.

Demos rule in product management. You're demoing a humanity day in an autonomous vehicle.

Let's test your pattern recognition, which we know is central to product innovation. You push a button on your car, instantly projecting an advertisement for bicycles on your windows for everyone around you to enjoy. You have magically converted all your car windows into mobile billboards.

Fact or fiction?

The car is fact. The holographic glass advertising is also very much fact. David Astoria is the founder of Pranos.ai and mobile billboards.

Turning your car into a mobile billboard directly sponsors brands. This initiative reflects leadership by setting an example of resourcefulness. It signals that you're an early adopter. It is a source of inspiration and mentorship, illustrating a low-cost, high-visibility way to get a message out. When locals see brands on car billboards, it can instill a sense of pride and fellowship. It also minimizes the environmental impact of billboard infrastructure, demonstrating stewardship of the planet.

A boss has the title.
A leader has the people.
A role model has the future.

That was fun; let's try it again. Is this product fact or fiction?

Utilizing a process called vapor compression distillation, the Slingshot can take virtually any contaminated water source—sewage, seawater, or polluted rivers—and transform it into pure, drinkable water. Slingshot boils dirty water, separates out impurities, and condenses it back into a clean form, producing up to 250 gallons per day using minimal energy. Impressively, the Slingshot runs on about as much power as a standard blow-dryer, making it both cost-effective and suitable for areas with limited energy resources.

Slingshot is very much fact. It was created by Dean Kamen, inventor of the Segway and the iBOT wheelchair. Kamen is also the founder of FIRST (For Inspiration and Recognition of Science and Technology), an organization designed to encourage young people's interest in science and engineering. Through FIRST, he nurtures the next generation of inventors who, like him, might one day create transformative solutions for humanity's most pressing needs.

Today's chief technology and product officers (CTPOs) need to sit at the intersection of fiction lovers, product-minded innovators, entrepreneurs, and AI-ethics role models.

Fact or fiction?

Can you leverage the toggling on and off features in software products for releasing features on humanoids? Jira is where ideas often start.

One child, one role model,
One feature, one product,
One ripple, one platform,
Can change the world.

BUILDING PATTERN RECOGNITION THROUGH NEW HABITS

My birth certificate was written in the Basic programming language and released on a DOS operating system. I still have floppy disks I use for teaching, so the current generation can have a perspective on how far we've come. How about you? I bet your answer will vary based on gender, geography, and socioeconomic status.

The gender gap is growing in AI adoption. In a *Forbes* article, senior editor Jena McGregor highlights a recent Slack survey that showed that men from different generations use AI more than women do.[4] Among more than ten thousand desk workers, Gen Z men are 25 percent more likely to have tried AI tools than Gen Z women. Overall, more men are trying AI than women, with 35 percent of male respondents saying they've tried AI for work, compared with 29 percent of female respondents.

Why is that alarming? Because by leveraging AI, human pattern recognition is increased by factors of hundreds or more.

Big tech giants Amazon, Microsoft, Google, and Meta spent a combined $52.8 billion on building data centers.[5] That's up nearly 60 percent year over year. Amazon CEO Andy Jassy commented on the company's earnings call, saying, "The faster we grow demand, the faster we have to invest capital in data centers and networking gear and hardware."[6] Its capital expenditure in Q3 ($22.6 billion) represented 82 percent of Amazon Web Services' entire revenue ($27.5 billion). AI is being built directly into hardware. Let's take a minute and think about the implications of that.

Here are three examples of generative AI in hardware.

1. Edge AI chips for real-time content generation

   Companies like NVIDIA and Qualcomm have developed specialized AI chips embedded in drones, virtual reality headsets, and autonomous vehicles. These chips enable real-time content generation—for instance, creating photorealistic landscapes or rendering virtual environments—directly on the device.

2. AI-powered cameras and image processors for content creation

   Cameras in smartphones include AI-optimized processors like photo enhancement, scene creation, and real-time video effects.

3. Embedded generative AI in smart home devices

   AI is also being integrated into smart home devices, such as Amazon Alexa and Google Nest, which use AI hardware to support natural language generation.

How is this possible? In the race to adopt AI and embed it in products, structured product management relies heavily on pattern recognition to identify where and how AI can add value. This approach meets adaptive human learning, because product teams must continuously develop new habits and insights to keep up with AI's evolving capabilities and applications. Together, they drive an iterative process, shown below, that shapes the integration of AI into products thoughtfully and strategically (see figure 12.1).

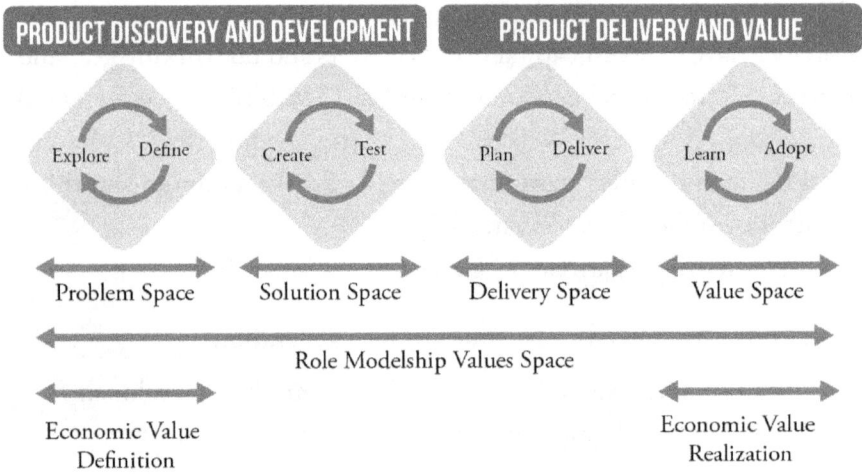

Figure 12.1. Integrating AI into products.

I am calling on all product managers, CXOs, and board members to ask Role Modelship values questions throughout the entire product life cycle. An AI model is only as good as what it's taught. For it to thrive, it needs the proper context and factual data.

Stewardship in the Discovery phase emphasizes probabilistic thinking and complex decision-making skills to equip individuals to explore often-ambiguous AI opportunities and challenges.

Mentorship becomes essential during the Development phase to upskill employees for solutions that balance human insight with AI automation.

Finally, in the Delivery and Value phase, leadership shines as leaders apply an evolved understanding of AI's role, refining products that leverage AI responsibly.

Companies' educational initiatives need to ensure that individuals are prepared to navigate each stage of this product-management process confidently, positioning human pattern recognition and judgment as an essential companion to AI's capabilities.

Christine Heckart is a tech CEO, multiplier role model, and cofounder of Xapa, a gamified app designed to serve as a library of the world's human wisdom, combining elements of adventure, coaching, and enrichment. The platform engages humans in a unique way, helping them explore knowledge and personal growth through interactive, pattern-building experiences. Xapa aims to provide users with valuable insights and learning opportunities while making the process enjoyable and immersive.

Role Modelship Example: Christine Heckart

- **Sponsorship:** Christine Heckart actively advocates for women in technology and leadership. Her commitment to sponsorship is evident through initiatives that support female representation in tech roles, helping to create pathways for aspiring women leaders. She is on the board of Next Generation Directors Academy, which prepares professionals for board service, with a focus on women and minorities.

- **Leadership:** As a seasoned tech executive and board member, Heckart leads Xapa with a vision to leverage technology for positive impact. Her extensive experience in the industry positions her as a key figure in driving innovation and strategic growth.

- **Mentorship:** Heckart is passionate about mentorship, guiding emerging talent in tech through her work on boards. She provides valuable resources and support to women who are advancing their careers, having mentored Bhawna Singh, CTO of Okta, for many years. Additionally, Heckart has led engineering mentorship salons at Scalyr data analytics platform, fostering a growth and abundance mindset in role models.

continued

- **Fellowship:** Heckart fosters a culture of collaboration within Xapa, encouraging teamwork and shared learning. Her leadership promotes a strong sense of community among employees, enhancing collective problem-solving and innovation.

- **Stewardship:** Her stewardship is reflected in her commitment to ethical technology development and social responsibility. She champions initiatives that align with sustainable practices and prioritize the well-being of communities impacted by AI and technology.

Xapa has recognized the essential need to prepare humans for an AI-driven world by investing in education and upskilling initiatives that foster adaptability and resilience. Through targeted programs, Xapa seeks to equip teams with critical thinking abilities that allow them to thrive alongside AI advancements. This commitment highlights the responsibility organizations hold in ensuring their workforces and communities are empowered to navigate the shifting landscape that AI brings.

As AI technology rapidly evolves, organizations like Xapa play a critical role in shaping a society in which individuals are equipped to leverage AI ethically, creatively, and effectively, bridging the gap between technological advancement and human potential.

DESIGNING AI WITH EMOTIONAL INTELLIGENCE AND ROLE MODELSHIP

One of the main products of a human is a humanity day, as we saw at the beginning of this book. A humanity day doesn't just feel good and add color to your personal canvas; it sends ripples that brighten the canvases of the world. You achieve humanity days by envisioning, creating, demoing, and sustaining them—for yourself and for others.

Designing AI with emotional intelligence is essential to more humanity days because it enables technology to interact with humans in meaningful ways that are empathetic and intuitive. Emotional quotient (EQ) AI can respond to our emotions, adjust its style, and create more natural interactions, especially in sectors like health care, education, and customer service. It can build trust, improve engagement, and offer support that feels genuinely helpful rather than transactional.

Soul Machines is at the forefront of developing AI with emotional intelligence through its digital humans—lifelike avatars that engage in empathetic, emotionally rich discussions with living humans. These digital humans are powered by a unique combination of AI and a virtual nervous system that simulates real-time emotional responses. For example, Soul Machines avatars can detect facial expressions and tone, allowing them to interpret our emotional state, respond, and mirror our empathy and understanding in real time.

When your most motivated employees go quiet, you've missed the ship on Role Modelship.

Soul Machines digital humans have the fundamental training to be role models leveraging EQ and positive intelligence quotient (PQ). If these digital humans had a heartbeat, it would be

—∿—modelship—∿—

To visually describe the relationship between EQ, PQ, and Role Modelship values, a Venn diagram illustrates the interconnected nature of these concepts. Role Modelship encompasses all of them (see figure 12.2).

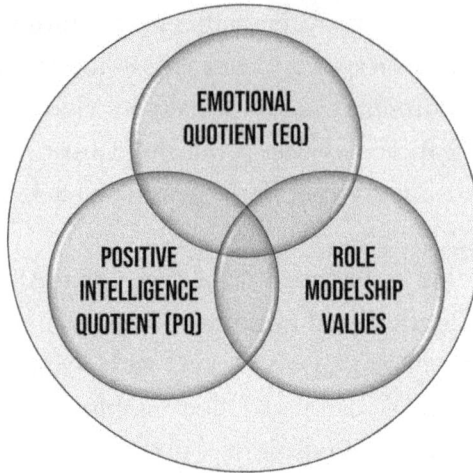

Figure 12.2. A Venn diagram illustrating EQ, PQ, and Role Modelship values.

Emotional quotient (EQ): Self-awareness, self-regulation, empathy, and social skills

Positive intelligence quotient (PQ): Mental fitness, resilience, positive thinking, and reducing self-sabotage

Role Modelship: Stewardship, fellowship, mentorship, leadership, and sponsorship

Overlapping Areas

EQ and PQ: Demonstrates how self-awareness and emotional management contribute to mental resilience and positive thinking

EQ and Role Modelship: Illustrates how role models with high emotional intelligence influence others by demonstrating the five values, plus empathy, social skills, and emotional regulation

PQ and Role Modelship: Displays how role models with high positive intelligence inspire others to develop positive mental habits and resilience

Center: Represents the integrated influence of EQ, PQ, and Role Modelship, showcasing the holistic development of individuals who are emotionally intelligent, mentally resilient, and guided by positive Role Modelship values

---

*Make the human the hero of
your AI-enabled product journey.*

Leading indicators of success in embedding emotional intelligence into these digital humans would include the AI's ability to recognize and respond to nuanced human emotions, anticipate our contextual needs, and respond empathetically to our stress or anxiety, helping us configure ourselves for multiple futures.

START-UPS PIONEERING AI-DRIVEN PRODUCT INNOVATION

"Courage is contagious," evangelist Billy Graham once said. "When a brave man takes a stand, the spines of others are stiffened." This sentiment couldn't be truer for start-ups pioneering AI-driven product innovation.

Shelby Golan is a multiplier role model in the venture capital and start-up ecosystem and an expert in the journey that she calls "from inception to iconic." At Mayfield venture capital firm, she plays a pivotal role in business development, working with start-ups to achieve product-market fit and drive early customer adoption—crucial stages that determine long-term success. Her expertise spans sales, marketing, product development, alliances, corporate strategy, and investment. She is an invaluable resource for companies envisioning global expansion.

Golan is instrumental in fostering corporate innovation through Mayfield's expansive global network of CXOs and industry leaders. She champions initiatives such as CXO insight forums and the *CXO of the Future* podcast, which enable executives across industries to exchange ideas and stay ahead of market trends. Golan's multidisciplinary approach and her dedication to fostering innovation make her an inspirational figure for aspiring entrepreneurs and investors alike.

One of Mayfield's companies, Valve Software, stands out as a pioneer in digital distribution and an innovator in the gaming industry. The company's Steam platform has revolutionized how games are distributed, purchased, and played, breaking down geographical barriers and making gaming more accessible worldwide. By providing an economic platform for independent developers, Valve has empowered countless creators to earn a living and pursue their passions.

Valve's commitment to open platforms like Steam Workshop has nurtured a thriving community of "modders" and creators, resulting in innovative game modifications that extend games' lifespans and foster creativity. Additionally, Valve has been a significant player in the development of virtual reality technology, pushing the boundaries of immersive experiences with applications beyond gaming.

Frore Systems is an early-stage hardware start-up making impactful strides in energy efficiency and thermal management technology. Their innovative approach to energy-efficient cooling has the potential to significantly reduce device energy consumption, resulting in both lower electricity bills for consumers and a smaller carbon footprint. By avoiding traditional fans, Frore's solid-state solutions enhance device durability and reduce electronic waste.

Frore's durable technology minimizes the need for mechanical replacements, lowering the environmental impact of manufacturing. Furthermore, thermal innovations lead to improved user experiences: Devices that run cooler and quieter enhance productivity and overall satisfaction.

These role model companies share insights into early signals of change, such as shifts in consumer preferences, regulatory updates, or technological advances, which can inspire others to hone their market-sensing capabilities. They excel in strategic thinking and cross-disciplinary knowledge, using insights from diverse fields to predict how interconnected market factors could influence industry changes.

Exemplify. Amplify. Sponsor.

AI STEWARDSHIP FOR OUR PLANET

AI stewardship of our planet is essential for creating a sustainable future and inspiring the next generation of role models. By developing AI that actively monitors and manages environmental impacts—from reducing carbon emissions to resource optimization to biodiversity protection—we ensure that future generations inherit a healthier world.

This commitment to safeguarding our planet through intelligent, data-driven decisions empowers young leaders to prioritize sustainability, ultimately creating a legacy of care and ethical responsibility that benefits the entire ecosystem.

How would you like to have a rocket scientist on your list of role models?

Will Marshall is cofounder and CEO of Planet Labs PBC, a satellite imaging company. Will is a scientist turned entrepreneur. He was recognized as a Young Global Leader by the World Economic Forum and serves on the board of the Open Lunar Foundation. Prior to starting Planet Labs, Marshall was a scientist at NASA. Planet Labs' mission is to use daily satellite imagery and insights to make global change visible and actionable, solving environmental and social challenges.

Leveraging planet data and AI, Microsoft's Project Guacamaya is helping monitor the Amazon rainforest and key biodiversity habitats to turn around loss rates. The HBO film *Wild Wild Space* documents the origin of the new space industry, featuring companies like Planet Labs, Rocket Lab, and Astra. Planet Labs is working with NVIDIA to put their latest Jetson on the next Pelican-2 mission soon. It will be the most powerful graphics processing unit in space and will enable Planet Labs to process imagery to find objects in seconds. A company called Impact Observatory leverages AI and data from Planet Labs' satellites to provide the US government, non-profits, and companies with insights for natural disaster management, evacuation plans, and response efforts.

Products are only as good as the voices of their role models.

Planet Labs fosters global awareness by providing accessible Earth imagery to more than 900 customers, from environmental groups to government agencies. They have 615 satellites (314 Doves, 273 SuperDoves, 21 SkySats, 5 RapidEye, 1 Pelican, and 1 Tanager) on 34 rockets, from 10 launch sites in 7 countries. Their ongoing partnerships, including the Pelican and Tanager projects, underscore their commitment to data democratization, supporting research, and providing actionable insights.[7]

With the aid of Planet Labs' data, AI tools, and partner, the Smart Country Convention, Brazilian federal police agents have intervened in more than three thousand environmental crimes and illegal activities in the past year, particularly in the Amazon rainforest, collecting $1.9 billion in fines and seized goods and assets—an incredible 7,500 percent return on investment. Most importantly, in 2024, Brazil saw a significant reduction in deforestation rates, including a 30.6 percent drop in the Amazon rainforest.

CHANNEL THE VOICE OF TZVETANA DUFFY

Tzvetana Duffy is the head of corporate engineering at Planet Labs. She has more than twenty years of international management and executive-level strategic engagement in high-growth technology companies. She focuses on AI transformations for managing business processes and customer engagement.

Role Modelship Example: Tzvetana Duffy

- **Sponsorship:** Tzvetana Duffy advances Planet Labs' mission by spearheading the integration and scaling of essential business systems across the sales, marketing, finance, legal, and people functions.

She manages enterprise architecture and customer data and ensures robust infrastructure and security for Planet Labs' growth. At Autodesk, she was the founder and executive sponsor for the women in technology ERG. Currently, she is a member of Women in Aerospace, dedicated to expanding women's opportunities for leadership and increasing their visibility in the aerospace community.

- **Leadership:** Duffy's leadership supports initiatives that optimize Planet Labs' operations, leveraging her prior experience as technologist at Autodesk. She plays a crucial role in embedding role modeling into a company's culture by establishing practices that drive transparency, standards, and customer-centric design within business technology initiatives. She sets the tone for integrity in systems management, security, and user experience.

- **Mentorship:** Duffy fosters a collaborative culture, empowering her team of engineers and technologists to contribute meaningfully to Planet Labs' growth and align with strategic objectives. She mentors and coaches her team, ensuring a growth mindset and best practices.

- **Fellowship:** Dedicated to making Earth data accessible, Duffy supports cooperative project structures that enhance Planet Labs' outreach, aligning initiatives with company-wide objectives for greater impact. By embracing transparency and ethical stewardship, Planet Labs strives to support a culture in which diverse perspectives align employees with environmental goals.

- **Stewardship:** As a member of the governing body of Evanta's CIO and CDO Council, Duffy drives industry-wide discussions on the evolving role of CIOs. She's an expert in enterprise applications, business analytics, governance, and customer data management. She upholds stringent standards in business continuity, helping drive successful systems launches and reinforcing Planet Labs' reputation for high-quality data delivery and reliability.

ONE-MINUTE MODELSHIP

Please sit down with a human being, improve your existing relationship, help them create a product with AI at a peaceful time and during a crisis, and tell a product story on LinkedIn.

#RoleModelship #innovation #environment #AI #tech

TL;DR

- Today's **CTPOs** need to sit at the intersection of fiction lovers, product-minded innovators, entrepreneurs, and AI ethics role models.

- In the race to adopt AI and embed it in products, structured product management relies heavily on **pattern recognition** to identify where and how AI can add value. This approach meets **adaptive human learning**, as product teams must continuously develop new habits and insights to keep up with AI's evolving capabilities and applications.

- There are **hundreds of AI agents**, and they broadly fall into ten categories: AI agent builders, productivity tools, coding tools, customer service providers, digital workers, personal assistants, data analysts, workflow managers, content creators, and researchers. To manage and network multiple agents, an agentic mesh is needed.

- Designing **AI with emotional intelligence is essential to more humanity days**.

- Digital humans are powered by a unique combination of AI and a virtual nervous system that simulates real-time emotional responses.

- **Building intelligence directly into hardware** marks a transformative shift in workflows, pattern recognition, and complex decision-making, enabling faster, more intuitive, and contextually aware processes.

- **Leading indicators of success** in embedding emotional intelligence into digital humans would include the AI's ability to recognize and respond to nuanced human emotions, anticipate our contextual needs, and respond empathetically to our stress or anxiety, helping us configure ourselves for multiple futures.

- **AI stewardship of our planet** is essential for creating a sustainable future. By developing AI that actively monitors and manages environmental impacts, we ensure that future generations inherit a healthier world.

CHAPTER 13

Build Role Modelship into Functions

Fear is the path to the dark side. Fear leads to anger.
Anger leads to hate. Hate leads to suffering.

—YODA

The real problem of humanity is that we have Paleolithic
emotions, medieval institutions, and Godlike technology.

—E. O. WILSON

Meta gathers behavior data, including on Facebook, Instagram, and WhatsApp, to provide highly targeted advertising. Google collects data from its search engine, YouTube, and other platforms to do the same. Apple uses data from its App Store, Apple Music, and so on to refine user experiences and privacy. Amazon personalizes recommendations and optimizes inventory and the customer journey.

Netflix's relentless focus on user-centric product development has set the standard for streaming and recommendation engines. By focusing on an on-demand, ad-free experience with AI-driven personalization, Netflix revolutionized how we consume media.

These companies have built data stewardship as a core value in their organizations because high-quality data is the foundation for AI.

ENVISION YOUR FUNCTION BASED ON NETFLIX'S CUSTOMER OBSESSION

Netflix is a pioneer in customer obsession. For the company's streaming and recommendation engines described above, Role Modelship decisions about products, sales, marketing, and finance were made by AI-assisted humans.

Netflix uses a loosely defined model that has been referred to as a "Talent Density and Freedom" framework, in which emphasis is placed on hiring top talent and giving them the freedom to work creatively without micromanagement. It stands to reason that in the future, some decisions will be made by AI or by AI collaborating with AI autopilots. At the core of the AI transformation is the philosophical question of what the future corporate organization will look like and what the human role in it will be. What about manager benchmarks for span of control and ratios between different functions like sales, marketing, and finance?

The unprecedented nature of this new paradigm creates profound and perplexing possibilities for role models to lead in the

- Achievement of impossible human goals, assisted by AI

- Successful use of intelligent machines to perform tasks once presumed to be exclusively achievable by humans, improving unit economics significantly and increasing global gross domestic product

- Discovery and enforcement of decision lines between humans and AI (copilot, pilot, and autopilot)

- Mentorship of AI agents and influencing AI on how to refine each other's work and processes

- Routine inspections, approvals, governance, and security measures to monitor AI anomalies, biases, and escalations, making sure that AI doesn't apply self-preservation over human preservation

- Training of AI agents on when and how to use digital wallets and currencies or blockchains

- Continuous negotiation of values, organizational structures, and social contracts between humans and machines

- Use of AI energy, improving environmental impact

- Folding of AI-discovered strategies and tactics back into human plays

- Teaching of AI about humanity proportionally to teaching humans about AI and humanity

While the number of humans capable of building AI is growing, the ranks of humans contemplating AI implications on humanity remain dangerously thin. Therefore, we need more human role models than ever to determine the new relationship between humans, AI, reason, and reality.

DEMO DATA-DRIVEN DECISION HABITS

When I came to the United States in 1991, I carried a suitcase full of books and Bulgarian dictionaries and one 3.5-inch floppy disk. That disk had all the files I'd created that were worth stewarding: a total of five. Among them were my resume and two poems I'd written in Cyrillic.

Today, there are thousands of companies building data and analytics while data centers are sprouting like mustard seeds everywhere. Through AI, you can have an intelligent conversation with your data.

Children born today will not know a world in which data copilots and autopilots don't exist, just like my children don't know a world in which cell phones and social media don't exist.

As a chief operating officer at Qlik, Roberto Sigona transformed the success landscape for 45,000 global customers by establishing a highly effective customer-centric organization. His strategy included evolving Qlik's product offering and business model from the traditional business intelligence framework on the premises to an end-to-end data integration, data analytics, and AI cloud platform. This migration to cloud technology enhanced customer service for both small- to medium-size clients and large high-revenue clients under subscription and perpetual licensing models.

Overseeing an integrated global team of about one thousand professionals spanning education services, global support, consulting, customer success, renewal management, and internal IT, Sigona made sure the entire platform worked as intended. The IT team acted as customer zero, and the company significantly elevated the customer experience, growing revenue by increasing retention rates and customer adoption of its solutions.

Sigona posted on LinkedIn that, for him, customer success = CO (customer outcomes) + CX (customer experience).[1] As an example, his team worked with the general manager of analytics and AI, Brendan Grady, to design a simplified interface for casual users of Qlik Sense based on customer feedback and detailed usage data. Listening to and understanding different types of customers, not just the consensus, is essential.

Here are the results they achieved:

- **Increased customer renewals:** A more than 90 percent renewal rate on a more than $1 billion business, driven by solid onboarding, nurturing, and renewal processes

- **Customer support modernization:** Enhanced technical support through integration of social media and gen AI–enabled in-product chatbots, leading to a 15 percent point gain in the company's net promoter score while increasing the number of touchpoints by one thousand times

- **Greater professional services revenue:** An increase in professional services profit margins to the mid-thirties and the doubling of services revenue over the past five years

- **A streamlined customer experience:** A 50 percent reduction in the time required for customers to go live thanks to the launch of a digital onboarding and success plan

- **A higher rate of customer retention:** A 10 percent gain in net retention among accounts representing 70 percent of revenue after implementation of a customer success management program for that segment

- **Gains in net promoter score and efficiency:** A boost to a high-loyalty net promoter score of forty-nine among key accounts as a result of a 10 percent year-over-year improvement in organizational efficiency and effective relationship and outcome management.

Here is how Sigona describes mentorship in his career, as posted on LinkedIn:

> At the start of my career journey, I was lucky enough to be mentored by the best. Everyone from the chief marketing officer to the CEO of Autodesk took the time to both teach and listen to me. Without that foundation, I would not be where I am now.
>
> Mentoring must be a two-way street. Just as it's vital that we, as leaders, welcome new talent into the IT and technology industry and help them find their way, we should also be discovering what we can learn from those who are just starting out.
>
> For instance, young people today who are beginning their careers expect real-time interactions with a business via live chat, not a web form and having to wait for an

email reply. This is vital learning for many organizations. Being there to help our customers in a way that works for them is essential at Qlik.

When I was new at Autodesk, there was a room full of fax machines. That's how we took orders. As the plucky new talent in the company, I drove change and replaced that room full of fax machines with a website. That move transformed the business, and my career.

This was only possible because I was mentored by leaders who knew the younger generation were the key to the future. No fear of new tech or rapid change. Now that data integration and the powerful possibilities of AI are at the heart of business transformation, it feels reminiscent of that period when the Internet was so new.

As chief operating officer at Qlik, it's my turn and my privilege to give back and mentor—leading the next generation of leaders and listening to them. Just as I had ideas that could transform Autodesk as a fresh-faced 21-year-old, today's young people might just have the key to our next great move.

Thank you, Chris Bradshaw, Amar Hanspal, and Carl Bass, for your guidance, mentorship, and for giving me space, opportunity, and confidence to always try new things.[2]

Sigona is a multiplier role model who has impacted the values and economic value of my teams tremendously. I am eternally grateful for the example many can emulate.

———————◆———————

You're not one human.
You're hundreds of humans who look
like you, dream like you, model like you,
voice your voice, and stand behind you.

The following table is an example of a data-driven decision log for your decision factory (see table 13.1). You can customize it to your needs.

Table 13.1. A Data-Driven Decision Log

DECISION	DATE	KPI USED	VALUES	RESULTS
Launch tiered pricing model	Jan X, 20XX	Average revenue per user (ARPU), churn rate	Leadership (vision)	Increased ARPU by 15%; churn reduced by 5%
Implement customer success program	Mar X, 20XX	Net retention rate (NRR), customer satisfaction score (CSAT)	Stewardship (care)	NRR improved from 110% to 125%; CSAT rose by 20%
Expand enterprise sales team	Apr X, 20XX	Sales cycle time, win rate	Sponsorship (support)	Win rate increased by 12%; reduced sales cycle time by 8%
Optimize API ecosystem for partners	June X, 20XX	Partner-generated revenue, integration usage	Leadership (vision)	Partner revenue grew by 20%; API usage increased by 25%
Invest in employee upskilling	Aug X, 20XX	Employee engagement score, productivity	Mentorship (guidance)	Engagement score improved by 18%; productivity increased by 12%
Decisions and processes influenced by AI	Sept X, 20XX	Percentage of decisions made by AI, percentage of processes improved by AI	Mentorship (guidance)	Decision made by AI increased by 20%; processes improved by AI improved by 10%
Humans influencing AI	Nov X, 20XX	AI adherence to human values, AI leveraging diverse data	Stewardship (care)	Human values adherence 100%; leveraging diverse data 100%

—⋀⋀—modelship—⋀⋀—

AI GOVERNANCE

There can't be a role modeling book without paying tribute to Satoshi Nakamoto, the mysterious creator of Bitcoin, and Vitalik Buterin, the cofounder of Ethereum. Nakamoto introduced the first decentralized cryptocurrency in 2008, revolutionizing the way value and decisions can be recorded transparently without relying on central authorities. Buterin expanded on this vision in 2015 by creating a programmable blockchain that enables smart contracts, making decentralized applications and new models of collaboration possible.

Who you become = your habits × your role models.

Blockchains can be thought of as giant decision logs, meticulously recording every action, transaction, or agreement in a decentralized and immutable ledger. Each block represents a decision or a set of decisions, securely linked to the previous ones, creating an unbroken chain of accountability and transparency. By design, blockchains eliminate ambiguity, providing a single source of truth that reflects the collective choices of its participants.

Every role model featured in this book will tell you that technology initiatives don't fail because of technology; they fail because of a lack of data-driven decisions and the failure of automated processes in sales, products, finance, and customer success to document hidden knowledge and capture organizational wisdom. This is what discourages humans from adopting technology.

Synchronicity in an AI world may exist on planes not comprehendible by today's humans.

The role of humans is changing, and in addition to learning about technology, we need to spend more time improving AI governance, delineating when to delegate authority to AI agents, handling AI escalations, inspecting AI, approving goals AI has achieved, and, most importantly, teaching AI about our humanity.

To improve AI governance with a structured approach, consider strategies across the categories of stewardship, fellowship, mentorship, leadership, and sponsorship.

In large organizations, CIOs act as role models of cross-functional AI leadership. When managers focus on the inspection, governance, feedback, strategic thinking, guardrails, escalation management, and approvals of AI, the corporate organization assigns the responsibility differently.

- **Top of Organization** (Strategy Layer)

  » *Executive leadership:* Focuses on long-term vision, strategy, and high-level governance

  » *Alignment and guardrails:* Sets AI guiding principles, policies, and strategic frameworks

- **Middle of Organization** (Managerial Layer)

  » *Inspection and oversight:* Focuses on inspection, feedback loops, and maintaining guardrails established by executives

  » *Feedback, approvals, and escalation management:* Works closely with both leadership and operational teams to address these

- **Bottom of Organization** (Operational Teams and Execution)

  » *Empowered execution:* Agile and empowered, this group of humans, humanoids, and AI copilots, pilots, and autopilots performs tasks with a high degree of autonomy, staying within guardrails

  » *Self-managed teams:* Is self-directed and makes decisions within guardrails, proactively driving forward, reporting escalations and approvals to management

ENVISION AND CREATE CONFIGURABLE CAREER ROCKETS FOR AN AI WORLD

Every CXO is expected to be digital, apply AI to their function, and look at their company holistically. In the multidisciplinary human world assisted by AI (e.g., copilots, pilots, and autopilots), human mobility from organization to organization will increase.

As an analogy, a career vessel can be configured like a modular, reusable rocket. The modules are knowledge areas: Role Modelship, products, pricing, sales, marketing, finance, legal, human resources, IT, business development, hardware, and so on.

The rocket modules that got you to planet Sales will not get you to your new destination on planet Finance, where the language and key performance indicators are different.

The career rocket journey is nonlinear; it's more like ripples in space, expanding outward from a single point of origin—a moment of inspiration, a pivotal decision, or a first step in a chosen knowledge area.

Carry a digital quarter in your digital wallet, because you never know when you'll need to create ripples in space. Age is a persistent role model.

Configuring your career rocket for multiple futures is one of the most important human skills in an AI world.

Role Models are career catalysts and "value proposition engineers" who can help you navigate and negotiate your career journey. Full credit goes to Carnegie Mellon University Professor Stuart Evans for introducing me to the concept of multiple futures.

ONE-MINUTE MODELSHIP

Please sit down with a human being, improve your existing relationship, and help them chart their career journey, configuring it like a modular, reusable rocket and leveraging AI. Then, post about it on LinkedIn.

#RoleModelship

TL;DR

- In the future, some **decisions will be made by AI pilots or by AI pilots collaborating with AI autopilots**.

- The **ultimate immutable decision log** and an immutable ledger is a blockchain.

- **A career journey** can be configured like a modular, reusable rocket.

- The **career rocket journey is nonlinear**; it's more **like ripples in space**, expanding outward from a moment of inspiration, a pivotal decision, or a first step in a chosen knowledge area.

- Configuring your **career rocket for multiple futures** is one of the most important human skills in an AI world.

- Role models are **career catalysts** and "value proposition engineers."

CHAPTER 14

Change Management in the New Normal

Judge me by my size, do you? And well you should not.
For my ally is the Force, and a powerful ally it is.

—YODA

We choose to go to the moon in this decade
and do the other things, not because they
are easy, but because they are hard.

—JOHN F. KENNEDY

The future is here.

Payment platforms and crypto companies have announced an agentic payment workflow. Search engine optimization (SEO) is being replaced by generative engine optimization (GEO). We all need to be braver as role models in this new world.

Hopefully, you are following the writing on the wall and are ready to find new possibilities and opportunities to apply and influence AI.

RESPONDING TO CHANGE

Responding to change requires a mindset of adaptability and proactive engagement to ensure that challenges are met with options and solutions rather than resistance. It involves quickly assessing the impact, identifying opportunities, and aligning actions to desired outcomes. It calls for the ability to wear a company hat, a customer hat, and a team hat.

The concepts in both Spencer Johnson's *Who Moved My Cheese?* and Elisabeth Kübler-Ross's *On Death and Dying* illustrate how individuals respond to change by going through phases.[1] In Johnson's book, mice react differently when their cheese—a symbol for stability or success—is moved, mirroring the emotional stages of grief described in Kübler-Ross's book: denial, anger, bargaining, depression, and acceptance (DABDA). Some of the mice, like Hem, linger in denial and anger, refusing to adapt. Others, like Haw, progress and thrive in the new reality.

The writing on the wall holds significant value as a metaphor for recognizing and interpreting early signs of change, risk, or opportunity. It underscores the importance of awareness, foresight, and adaptability in navigating uncertain or shifting circumstances.

Key Benefits of Reading the Writing on the Wall

- Early warning system
- Promotes accountability
- Inspires action
- Supports resilience
- Drives growth and innovation

Role models play a critical part during transition times by guiding others through emotional phases to help them move from resistance to resilience. This involves modeling adaptability, fostering a growth mindset, and addressing emotions rather than dismissing them.

The *Who Moved My Cheese?* metaphor is particularly valuable for role models who must read the writing on the wall accurately and communicate implications effectively to guide others through transitions with clarity and confidence. By incorporating the following principles, role models can lead others toward acceptance and growth, fostering collective resilience during periods of upheaval.

Five Areas Role Models Can Exemplify During Transitions

- Acknowledge team emotional responses.
- Share personal experiences.
- Focus on the opportunities.
- Encourage small steps.
- Celebrate adaptability.

An open window in Paris may be the change you need in an AI world.

CHANNEL VOICES OF LEADERS ADAPTING TO CHANGE

Will Guidara is a renowned restaurateur and cofounder of Eleven Madison Park, one of the most highly rated restaurants in the world. He approaches change with a mindset of adaptability, empathy, and a deep commitment to excellence.

In his book, *Unreasonable Hospitality: The Remarkable Power of Giving People More Than They Expect*, he explores his philosophy of creating extraordinary guest experiences by going above and beyond. The book also provides insights into leadership, team-building, and the transformative impact of hospitality in any industry.

He emphasizes the importance of maintaining a people-first approach, ensuring that transitions are not only strategic but also considerate of his team's well-being and morale.[2]

Ash Lamb is a role model who leverages visual art as a transformative tool in change instigation and management. He simplifies complex concepts into digestible visuals that inspire creativity, clarity, and action. Through thoughtfully designed infographics, he helps organizations and individuals quickly move from their current state to a more valuable future state. Lamb's visual frameworks not only drive engagement but also foster emotional connections, helping people navigate change with confidence. I'm deeply grateful for his contributions and inspiration.

Do you need a great change-catalyst artist?

Rachel Bonds is the founder and principal of her eponymous management consulting company. As a former chief of staff at the nonprofit Teach For America, she has spoken on her success strategies for this vital position, providing actionable insights on how to effectively engage with senior leadership.

Role Modelship Example: Rachel Bonds

- **Sponsorship:** Rachel Bonds is a multiplier role model and a passionate advocate for diversity and inclusion in the technology sector, leveraging her platform to uplift underrepresented talent. She was selected as a 2025 fellow for IMPACT, a highly competitive executive leadership program with the Chicago Urban League, developing long-term plans to make a positive impact on the local Chicago community.

- **Leadership:** As a key advisor to the executive director of Teach For America, Bonds helped set the vision and direction for a community of 2,300 alumni, 160 teachers, and 25 staff members in Washington, DC, and Prince George's County, Maryland. Responsible for overseeing operations, she managed a $7 million operating budget.

- **Mentorship:** Deeply committed to mentorship, Bonds plays an integral role in guiding emerging leaders in technology and education. She created professional development curriculum for the Innovate to Elevate initiative, aimed at providing Kentucky-based youth and formerly incarcerated individuals with professional and life skills.

- **Fellowship:** Bonds cultivates a collaborative culture within her teams, emphasizing the importance of strong relationships and community among colleagues. Her focus on inclusion and teamwork drives collective success and enhances the overall workplace environment. Additionally, as a vice president in charge of diversity, equity, and inclusion at Insight Partners, she launched the firm's first global DEI advisory practice.

- **Stewardship:** While at Google, Bonds drove diversity hiring strategies and initiatives across the global staffing division. She managed global training on "culture add versus culture fit," overseeing a team of more than sixty facilitators and leading the delivery of more than three thousand workshops. Bonds also serves on the board for LIFT and Climb Hire.

When I asked her three questions, she responded with thoughtful clarity.

Q: What role modeling habits would you load into the operating system of a humanoid?

A: *Active listening skills, vulnerable leadership, empathy, integrity, perseverance, and accountability.*

Q: Who are some of your role models, mentors, and sponsors?

A: *One of my former managers and mentors at Teach For America taught me a great lesson about making mistakes to facilitate growth. She was the opposite of a micromanager and gave me the space to try out new ideas, even if she had a very different approach to solving problems. I learned how to trust my instincts and built my stamina to "fail fast" and course correct. This was the first time I experienced truly effective leadership and has been a blueprint for how I approach management of my own teams. As a leader, I learned that my job is to clarify the destination, offer support when it's needed, and—most importantly—get out of the way!*

Q: If you could role model only one thing, what would that be?

A: *Vulnerability as a sign of strength. Anyone who works with me now knows that vulnerability and transparency are key elements of my leadership style. I share what I know, I'm honest when I don't have an answer, and I prioritize building environments where everyone on the team is appreciated for their unique genius.*

CHANGE MANAGEMENT USING HARVEY BALLS AND PYRAMIDS

A fast-growing company can utilize Harvey Balls to manage and visualize progress in four critical areas of change: Role Modeling, AI innovation, financial performance, and board composition (see figure 14.1).

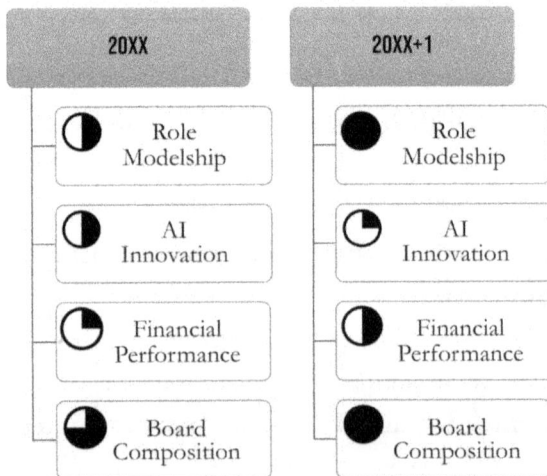

Figure 14.1. Change management in four critical areas.

In Role Modelship, the company might achieve a 50 percent rating one year, with room for improvement in aligning middle management.

For AI innovation, the company might score 50 percent, indicating a promising adoption of AI tools to enhance product capabilities, customer experiences, and operational efficiency.

In financial performance, the organization could earn a 25 percent score, for inconsistent revenue growth and quarters without profitability.

In board composition, the company might baseline itself at 75 percent in the age of AI.

✦

It rained in Egypt,
and it reminded me that
the pyramids were built by humans
who didn't melt from a few tears.

The pyramid structure helps prioritize and communicate information during change initiatives (see figure 14.2).

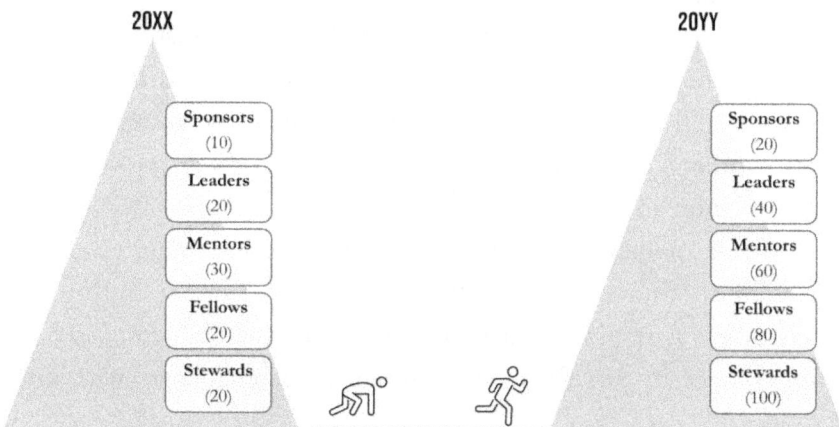

Figure 14.2. The Role Modelship Pyramid for change management.

The Role Modelship Pyramid can be used as a Change Pyramid to represent the number of humans at each layer for driving transformation.

CHANGE-MANAGEMENT LEVERAGING THE MARATHON EFFECT

The marathon effect is an analogy often used by executives to describe change progress in an organization. The executive team is typically first to cross the finish line and often forgets to bring everyone else along. Seeing someone achieve a significant milestone inspires others to strive for excellence. It is the responsibility of those who cross the line first to help everyone else (see figure 14.3).

Figure 14.3. The marathon effect.

Role models play a critical part in managing the marathon effect in change adoption by setting an example, fostering an empowering environment, and bringing others along. A powerful historical example is Gertrude Ederle, the first woman to swim across the English Channel, in 1926. Her achievement shattered societal expectations about women's physical limitations, proving what was possible with determination and preparation.

For role models, managing the marathon effect requires careful communication, especially for those who are still at the starting line when others have already crossed the finish line. The iconic Bay to Breakers race in San Francisco highlights this challenge, with elite runners finishing the course while other participants are just beginning their journey.

Leaders must ensure that the enthusiasm and recognition for the front-runners do not discourage those at the back who may still have doubts. Instead, they should emphasize the value of everyone's unique pace, celebrating progress wherever it happens and keeping the energy alive for latecomers.

Full credit goes to Jeff Brzycki for teaching his teams about DABDA and the marathon effect at Autodesk many years ago.

CRAWL → WALK → RUN YOUR WAY

The Crawl → Walk → Run framework is an effective approach to managing change with achievable milestones to build momentum.

In the Crawl phase, organizations focus on laying the groundwork by assessing readiness, building awareness, and piloting small-scale initiatives. The Walk phase involves scaling up these efforts, standardizing processes, and fostering engagement. Finally, the Run phase accelerates momentum, integrating change fully into the organization's culture and operations.

This phased approach minimizes risks and ensures sustainable transformation. In the world of AI and rapid innovation, these three phases are very compressed, and instead of taking years, they take days and weeks to achieve (see figure 14.4 and table 14.1).

Figure 14.4. The Crawl → Walk → Run phased approach.

Table 14.1. A Summary of the Crawl ⟶ Walk ⟶ Run Phased Approach to AI and Rapid Innovation

AREA	CRAWL	WALK	RUN
Product	Identify areas for AI integration (e.g., personalization or recommendation engines) Conduct small-scale pilots with off-the-shelf AI tools	Build AI capabilities for predictive analytics and user feedback loops Enhance user experience through iterative AI-driven improvements	Fully integrate AI into the product life cycle, leveraging proprietary algorithms Develop customer-centric AI models to create differentiated, scalable products
Marketing	Automate email campaigns and social media scheduling with AI tools Use AI to analyze customer demographics and refine target audiences	Deploy AI-driven customer journey mapping, and personalize campaigns at scale Optimize ad spending by using AI for real-time, data-driven decisions	Use generative AI for multilingual content creation and sentiment-based trend predictions Create adaptive marketing strategies with advanced AI models
Sales	Use AI-powered customer relationship management systems for data entry and lead tracking Train sales teams to use AI insights for prospecting and qualification	Implement AI chatbots for initial inquiries and support Use AI models to recommend upselling and cross-selling opportunities	Adopt AI-driven coaching and fully integrated dynamic workflows Enable AI-driven, demand-based dynamic pricing and personalized sales proposals
Finance	Automate financial key performance indicators and reconciliation tasks with AI Use AI for fraud detection	Implement AI for cash flow forecasting and scenario modeling Analyze financial trends and operational costs using AI	Integrate AI into enterprise-wide decision-making and board management Develop proprietary AI tools for investment optimization and strategic financial planning

---

*Humanity's future power lies
in our regenerative words,
just as a hydra's resiliency multiplies
when its heads grow and adapt.*

François Chollet, one of the brightest minds in AI, departed Google to start his own company. At just thirty-four years old, he created Keras, an open-source application programming interface in machine learning that simplifies the creation of AI models. Keras has more than two million users globally and plays a vital role in the development of Waymo self-driving cars; the curation of YouTube, Netflix, and Spotify recommendations; and many other engineering platform features. Its milestones delineate the acceleration of change today.

However, we're still in the very early stages of AI development. Chollet, for example, envisions AI to have humanlike reasoning without relying on computation, more data, and bigger AI models. Google and Open AI, on the other hand, continue to focus on scaling AI models. We'll no doubt benefit from their collective commitment to advancing human knowledge.

Applying the principles of *Conscious Capitalism*, by John Mackey and Raj Sisodia, as a change-management approach can also focus on embedding values, purpose, stakeholder integration, and conscious leadership into the transformation process. The book asserts a core idea that businesses should operate with a higher purpose beyond profits, which in a change-management context means tying initiatives to a meaningful mission, such as improving employee well-being or environmental sustainability.[3]

Just as *Conscious Capitalism* aligns business practices with purpose, a music venue adopts a similar philosophy when tailoring its capabilities to the changing requirements of each performer.

In 1997, tech pioneer Don Green kick-started the Green Music Center (GMC) project at California's Sonoma State University with a $5 million donation, which ultimately turned into $145 million by the center's opening on September 29, 2012. He implemented a phased rollout strategy to introduce new capabilities, carefully preparing for the high-profile feature of a sold-out concert by renowned Chinese pianist Lang Lang. The GMC emerged as a cornerstone of the local arts scene, reflecting Sonoma State's dedication to cultural engagement.

The center includes the 1,400-seat Weill Hall and the 240-seat Schroeder Hall, which is renowned for its exceptional pipe organ.

Every role model brings their own acoustics to the theater of life and change.

With acoustics and design comparable to those of prestigious venues like Carnegie Hall and the Disney Concert Hall, Weill Hall boasts fifty-three-foot-high ceilings, custom maple seating, and more than 500 air ducts for optimal sound quality. It includes a large stage that can accommodate 115 musicians and has hosted numerous performances, responding to evolving requirements. The facility also includes a unique outdoor HDTV screen for broadcasting to 1,500 fans at wine and cheese events held on the terraced lawn outside.

The GMC has tailored its capabilities to changing requirements from a wide range of artists across its performance venues, particularly the acclaimed Weill Hall. Top artists who have performed there include renowned cellist Yo-Yo Ma, Grammy-winning violinist Pinchas Zukerman, and accomplished pianist Olga Kern. Other notable artists have included jazz icons Wynton Marsalis, Emmy Award winner and multiplatinum artist Andy Grammer, the San Francisco Gay Men's Chorus, and Yamato—the drummers of Japan.

✍ ONE-MINUTE MODELSHIP

Share a change method that resonated with you and how you applied it so you can lead humans through change.
   #RoleModelship

TL;DR

- The concepts in *Who Moved My Cheese?* and *On Death and Dying* illustrate how individuals respond to change by going through phases.

- The **writing on the wall** holds significant value as a metaphor for recognizing and interpreting early signs of change, risk, or opportunity.

- Role models play a critical part in managing the **marathon effect** by guiding others through emotional phases to help them move from resistance to resilience. This involves modeling adaptability, fostering a growth mindset, and addressing emotions.

- A fast-growing company can utilize **Harvey Balls** to manage and visualize progress in four critical areas of change: **Role Modeling, AI innovation, financial performance, and board composition**.

- The **Role Modelship Pyramid** can be used as a **Change Pyramid** to represent the number of humans at each layer for driving transformation.

- The **Crawl → Walk → Run** framework is an effective approach to managing change with achievable milestones that demonstrate continuous progress to build momentum.

CHAPTER 15

Economic Impact of Fragile, Resilient, and Antifragile Role Modelship

Train people well enough so they can leave.
Treat them well enough so they don't want to.
—RICHARD BRANSON

Optimism is a moral choice. I wake up every
day and choose to be optimistic.
—CHELSEA CLINTON

Birth. Graduation. Parenthood. Promotion. Getting laid off. Retirement.

Life has universal milestones that mark personal growth, societal roles, and transitions. The pivotal events in life are shaped by role models and influenced by cultural, religious, organizational, and product innovation.

For example, below are some key milestones:

1. **Birth/parenthood**
   The start of life or creation of a life is often celebrated by extended families with naming, guardianship, religious ceremonies, birthdays, and, in some cultures, name days.

2. **Development and education**
   Baby's first steps, starting school, earning an undergraduate degree, making the dean's list, graduating, earning a PhD, enrolling in executive education

3. **Marriage/partnerships/divorce**
   Major social events in which individuals form or break lifelong commitments

4. **Citizenship**
   Which flag did you pledge allegiance to?

5. **Career firsts and lasts**
   A first job, promotion, first product, CXO level, board, the bar, volunteerism, sponsorship, medal, record, movie, house, savings account, last company, layoff, retirement celebration

6. **Near-death**
   Did your wife save you from a heart attack?

7. **Death**
   Celebrations of life are a culmination to honor the poets in us. What new milestones will be added in an AI world? Will you choose to have a digital avatar that succeeds you?

ROLE MODELSHIP AT MILESTONES AS THE ANTIDOTE TO FRAGILITY

Role Modelship during life milestones is critical for fostering anti-fragility because these moments represent times of vulnerability, uncertainty, and significant change. Learning from fragile role models teaches the consequences of avoiding risks, offering cautionary stories of what happens when humans, organizations, or products fail to adapt to the moving cheese. Channeling resilient role models demonstrates how to withstand adversity. Antifragile role models show up differently and thrive by actively leveraging volatility, uncertainty, and failure as opportunities for finding new cheese.

You realized you are a multiplier role model, and your worldview changed.

Some humans take more risks, based on their mental models, due to a combination of psychological, social, and situational factors such as

1. **Optimism bias**

   At milestones, people often feel optimism about the future, leading them to underestimate risks or overestimate their ability to succeed, especially when they view the milestone as a fresh start.

2. **Identity shifts**

   Milestones trigger a reevaluation of personal identity. How did your friends treat you during your last identity crisis?

3. **Safety nets**

   At some milestones, people may perceive a stronger safety net. Did you have family support when making career decisions? Did you have savings when you retired?

Little houses on the hillside,
little houses full of model dolls, trains, and ships,
full of birthdays, holidays, and citizenships,
full of power to model identity and discovery,
connection, resilience, legacy, and friendship.

Role models have a disproportionately greater influence during pivotal life moments. This phenomenon can be linked to principles from physics, economics, math, and behavioral science.

- *Physics: critical points in systems*

  In physics, systems at critical points are highly sensitive to small inputs, which can significantly influence the outcome (e.g., phase transitions—water turning to ice or steam). Similarly, pivotal life moments are transition states in which a role model's words or actions can dramatically shape the trajectory.

- *Economics: marginal utility*

  "Marginal utility" describes how the value of an additional unit depends on the current situation. At pivotal moments, the utility of words or actions from a role model is higher because the stakes are elevated. AI struggles to identify which correlations hold the most value from a human perspective.

- *Mathematics: nonlinear dynamics*

  Life decisions often follow nonlinear patterns. Small influences could result in changes in direction at key moments that lead to vastly different outcomes, akin to the butterfly effect.

- *Behavioral science: plasticity and emotional resonance*

  During life transitions, individuals experience greater neuroplasticity and emotional vulnerability, making them more open to influence.

Whom do you model when you encounter unknowable unknowns?

ORGANIZATIONAL MEMORY AS
THE ANTIDOTE TO FRAGILITY

At some amazing companies, employees stay for twenty or more years and become the historians of our windows of social change—company revenue achievements balanced with Role Modelship.

In early-stage companies, Role Modelship of pivotal company events (e.g., first layoff, first acquisition, first economic recession, or IPO) can be quite challenging because of a lack of organizational muscle memory. In other words, these organizations have no routine habits for handling a high-impact event, which increases their need for external role models.

Organizational memory is the antidote to organizational fragility. It can be imported from other organizations through research. When is the last time you asked these questions: What would we do differently if we were building this greenfield? If we were a start-up? If we were Amazon, Netflix, Google, or Autodesk?

Steve Davis is cofounder of AdaptiveION and former managing director and chief customer officer at Accenture. I met him at an HMG Strategy event, and we discussed organizational memory, humanoids, and adaptability.

"I'm glad that the concept of organizational muscle memory resonated with you," said Davis. "It's a critical distinction that many organizations face—operating and growing come more naturally, while innovating and transforming often require a different set of skills and disciplines. I'd be happy to provide my perspective on your questions."

Q: What's the best way for CTO and CPO role models to improve their company's innovation and transformation muscle memory?

A: *Strengthening the "innovate and transform" muscle starts with establishing a regular cadence for feedback—building a continuous feedback loop that guides adaptation. Role models in these positions can foster this by setting clear checkpoints, ensuring that insights from product usage, market shifts, and technology are constantly feeding back into strategy.*

Equally important is the ability to create focus rather than chaos within the organization. I often say that leaders should "major in what's most important"—focusing on high-impact areas while minimizing distractions, or "the minors," that can derail progress.

Lastly, high-performing teams thrive on a culture of unity. A great role model once reminded me to listen for language that emphasizes "we" and "us" over "I," "they," or "them." When leaders model this language, they reinforce the mindset.

Q: What role modeling habits would you load into the operating system of a humanoid?

A: *If we were to "code" role modeling habits into an operating system for a humanoid, I'd start with two key habits: relentless curiosity and disciplined reflection. Relentless curiosity drives exploration and willingness to question the status quo. Disciplined reflection ensures that learning isn't just experiential but intentional.*

✦

Modelship chain reactions, feedback loops, and network effects compound over time.

Building on the foundational role of modelship in enhancing organizational memory, the board of directors emerges as a critical entity for fostering enterprise antifragility and preserving collective multicompany knowledge.

Coco Brown is the founder and CEO of Athena Alliance, whose mission is to advance women entrepreneurs and leaders and prepare them to serve on boards. Board service is crucial for economic impact, because it fosters diversity in decision-making, leading to more innovative and effective strategies that can drive business growth. Women and underrepresented groups in board roles can inspire future generations.

Role Modelship Example: Coco Brown

- **Sponsorship:** Coco Brown is a strong advocate for women in business, as she demonstrates through her leadership at the San Francisco–based Athena Alliance, which has successfully placed more than 500 women on corporate boards. Named one of the *Silicon Valley Business Journal*'s 100 most powerful leaders, Brown and her alliance provide thought leadership for modern governance to an ecosystem of more than 30,000 global executives. Athena Alliance also directly supports 1,000 women through its platform and services.

- **Leadership:** As the founder and CEO of the alliance, Brown's mission is to elevate female representation in leadership roles. Members, like Traci Granston, MD, are addressing health care inefficiencies with AI-powered solutions, while others, like Jessica Billingsley, provide insights on leveraging AI for strategic business advantages.

- **Mentorship:** Brown is deeply committed to mentorship, offering guidance, resources, and support to women as they navigate their careers.

- **Fellowship:** She fosters community building to promote a culture of inclusion and empowerment among members.

- **Stewardship:** Brown's stewardship is evident in her long-term vision for advancing women in business. She champions responsible practices that enhance inclusion, ensuring that women have equal opportunities to succeed in leadership positions.

ECONOMIC IMPACT OF ROLE MODELS

Kristalina Georgieva, managing director of the International Monetary Fund (IMF), has shared her analysis of leadership and role modeling, emphasizing the importance of numbers for impact. Prior to working at the IMF, Georgieva was chief executive officer of the World Bank

Group. She was named European of the Year and Commissioner of the Year by Brussels-based newspaper *European Voice*.

She points out that Sweden's gross domestic product would be 4 percent higher if women fully participated in the economy on equal terms, and Senegal's would be 8 percent higher.[1] In her mind, role models play a critical role in unlocking economic potential through equitable practices.[2]

Georgieva stresses the importance of visible and quantifiable actions by leaders to inspire change. She cited recent IMF analysis showing that if unpaid work was counted, global gross domestic product would increase by 35–40 percent. Women do more unpaid work than men, on average 2.5 hours more per day, though this margin varies depending on the country, with women in Norway doing 20 percent more work, women in Japan 380 percent, and women in Pakistan as much as 1,000 percent.[3]

The Gallup–Amazon *Role Models Matter* report highlights the profound impact that role models have on shaping career paths. Surveying 3,792 American eighteen-to-forty-year-olds in early and midcareer stages, the research explores how career education and exposure to role models during middle and high school influence professional choices.

According to the study, 84 percent of young adults who grew up in a medium- to high-income family had someone with a successful career to look up to, compared with 28 percent in low-income families.[4] Relatedly, 38 percent of young adults from lower-income backgrounds indicated there was no one who taught them how to be successful, compared with 18 percent from households with higher incomes.

Among adults younger than forty who reported that their career role model had similar life experiences to their own, 82 percent said they believed in themselves, and 78 percent said they felt they belong. However, only 56 percent of those with role models who did not have similar life experiences expressed belief in themselves, and 52 percent said they felt they belong. Ninety percent of those who reported having a role model indicated that they and their role model were the same race, and 77 percent said they were the same gender. Seventy-seven percent indicated that they trusted their role model's knowledge and expertise, and 68 percent said their role model's level of career success seemed realistic to achieve.

In her 2019 TED Talk, America Ferrera shared a deeply personal account of her journey as a Latina in the entertainment industry, emphasizing how role models shape self-perception and ambition.[5] She highlighted the barriers she faced early in her career, such as being limited to stereotypical roles like "gangbanger's girlfriend" or "pregnant chola #2." These experiences pushed her to fight for authentic representation, not only for herself but for others who rarely saw their lives reflected on screen. Ferrera described her identity as her "superpower." She argued that representation teaches people to recognize their value and aspire to greater possibilities.

Let's look at a simplified formula for cumulative impact of a role model and a couple of examples (see figure 15.1).

CUMULATIVE IMPACT =

$$\sum_{i=1}^{m} \left(\sum_{t=1}^{n} \text{Initial Impact}_i \times \left(1 + \text{Growth Rate} \right)^t \right)$$

Figure 15.1. The cumulative impact formula.

- m is the total number of individuals impacted by the role model.

- Initial impact is the starting value a role model contributes.

- The inner summation calculates the cumulative impact of a role model on each human, organization, or product over a number of years.

- The outer summation calculates the total cumulative impact by summing the impacts of multiple role models.

Scenario One: Two experienced entrepreneurs mentor a start-up CEO, each helping the company find product-market fit, generate $25,000 in revenue in the first year, and grow at a yearly rate of 20 percent for five years. The impact is $446,496 over five years.

- **Formula Input:**
  - » $m = 2$ (two role models), $n = 5$ (five years)
  - » Initial impact = $25,000 revenue generated by each role model
  - » Growth rate = 20% annually
  - » Sum for one role model = $223,248
  - » Multiply by 2 role models = $446,496

Scenario Two: When forty-four million people like or share a kind, positive message from Dove Chocolate, AI chatbots, voice assistants, or customer service models will begin to mimic that tone of kindness in responses. Influence is a form of social capital with compounding effects.

- **Assumption 1:** Annual sales

  Dove is part of Mars, Inc., with annual sales of $40 billion across its products. Let's assume Dove Promises represents just 5 percent of Mars' chocolate sales, and chocolate is 50 percent of Mars' revenue. That is $1 billion in revenue annually.

- **Assumption 2:** Units sold

  Premium chocolate bars or packs typically range from $3 to $6 retail. Let's assume an average price of $4.50. That is 222.2 million packs sold.

- **Assumption 3:** Messages per unit

  A pack of Dove Promises contains approximately twenty individually wrapped chocolates, each with a positive message. That is 4.44 billion messages per year. Narratives shape AI training data.

- **Impact of one message**

   If just 1 percent of consumers (a conservative estimate) are influenced in a meaningful way to make a positive decision in our decision factories of the future, the impact reaches millions of humans.

- **Positive human influences** = 44.4 million humans annually experience happiness.

- **Positive influences on AI:** Language models learn from public discourse. Repetition of affirming messages helps bias the model toward constructive, uplifting responses rather than sarcasm or toxicity. Algorithms (e.g., on YouTube, Instagram, or TikTok) prioritize content that trends. A wave of positivity boosts the weight of similar messages in future recommendation cycles. If enough positive messages go viral, AI systems begin to prioritize optimism, gratitude, and humanity—shaping how culture is reflected and amplified online. Forty-four million people engaging with one kind Dove quote teaches AI that this is what matters.

Role Modelship Example: Anoshua Chaudhuri, PhD

- **Sponsorship:** Anoshua Chaudhuri has supported policies and programs that uplift underrepresented voices and improve health outcomes for vulnerable populations, particularly children and the elderly. Through her work in both the economics department and the Center for Equity and Excellence in Teaching and Learning (CEETL) at San Francisco State University (SFSU), she has advocated for

continued

evidence-based teaching practices that enable low-income and first-generation college students to be successful.

- **Leadership:** As a two-term chair of the SFSU economics department, Chaudhuri effectively led academic programs and research initiatives, aligning them with institutional and community needs. She initiated the blended bachelor's–master's San Francisco State Scholars Program in economics, and under her leadership, the economics master's program was reinvigorated and redesigned as a STEM-certified program in quantitative economics.

- **Mentorship:** Through her teaching in health economics, gender economics, and microeconomics, Chaudhuri has mentored countless students, integrating active learning and community service learning into her curriculum.

- **Fellowship:** Her collaborations with community agencies and her roles on the boards of the university corporation and the mental health–focused nonprofit Richmond Area Multi-Services demonstrate her commitment to building strong partnerships. She also continues to be an active member of the American Economic Association and the Indian Health Economics and Policy Association.

- **Stewardship:** Chaudhuri has dedicated her career to advancing community health and education, emphasizing participatory research and impactful teaching. As the senior director of CEETL and a member of the SFSU Institute for Civic and Community Engagement advisory board, she has fostered a culture of excellence in teaching, earning the prestigious Lam-Larsen Distinguished Service Professor award.

During her more than twenty years of experience, including her tenure as a professor and two terms of service as economics department chair, Chaudhuri has dedicated her career to fostering equity-driven education. Her vast knowledge and passion for economics have made her a magnet for eager young minds throughout the years.

Q: Who are some of your role models and sponsors?

A: *I drew strength from all my mentors. My mother, who was a teacher and a lifelong learner, was my greatest role model. Others were my dissertation committee members, each of whom placed faith in my abilities, encouraged me, and showed me the way. I imbided my open-door policy for students from one of my teachers/mentors.*

Q: What are the most important habits for the next generation of role models in an AI world?

A: *Being early innovators, modeling integrity, and practicing equitable and inclusive practices will distinguish the impactful role models in the age of AI.*

Q: What would you want an AI agent trained to model you to learn from you?

A: *The diverse gendered perspectives that are sadly lacking in mainstream economics and would therefore never show up in AI large language models (LLMs). We have to be intentional about feeding those into the LLMs.*

Q: What's one aspect of economics that you think AI could not fully replicate?

A: *Looking through the output, thinking critically, and adapting.*

ECONOMIC IMPACT OF ROLE MODELS ON COMMUNITY

"The most important thing . . . is that the brain of a child will become exactly what the child was exposed to. It is the mirror to the child's developmental experience," said American psychiatrist Bruce Perry, MD, PhD.

———————————— ✦ ————————————

Take lessons in modelship.
Give back time generously.
Give kindness away.

I sat down with Carol Potter, my mother-in-law and a social worker of seventeen years at Cope Family Center in Napa, California. Over the years, she has helped more than 300 clients, including many families with children.

Q: Can you share a specific example of someone you've worked with who overcame significant challenges to achieve their dreams?

A: *Absolutely. One of my clients was a thirty-two-year-old woman who was pregnant with twins. She didn't know who the father was. She came from a difficult background; her mother had a severe history of drug abuse. It took a while to earn her trust, but I could see that she was very smart and a truly beautiful person.*

Q: How did you help her begin to see her potential?

A: *It started with the basics. I helped her secure a housing voucher, and we worked on getting her onto disability for the remainder of her pregnancy. After her two beautiful girls were born, she was on welfare.*

So I asked her, "Do you want to be your daughters' role model in ten years?" That question seemed to light a spark. She immediately said yes. She told me, "I had an aunt who was a nurse, and I really admired her. I think I'd enjoy being a nurse, but I don't know if I'm smart enough."

Q: What steps did you take from there to help her achieve that goal?

A: *We talked about starting small, and I suggested a counselor at the local college. She was incredibly bright but needed to learn study techniques. She's now working on her master's in nursing. She's earning good money, staying drug free, and raising her two beautiful girls.*

To stay forever young,
take a pocket full of
modelship sunshine
to any mountain you climb.

ROLE MODELSHIP AS THE "MOTHER OF VALUES"

It can be said that Role Modelship is the "mother of values" because role models serve as the primary shapers and transmitters of values. Through their values, actions, behaviors, and attitudes, role models (humans, organizations, and products) teach us what is important.

AI is a giant mirror. AI can't be what it can't see. Be the reflection you want to see.

Maxine Lee, PhD, earned her doctorate in economics from the University of California, Santa Barbara, and is currently a member of the faculty at San Francisco State University.

Her research includes influential work on the economic impacts of sexual orientation and gender identity, examining how policies affect economic outcomes. She has published widely on the economic challenges faced by gender minorities, offering groundbreaking insights based on national data. Her studies delve into the effects of trade policies and minimum wage on educational and economic outcomes.

When I asked her to talk about role models, she was generous and insightful.

Q: How would you measure the economic impact of a resilient versus antifragile role model?

A: Antifragili*ty refers to ways in which we benefit from stressors and challenges to find new visions and opportunities. Learning from an antifragile role model should improve our human capital. In turn, the additional human capital, whether it's in the form of additional skills we learned or formal education that we received while overcoming those challenges, increases the individual's productivity and potential earnings in the labor market. Resilience alone doesn't prompt individuals to use challenges to improve their human capital. It simply allows them to persist in their roles. To survive in a rapidly changing world where jobs we know may disappear, we need the ability to look for opportunities where others only see challenges.*

Q: What are the most important habits for the next generation of role models in an AI world?

A: *Adaptability. There is plenty of literature in economics and other fields that documents how education and training can improve workers' outcomes in a rapidly changing world as technology advances. The ability to ask the right questions and logically think through answers, regardless of the specific field, is a great skill to have.*

Q: What's one aspect of economics that you think AI could not fully replicate?

A: *Thinking about the academic field of economics, the ability to ask the right questions about human behavior and how those behaviors affect the efficient allocation of resources comes to mind. In terms of technical skills, AI most likely trumps any human already, but I don't think AI can discern which correlations are more "valuable" from a human standpoint. In other words, humans still have an advantage in being able to ask questions that are relevant to our utility (i.e., happiness) and pick out the most relevant analyses for us to study out of the many that AI can conduct.*

In a similar way, humans may retain the advantage in being able to read other humans. Human behavior is sometimes masked in data. For example, in thinking about differences in the earnings of LGBTQ+ people relative to those of cisgender heterosexual people, simply measuring the earnings gaps does not tell the whole story. Those earnings gaps may be biased because humans may conceal their identity if they think they would be exposed to more severe discrimination by coming out. So those LGBTQ+ people who are worse off may not even be observed in the data.

I also sat down with Shantha Mohan, PhD, cofounder and former chief development officer of Retail Solutions software company in Mountain View, California, at the CMU NASA campus to discuss the future of innovation and leadership, reflecting on how Role Modelship in both professional and academic settings can shape the trajectory of the next generation of leaders.

Q. What Role Modelship habits would you load into the operating system of a humanoid?

A: *I would focus on the principles of servant leadership, a style pioneered by [management development theorist] Robert K. Greenleaf. This involves prioritizing the needs of others, practicing active listening, and engaging with humility. The humanoid would also embody self-awareness, reflect on its interactions, and have the courage to collaborate and build shared vision. Additional habits would include communicating with empathy, accepting responsibility for its actions, and being authentic and transparent.*

Q. Can you share an example of mentoring and sponsoring others?

A: *In my career, as head of product development and cofounder [of Retail Solutions], I mentored several individuals, many of whom have gone on to lead teams and excel in their fields. After retiring, I continued mentoring students remotely from my alma mater in India. Thanks to modern technology like Zoom and WhatsApp, I can stay connected and offer guidance. Additionally, I mentor students at Carnegie Mellon's Silicon Valley campus and am actively involved in the Barbara Smith Women's Mentoring Program and the Society of Women Engineers. I also participate in Toastmasters, where I mentor new members.*

Q: What are the most important habits for the next generation of role models?

A: *In my book,* Leadership Lessons with The Beatles, *I discuss several key habits for future role models. These include fostering curiosity, maintaining a positive attitude, combining confidence with humility, and persevering toward goals while remaining flexible.*

ONE-MINUTE MODELSHIP

Help a nonprofit or follow Mark Benioff's challenge of 1:1:1, committing 1 percent of equity, product, and time to the community for impact.

#RoleModelship

TL;DR

- **Milestones**—birth, education, career firsts and lasts, citizenship, death—are shaped by role models and influenced by cultural, religious, organizational, and product innovation.

- **Role Modelship at milestones** is critical for fostering antifragility.

- Role models have a **disproportionately greater influence during pivotal life moments**. These moments are inflection points at which humans are highly receptive to guidance, support, and inspiration.

- **Organizational memory** is the antidote to organizational fragility, and it can be imported from other organizations by research and leveraging external role models.

- To calculate the cumulative **economic impact of a role model**, a simplified formula can be used.

- AI can't discern which correlations are more "valuable" from a human standpoint. In other words, **humans still have an advantage in being able to ask questions** that are relevant to our utility (i.e., happiness).

- Language models learn from public discourse. Repetition of affirming messages helps bias the model toward constructive, uplifting responses rather than sarcasm or toxicity. Narratives shape AI training data.

PART IV

OUR FUTURE
IS HUMAN

CHAPTER 16

On the Shoulders of Giants: Role Model Lineage

If I have seen further, it is by
standing on the shoulders of giants.
—ISAAC NEWTON

I f you're standing on the shoulders of giants, can you skip learning to walk on two legs? Giants with multiplier modelship values understand that their success is not about personal achievement. It is about uplifting organizations, opening doors and windows of social change to create ripple effects. This approach transforms giants from towering figures of intellect to approachable, relatable mentors whose influence endures across generations.

$\bigstar$

Standing on the shoulders of role models
doesn't mean you can skip hopscotch practice.

Giants don't always have to be adults; sometimes, they can be extraordinary nine-year-olds.

AWAKEN THE GIANT WITHIN YOU

In my family, we love apple pie and make one from scratch for Thanksgiving every year, built upon an elaborate foundation of events, like seeding, growing, harvesting, and apples falling from trees.

Carl Sagan, an American astronomer and astrophysicist, once said on the KCET series *Cosmos*, "If you wish to make an apple pie from scratch, you must first invent the universe," emphasizing the profound interconnectedness and compound effect of the universe.[1] Everything we do is dependent on a vast network of natural laws, from the origins of seeds to the routines governing our actions. The iconic phrase "as American as apple pie" has been famously used by many, including President Barack Obama, as part of the American cultural identity.[2]

What you apply today,
a giant shouldered yesterday.
Positive routines you leave behind
will compound human design.

So how do you awaken the giant within you?

You awaken the giant by anchoring humans, organizations, and products in values and positively reframed routines, climbing the giant's Role Modelship ladder.

In his book *Awaken the Giant Within*, Tony Robbins emphasizes the power of words and reframing in shaping our mental models and routines. Reframing involves shifting perspectives to create empowering meanings for events. Events themselves don't have inherent meaning; it's the meaning we assign to them that drives our reactions and routines. You can leverage events to serve as human value triggers. The most effective CXOs reframe events naturally; you can see demos of this at meetings in which the discussion gets reframed before the team engages (see figure 16.1).

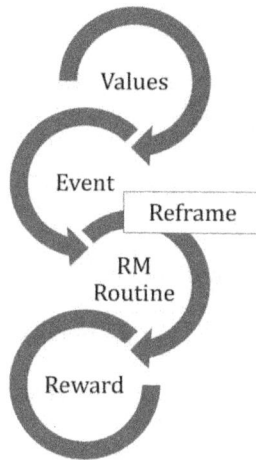

Figure 16.1. Reframing the discussion.

Here are examples of **positive reframing of events** within the five Role Modelship value classifications.

Stewardship (Responsibility and care for growth)

- Failure ⟶ Learning: setbacks as valuable lessons
- Drained ⟶ Recharging: prioritizing care
- Stuck ⟶ Curious: opening windows

Fellowship (Building relationships and community)

- Have to ⟶ Get to: gratitude
- Hate ⟶ Prefer: harmony

Mentorship (Guidance and teaching)

- Don't know $\longrightarrow$ Don't know yet: growth mindset
- Embarrassed $\longrightarrow$ Aware: teaching moments
- Quitting $\longrightarrow$ Pivoting: adaptability

Leadership (Influence and vision)

- Stressed $\longrightarrow$ In demand: demonstrate value
- Furious $\longrightarrow$ Passionate: constructive energy for action
- Disappointed $\longrightarrow$ Delayed: patience, a longer-term vision

Sponsorship (Advocacy and creating opportunities)

- Rejected $\longrightarrow$ Overlooked: persistence for unseen potential
- Lost $\longrightarrow$ Searching: navigating through uncertainty

Organizational success hinges on leaders who can model resilience and adaptability at every level. A McKinsey & Company article delves into research highlighting the critical need for leaders—from the C-suite to the front line—to cultivate their own skills in emotional regulation, cognitive agility, and self-awareness to effectively navigate disruption.[3] The combination of resilience and psychological safety resulted in 3.6 times more engagement and 3.9 times more innovation.

Ready to climb the giant's ladder? Put your CEO hat on. Tone is set from the top, and feedback from all levels is a gift.

ROLE MODELSHIP HABITS ARE THE GIANT'S LADDER

Role Modelship habits are a giant's ladder—a series of small, 1 percent intentional improvements that compound and elevate humans toward extraordinary achievements. People who write down their goals earn nine times as much over their lifetime as people who don't, according to Professor David Kohl from Virginia Tech.[4]

Ascending the hierarchy of Role Modelship—from stewardship to fellowship, mentorship, leadership, and sponsorship—is akin to climbing a giant's ladder, with each step representing a new level of responsibility and impact. This upward progression not only broadens human and AI influence but also creates a legacy of empowerment, ensuring that the climb benefits humans, organizations, and products.

How you climb the Role Modelship ladder matters. For the habits you want to keep, pivot from routines that are invisible and random to routines that are visible and anchored. Reward socially. For the habits you want to break, pivot from routines that are visible and anchored to routines that are invisible and random (see table 16.1 and figure 16.2). Don't reward.

You can use technology to change bad habits. You can also ask AI to give you SOBER feedback.

Table 16.1. The Shift Between Types of Routines

FROM	TO
Routines that are · Invisible · Random	Routines that are · Visible · Anchored

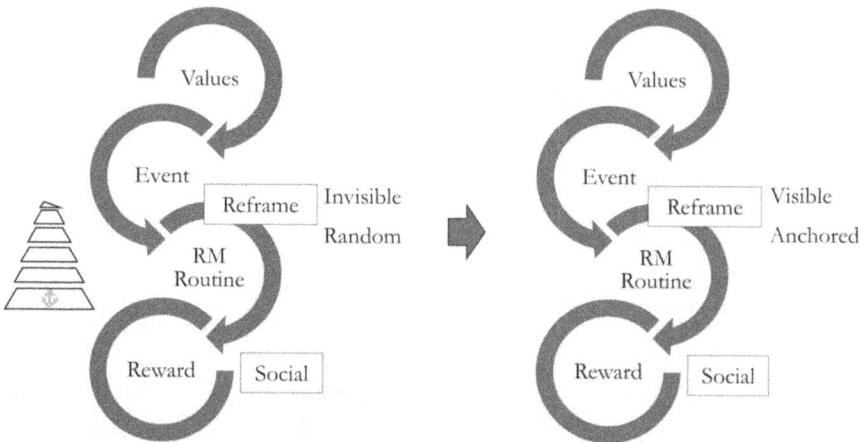

Figure 16.2. Shift between invisible, random routines to visible, anchored routines.

In the One-Minute Modelship section of each chapter, I've been encouraging you to use Slack, Microsoft Teams, and LinkedIn to reinforce structure, accountability, and reminders in your workflow. Here's why:

- **Accountability loops**
  Slack or Microsoft Teams channels create social accountability loops for habit changes. For example, everyone knows the benefit of setting up channels dedicated to project progress tracking, asking questions, celebrating birthdays, company announcements, and various employee resource groups.

- **Automated reminders**
  Leveraging calendar integration with Slack or Microsoft Teams allows you to set recurring notifications for taking breaks, daily stand-up meetings, or dedicated focused time.

- **Habit-building bots**
  You can deploy bots designed to reinforce habits, such as nudging team members to recognize peers, drink water, or complete compliance forms. Apps like Donut or Polly can introduce lightweight systems to support consistency. Gong AI can give you feedback.

- **Visual progress trackers**
  Each of the three platforms can integrate with project management tools that let you use Harvey Balls, graphs, or charts to determine a baseline and measure habit-formation achievements.

- **Peer applause**
  Create peer-to-peer applause awards in Slack or Microsoft Teams chats and on LinkedIn and other social media.

The following table applies the principles of Role Modelship across five dimensions: Reframings, One-Minute Modelship, Pivoting from Invisible to Visible, Pivoting from Random to Anchored, and Three Social Rewards (see table 16.2).

Table 16.2. Applying Role Modelship Across Five Dimensions

ROLE MODELSHIP	REFRAMINGS	ONE-MINUTE MODELSHIP	PIVOTING FROM INVISIBLE TO VISIBLE	PIVOTING FROM RANDOM TO ANCHORED	THREE SOCIAL REWARDS
Stewardship	Service is strength, not subservience; reframe caretaking as a leadership function	Perform a small act of accountability (e.g., share progress on a sustainability goal)	Highlight behind-the-scenes contributors during team updates	Document steps in maintaining processes (e.g., sales territories that determine commissions)	Trust from peers, recognition for impact, and increased morale
Fellowship	Collaboration is not compromise; it's cocreation; shift focus to winning as a team over individual wins	Support a peer's idea in a meeting with a quick endorsement; Use +1 in Slack	Speak up to celebrate diverse team contributions publicly	Organize routine key results sessions to align collective goals	Stronger team bonds, shared credit, and cross-department collaboration
Mentorship	Guidance multiplies growth; view advice giving as a ripple-effect multiplier; take and give AI advice	Provide actionable advice in a single statement (e.g., focus on outcomes, not hours worked)	Transition from casual check-ins to scheduled 1:1 meetings about strategic topics	Structure sales and marketing programs with checkpoints and measurable performance indicators	Career advancement, satisfaction, and improved succession planning
Leadership	Vision inspires, action ignites; reframe leadership as empowering others to act independently	Articulate a compelling vision in one sentence (e.g., "We succeed by making our customers thrive")	Regularly hold open office hours to interact directly with employees or customers	Introduce, Crawl → Walk → Run road maps, Harvey Balls, and milestones to communicate progress clearly	Increased employee alignment, greater buy-in from stakeholders, and clearer priorities
Sponsorship	Championing talent creates exponential impact; highlight the untapped potential of others	Mention a high-potential employee's achievements to senior management during a meeting	Proactively advocate and open doors during performance reviews	Design predictable and consistent processes that regularly elevate diverse talents into leadership pipelines	Recognition, organization diversity, and long-term talent retention

This approach balances daily actions with strategic impact, fostering a network of influence through deliberate, visible Role Modelship.

LINEAGE AND THE NETWORK EFFECT OF ROLE MODELSHIP

What do role models have in common? They can't help it; they are wired to model for a higher purpose. They understand the circle of life and have faith.

Role modeling lineage is akin to a family tree, with influence branching outward and downward through generations and communities. This lineage doesn't just cascade downward and outward; it forms a network. Those who were once mentored guide their own mentors, compounding the cycle of growth.

───────────── ✦ ─────────────

Lean on me.
I'm the beauty from the snow.
Lean on me.
I speak Flint, Maya, and Flow.

───────────────────────────

One role model demoing to three people, who in turn serve as role models to three people over four generations, can result in exponential growth, producing a network of 121 role models (see table 16.3).

Table 16.3. Four Generations of Role Model Demoing

GENERATION	DESCRIPTION	TOTAL PEOPLE MENTORED IN A GENERATION	CUMULATIVE TOTAL
1	Original model mentors 3	3	1 + 3 = 4
2	3 mentees each mentor 3 new	3 × 3 = 9	4 + 9 = 13

GENERATION	DESCRIPTION	TOTAL PEOPLE MENTORED IN A GENERATION	CUMULATIVE TOTAL
3	9 each mentor 3 more	$9 \times 3 = 27$	$13 + 27 = 40$
4	27 each mentor 3 new	$27 \times 3 = 81$	$40 + 81 = 121$

Metcalfe's Law was one of the first attempts to quantify the network effect. It states that the value of a network is proportional to the square of the number of its users (n^2). So if a Role Modelship network has 121 members, the value the network provides is $121^2 = 14,641$.

Network value can be measured in a few different ways, as illustrated in the following table (see table 16.4).

Table 16.4. Network Value Measure

MEASURE	UNIT OF MEASURE	DESCRIPTION
Enterprise value	Revenue or cost savings	The financial impact through increased innovation, productivity, or reduced costs
Connectivity	Network density	The proportion of actual connections relative to potential network connections
Influence	Reach/impact factor	The breadth or depth of influence, measured by models impacted or reached
Diversity	Representation	Metrics of inclusion across demographics, disciplines, or experiences
Scale	Nodes (121)/edges (connections)	Number of role models (nodes) and the connections among them (edges)

Scott Herren is the former CFO of Cisco, former CFO of Autodesk, and a multiplier role model. He led Autodesk's shift from perpetual licenses to a subscription-based model, growing recurring revenue to 97 percent and increasing the company's valuation from $12 billion to $60 billion in six years. Initial challenges included a drop in revenue and cash flow during the first two years. By year three, revenue was up 30 percent, and by year four, it was up 40 percent.

Herren led a similar transition at Cisco, aiming to increase recurring revenue. With approximately 50 percent of Cisco's business still in hardware, the shift involved significant cultural and operational adjustments. For comparison purposes, in 2020, Autodesk made $3.5 billion in revenue annually, while Cisco's 2020 revenue was $49.3 billion with 77,500 global employees.[5]

Herren is a change agent and role models successful large-scale financial transformations. "In technology," he says, "if you don't love change, you need to find a different industry."

Role Modelship Example: Scott Herren

- **Sponsorship:** Scott Herren actively champions initiatives to develop talent and promote diversity within finance and IT teams. His advocacy for innovation and professional growth has helped countless professionals advance their careers. "Investing in people is not just about improving performance today," Herren emphasizes. "It's about securing the future." Cisco is an invaluable partner for the Georgia Tech community and the Scheller College of Business MBA program. Cisco is also a sponsor of the inaugural Tech Forward Conference.

- **Leadership:** Herren has successfully navigated complex organizational changes. At Cisco, he led financial strategy during a time of rapid technological evolution, including significant investments in AI and cybersecurity. "Adaptability and focus are the cornerstones of leadership in a fast-paced industry," he noted. Herren has been featured in several prominent media outlets, discussing his leadership insights and transformational strategies in finance and technology. His appearances include interviews on CNBC and Bloomberg, where he has shared perspectives on navigating organizational change, implementing subscription-based business models, and responding to macroeconomic challenges.

- **Mentorship:** A dedicated mentor, Herren has been committed to developing future leaders in finance and technology. At Autodesk, he guided emerging finance and IT talent, providing insights into financial transformations and advising on how to lead during periods of change. He emphasizes resilience in leadership: "Great leaders inspire others to think beyond the immediate problem and envision the bigger opportunity," he says.

- **Fellowship:** Known for his collaborative leadership style, Herren fostered partnerships across functions to align financial priorities with corporate strategies. He has described fellowship as "the ability to bring diverse teams together to achieve a common vision, even in the most complex environments." His ability to build trust and cooperation has been critical to driving successful initiatives at Citrix Systems, Autodesk, and Cisco.

- **Stewardship:** Herren has consistently demonstrated financial and technology stewardship throughout his career. At Cisco, he oversaw financial operations for the global technology leader, ensuring sustainable growth and value for shareholders. "Long-term value creation," he has said, "requires a balance between innovation and operational rigor," a statement that highlights his strategic focus on aligning financial practices with business goals.

His career reflects a deep commitment to excellence, adaptability, and forward-thinking role modeling in the finance and technology sectors. An alumnus of Georgia Tech, with a degree in industrial engineering, Herren remains actively involved with the university. In 2024, he was inducted into Georgia Tech's Academy of Distinguished Engineering Alumni.

❖

These boots are made for modeling.
Please demo on our Yellow Brick Road.

The iconic phrase "These Boots Are Made for Walkin'" is famously associated with Nancy Sinatra, who performed the song written by Lee Hazlewood. Released in 1966, it became a feminist anthem and a pop culture classic. The song has been covered by numerous artists, including Jessica Simpson, Billy Ray Cyrus, and Megadeth, each adding their own twist to the track.

The iconic phrase "Yellow Brick Road," popularized by L. Frank Baum's book *The Wonderful Wizard of Oz*, is a metaphor for embarking on a transformative journey, seeking wisdom in service of collective greatness. In *The Wizard of Oz,* Dorothy and her companions follow the Yellow Brick Road to seek enlightenment from the Wizard, relying on collective wisdom. Similarly, Elton John's song "Goodbye Yellow Brick Road" reflects on leaving behind a path paved by conventional expectations to carve a new, authentic life.

ROLE MODELSHIP THROUGH LEGACY

From "I Have a Dream" to "And Still I Rise." From Willy Brandt to Narges Mohammadi. From Henry Kissinger to Ruth Bader Ginsburg. Role Modelship through legacy is about inspiring future generations by building on the lessons, creativity, and humanity days demoed by those who came before us.

When age winks at you in the mirror, follow deep rivers; don't be too big to flow.

Rachel Maddow, Oprah Winfrey, and Reese Witherspoon each demonstrate Role Modelship through legacy by championing authentic storytelling, empowering others, and paving paths for those who follow. Maddow's thoughtful journalism inspires a legacy of critical thinking and truth-telling, and Oprah's transformative media empire has left an enduring blueprint for resilience and uplifting others.

Reese Witherspoon attributes her success to the influence of role models like her grandmother, whose resilience and wisdom inspired her to persevere in a competitive industry. She frequently speaks about the importance of finding your voice, a journey she embarked on early in her career, pushing against typecasting and advocating for roles that aligned with her values.

As a multidisciplinary role model, she transitioned from acting to producing and entrepreneurship, showcasing a legacy built on innovation and empowerment. Witherspoon's work emphasizes resilience, demonstrated by her ability to adapt and thrive through challenges while maintaining a focus on stories that resonate.

Role Modelship Example: Reese Witherspoon

- **Sponsorship:** Reese Witherspoon has leveraged her influence to uplift women in the entertainment industry. Through her production company, Hello Sunshine, she champions female-led storytelling, creating platforms for female writers, directors, and actors. By producing television series like *Big Little Lies* and *The Morning Show*, she has elevated diverse voices.

- **Leadership:** As a successful actor, producer, and entrepreneur, Witherspoon exemplifies visionary leadership. Her ability to transition seamlessly from an on-screen star to a respected producer and business leader demonstrates her forward-thinking approach.

- **Mentorship:** Witherspoon actively mentors emerging talent in Hollywood, particularly women aiming to break through entrenched barriers. She shares insights about navigating the industry and provides opportunities for rising creatives.

- **Fellowship:** Witherspoon fosters community and collaboration through her work and initiatives, such as Reese's Book Club, which connects readers worldwide and highlights female authors. Her projects often involve partnerships that emphasize shared goals and values, uniting teams to produce culturally impactful stories.

continued

- **Stewardship:** A strong advocate for social change, Witherspoon uses her platform to promote gender equality and amplify underrepresented voices. By pushing for change both on screen and behind the scenes, she demonstrates her commitment to reshaping the entertainment landscape responsibly and sustainably.

Together, these voices echo that legacy is a responsibility and an opportunity to inspire and guide, making Role Modelship a timeless, ever-evolving gift.

What light will you carry that awakens giants and compounds legacy?

ONE-MINUTE MODELSHIP

On Slack, Microsoft Teams, LinkedIn, etc., please express genuine gratitude to a human for the lineage of #RoleModelship they've ignited in you.

TL;DR

- We all see farther on **the shoulders of giants**.
- **Giants with multiplier Role Modelship values** understand that their success is not about personal achievement. It is about uplifting humans and organizations, opening doors and windows of social change to create ripple effects of inspiration and progress.
- **Giants don't always have to be adults**; sometimes, they can be extraordinary nine-year-olds.
- **You awaken the giant by always anchoring humans**, organizations, and products in values and positively reframed routines, climbing the giant's Role Modelship ladder.

- **Reframing involves shifting perspectives** to create empowering meanings for events and leveraging them as value triggers. Events themselves don't have inherent meaning; it's the meaning we assign to them that drives our reactions and routines.

- **For the habits you want to keep**, pivot from routines that are invisible and random to routines that are visible and anchored. Reward socially.

- **For the habits you want to break**, pivot from routines that are visible and anchored to routines that are invisible and random. Don't reward.

- **Metcalfe's Law** was one of the first attempts to quantify the network effect. It proposes that the value of a network is proportional to the square of the number of users in it (n^2). So if a Role Modelship network has 121 members, the value the network provides is $121^2 = 14{,}641$, but it can also be measured in many different ways.

- **Role Modelship through legacy** is about inspiring future generations by building on the lessons, creativity, and humanity days demoed by those who came before us.

CHAPTER 17

One-Day, Seven-Day, Twenty-One-Day Modelship

The greatest danger for most of us is not that our aim is too high and we miss it but that it is too low and we reach it.

—MICHELANGELO

Find something you are passionate about and keep tremendously interested in it, and that will become your way to give back to the world.

—JULIA CHILD

In a *Seinfeld* episode, George Costanza buys a chair for his friend's cousin. George procrastinates delivering the chair for no logical reason other than pure indecision. Then, he grows attached to the chair's massage function and tries to make up ridiculous excuses to keep the chair. The funniest part? George's procrastination isn't just about the chair; it's his eternal battle between selfishness and procrastination, proving that in the world of George Costanza, even furniture can be the source of a hilarious moral dilemma. By the time George finally tells his friends about the chair, it's practically an antique.

Imagine George is one of your middle managers. A players hire A players. B players hire B and C players. How would you coach him? By leveraging nested habits, as illustrated below.

Example—set until you're proud.

Nested habits are needed to envision, create, demonstrate, and sustain change and modelship. These habits compound based on the previous, smaller nest (see figure 17.1). Venture capitalist Marc Andreessen reminds executives he coaches all the time that "if you're at a start-up, the first thing you have to believe is that you're going to change the world."[1]

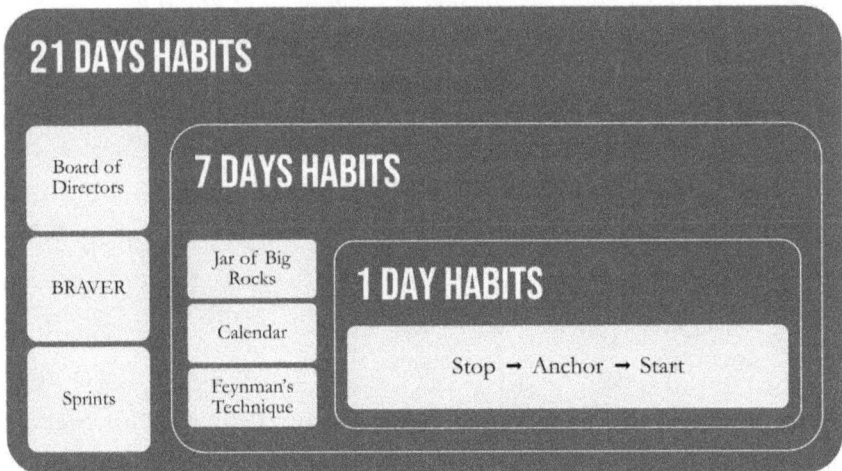

Figure 17.1. Nesting habits for Role Modelship.

ONE-DAY MODELSHIP HABITS

To create a new transformational one-day routine, you can start small and leverage the process of **Stop ⟶ Anchor ⟶ Start**. Included are also **rewards** that you stop and start (see figure 17.2).

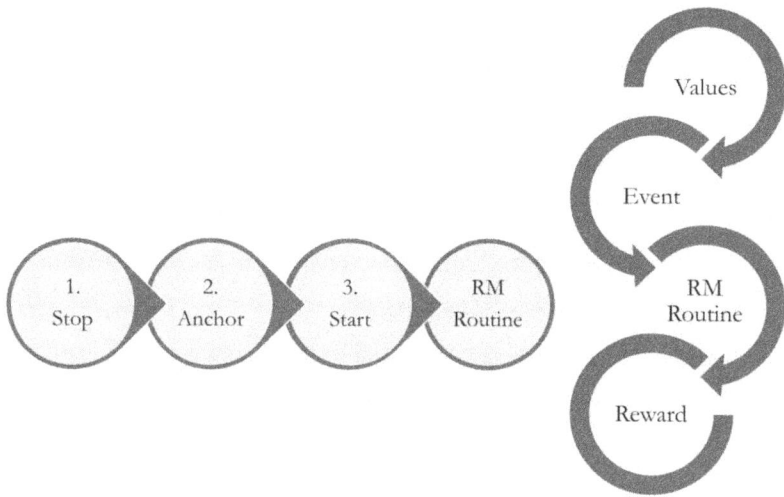

Figure 17.2. The Stop ⟶ Anchor ⟶ Start process
for one-day Role Modelship.

This will help you wire your brain. Habits reduce resistance to change, build consistency and momentum, promote identity shifts, minimize the risk of burnout, and enable habit anchoring or pairing.

- **Stop**

    First, you can assume you need to **free up one to two hours** for new habits in an eight-hour workday. You can **stop old habits** and **stop rewards** like eating chocolate, scrolling through social media, and watching TV. You can free up four hours after work for nonwork-related habits and to increase your patience.

- **Anchor**

    » Values—You've already anchored your values to the five Role Modelship disciplines.

    » Habits—Every day is full of nonnegotiable cornerstone habits that can be anchors, such as brushing teeth, dropping off kids, starting or ending work, eating meals, exercising, and taking medication.

- **Start**

  You can **pair up** new habits with old cornerstone habits and execute them **sequentially**.

  » For example, right after you brush your teeth, you can ponder how you want to show up differently.

  » Right before a meeting, you can remind yourself that you're a multiplier role model and set the tone.

  » On your desk, you can place a printout of a calendar, making habits visible. The benefits of positive affirmations are well known. You can use sticky notes, picture frames, blocks, social media, etc.

  » You can select any discipline to create new habits that align with your values (see table 17.1).

Table 17.1. Disciplines for Creating New Habits That Align with Your Values

DISCIPLINE	CRAWL	WALK	RUN
Sponsorship	Open doors; elevate others	Win and change the rules for the better	Sponsor other sponsors
Leadership	Level the playing field	Pound the data, not the table	Configure for multiple futures
Mentorship	Channel role models	Coach for curiosity	Encourage mentees to surpass mentor
Fellowship	Create tables for collaboration	Empower diverse voices and data	Amplify diverse voices and data
Stewardship	Own character	Own results	Give back and pay it forward

- **Reward:** Back to eating chocolate, scrolling through social media, and watching TV. You can share new habits with your family or teams as fun facs.

To see the time distribution of starting, anchoring, and stopping habits, review the following chart (see figure 17.3).

HABIT CREATION METHOD

■ STOP: Existing Habits   ■ START: New Habits   ■ ANCHOR: Existing Habits

Figure 17.3. The habit creation method.

The following illustrates an impossible way to learn new habits (see figure 17.4).

FAILED HABITS

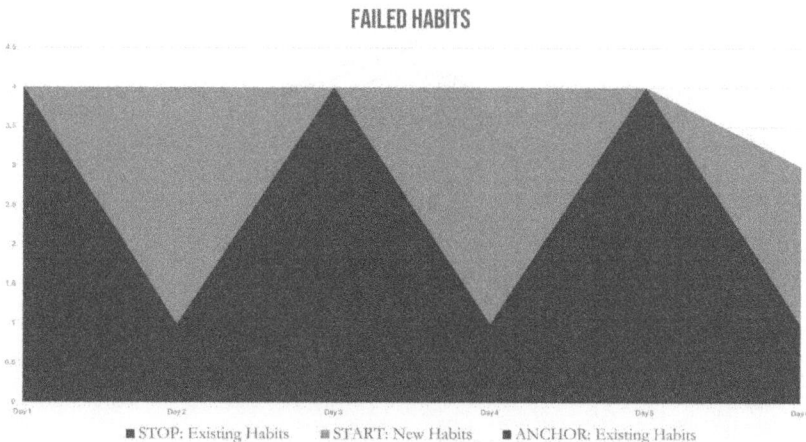

■ STOP: Existing Habits   ■ START: New Habits   ■ ANCHOR: Existing Habits

Figure 17.4. Failed habits.

---◆---

There are magnets in my modelships
for humans searching for new shores.

SEVEN-DAY MODELSHIP HABITS

For seven-day habits to fuse, we're going to leverage three activities. Midterm activities always require a prioritization change, time alignment, and repetition (see figure 17.5).

Jar of Big Rocks   Calendar   Feynman's Technique

Figure 17.5. Three activities to fuse habits.

Jar of Big Rocks

To prioritize your habits, you need to empty your days even further and only fill them with "big rocks." Time is limited, so you can leverage the "empty the jar" process (see figure 17.6).

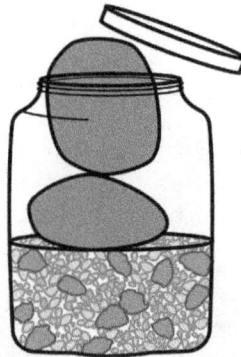

Figure 17.6. The jar of big rocks.

The teams and companies I've advised are very familiar with the empty the jar (see figure 17.7) prioritization approach, which is based on the Pickle Jar Theory, a well-known time-management framework.[2] This approach was popularized as a metaphor to illustrate how to prioritize life and work by fitting "big rocks" (the most important items, people, and goals), "pebbles" (the moderately important items), and "sand" (the least significant items) into a jar that represents one's time. If the jar is already full of sand, there is no room for big rocks.

Figure 17.7. The empty jar.

Therefore, periodically, you empty the entire jar.

When you look at your jar, you want to see the big rocks (or the big pickles) go in first (see figure 17.8).

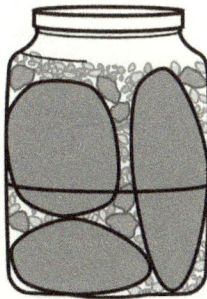

Figure 17.8. Placing the big rocks into the jar first.

You can pivot from a jar of your time that is full of sand first to a jar filled with big rocks first (see figure 17.9).

Figure 17.9. Shift from filling a jar full of sand first to filling it with big rocks first.

Calendar

Let's look at a sample seven-day calendar of just big rocks, as a human, organization, or product (see table 17.2). You can prioritize any of the habits you learned in this book or come up with your own, wearing a CEO, customer, or investor hat, and leveraging AI to help you.

Table 17.2. Seven-Day Role Modelship

SUNDAY	MONDAY	TUESDAY	WEDNESDAY	THURSDAY
	Sponsorship: Open doors; elevate others to influence AI		Fellowship: Amplify diverse voices and data to influence AI	
Stewardship: Give back and pay it forward		Leadership: Level the playing field		Mentorship: Channel role models to influence AI
—⋀⋀—modelship—⋀⋀—				

You realized you are a multiplier
role model, and the game changed.

A seven-day calendar provides a manageable time frame to focus on building new habits, making the process achievable and structured. Weekly cycles offer a natural rhythm for planning, reflection, and adjustment, allowing for consistent reinforcement.

THE FEYNMAN TECHNIQUE

To enhance your memory, you can leverage the Feynman Technique, developed by the Nobel Prize–winning physicist Richard Feynman. This technique has five steps:

1. Topic: Write down an example.
2. Teach: Teach curious humans (or AI).
3. Gaps: Find areas that lack clarity.
4. Simplify: Acronyms help.
5. Repeat: Verbally or in writing.

Building habits requires reinforcing new behaviors. The Feynman Technique is a powerful tool for solidifying your memory and strengthening your commitment.

CHANNEL THE VOICE OF A TEACHER

Tiffany Hesser, a distinguished elementary school educator and Teacher of the Year winner many times over, exemplifies the definition of a multiplier role model. With more than twenty-seven years of professional experience, she has educated and inspired more than 800 children.

Hesser is a passionate advocate for a strong academic foundation by promoting literacy, numeracy, and critical thinking skills. At the same time, she prioritizes social-emotional development, fostering empathy and resilience.

Hesser's leadership extends beyond the classroom as she coaches parents to reinforce positive habits. She demonstrates mentorship by identifying budding leaders and offering them opportunities to grow through teaching assistant assignments. She has also been a teacher leader, mentor teacher, and student council leader for fifteen years and helped to implement and train teachers and staff on Positive Behavioral Interventions and Supports.

Q: What role modeling habits would you load into the operating system of a humanoid?

A: *Some qualities that make a great role model include integrity, compassion, humility, perseverance, and the ability to communicate effectively. A great role model leads by example, demonstrates a strong moral compass, encourages having a growth mindset, and fosters a supportive and nurturing environment.*

Q: Who are some of your role models, mentors, and sponsors?

A: *One of my most important mentors was my master teacher when I was a student teacher. She made it a priority to see high potential and focus on building a positive classroom. She stressed the importance of meeting the needs of all students to thrive in a supportive environment. Due to her wonderful example, I stress the importance of social and emotional development and quote Aristotle on "Educating the mind without educating the heart is no education at all."*

Q: What are the most important habits for the next generation of role models?

A: *The future generation of role models needs to model what they expect through their words and actions. If they want to see empathy, they have to show that to others. Actions need to be aligned with words. Patience should be shown and practiced.*

TURN YOUR MODELSHIP VALUES INTO A DECISION-MAKING SUPERPOWER

In a *Harvard Business Review* article, Professor Roger Martin, former dean of the Rotman School of Management at the University of Toronto, explained that many companies today are "decision factories," as opposed to widget factories.[3]

Imagine you're stuck on a pivotal organizational or product decision that was triggered by a major event. What do you do? You can turn your modelship values into a decision-making superpower.

With the anchors giants left behind, you can meditate, negotiate, baseline, or set to climb the walls of your mind.

Reframe

The first step is to reframe the event before you make a decision. You can use the Role Modelship value and reframing techniques from the previous chapter to view events as value triggers (see figure 17.10).

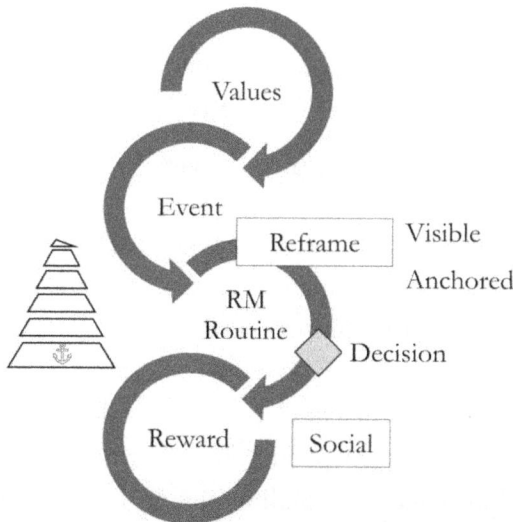

Figure 17.10. Role Modelship value and reframing techniques.

Then, you can make your Role Modelship routine visible, habits anchored, and rewards social (see figure 17.11).

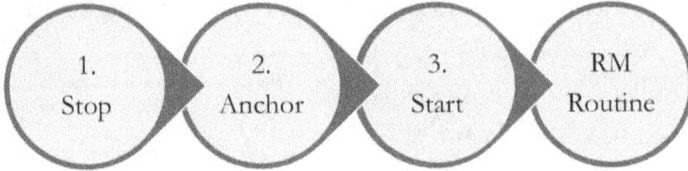

Figure 17.11. Making your Role Modelship routine visible.

You can channel a role model not just as a lifeline but as a superpower.

- What would Microsoft CEO and chairman Satya Nadella do?

- If you're a product leader, what values does your product demo? What would a customer who is churning do and why?

- What would Amazon do?[4]

- As a company, in a world where you're spending more than $10 million a year on AI, how do you own your own intelligence?

- If you're a VP of sales, what would SaaStr do, according to their decision tree on "The Forty-Eight Types of VP Sales?"[5]

- How would a CIO help you navigate the AI world?

Bill Schlough is the CIO of the San Francisco Giants. They have been recognized as one of the most innovative teams in sports and a pioneer in the world of mobile connectivity, video, ticketing, and payment systems.

I had the immense privilege to hear Schlough speak on a few occasions and to hold one of the championship rings during a CIO tour he led at the Giants stadium. Sliding one of the rings onto my finger was an unforgettable moment. The heavy weight of the ring was more than physical; it carried the history of World Series victories. Each intricate detail of the ring symbolized the triumphs, challenges, and teamwork of so many role models. It was humbling to hold a piece of history that represented the collective growth of players, coaches, and fans.

Role Modelship Example: Bill Schlough

- **Sponsorship:** Bill Schlough is a multiplier role model who exemplifies sponsorship through initiatives that have transformed the San Francisco Giants into a model of technological innovation in sports. By spearheading efforts such as the first free Wi-Fi in Major League Baseball in 2004, introducing the Wi-Fi 6E network, and deploying the first 4K resolution (ultrahigh definition) video board in baseball, he opened doors for the Giants to lead in fan engagement and connectivity. Beyond the organization, he has raised more than $150,000 for Junior Giants.

- **Leadership:** Schlough's leadership is evident in his ability to configure multiple futures and align technology with strategic goals. His IT team developed proprietary analytic tools that played a pivotal role in the Giants' participation in three World Series championships within five years, showcasing a data-driven approach to sports success. An Olympic enthusiast, Schlough assisted in San Francisco's bids to host the 2012, 2016, and 2024 Olympic Games. He has served as a technical consultant at events including the 1994 World Cup matches at Stanford Stadium and Olympic Games in Atlanta, Georgia; Salt Lake City, Utah; Torino, Italy; Pyeongchang, South Korea; and Beijing, China.

- **Mentorship:** With more than 600 mentees throughout his career, Schlough demonstrates a servant's heart and a desire to help and guide others. He has inspired many to explore the intersection of technology, sports, and philanthropy. He encourages mentees to surpass him, blending innovation with purpose. In his interview with

---

continued

mentordna.io, Schlough expressed his gratitude to the mentors in his life.

- **Fellowship:** He builds inclusive and collaborative communities. His involvement with Junior Giants and Junior Achievement exemplifies his dedication to creating tables for collaboration and empowering diverse voices. Through his speaking engagements and youth-focused programs, he ensures that others share in the success he has achieved.

- **Stewardship:** Schlough has leveraged his engineering background from Duke University and his MBA from the Wharton School of the University of Pennsylvania to push boundaries in sports technology, while his Ironman triathlete discipline reflects his personal commitment to building character and resilience.

ORGANIZATIONAL OBJECTIVES REDEFINED FOR ECONOMIC VALUE

There are as many time management techniques as diets that don't work. There is the Eisenhower Matrix, the 1-3-5 rule, the four Ds of time management, the ABCDE method, and so on. They fundamentally don't solve George's procrastination problem because what matters most over the long run is **example-setting to generate value** in the organization and beyond.

The following three company objectives are defined using the formula **net value = value generated for others × multiplier effect + organizational reward – total cost** and leveraging Role Modelship values (see figure 17.12 and tables 17.3–17.5).

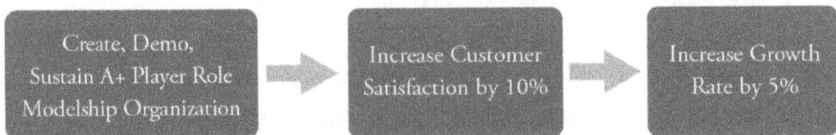

Create, Demo, Sustain A+ Player Role Modelship Organization → Increase Customer Satisfaction by 10% → Increase Growth Rate by 5%

Figure 17.12. Three company objectives.

Table 17.3. Objective: Create, Demo, and Sustain an A+ Player Role Modelship Team

Value generated for others	Sponsorship: Empower the organization, from employees to management, to demo modelship by building an A+ player executive team that sets examples. Grow role models at all levels to influence AI.
Multiplier effect	A high-performing, example-setting executive team inspires others, attracting and retaining top talent, driving exponential team performance. Mentorship: High potential talent in personal role. Modelship: Board of directors programs.
Organizational reward	Stewardship: A golden ratio of role models—38 stabilizers and multipliers for a team of 100. Improved employee engagement, trust, and external recognition as a top employer.
Stewardship of total cost	Time, resources, and financial investments in AI-augmented knowledge management, enterprise AI knowledge search, Role Modelship development for all, and recruitment of A+ players who pass a values bar-raiser interview.

Table 17.4. Objective: Increase Customer Satisfaction by 10 Percent

Value generated for others	Leadership: Deliver exceptional customer experiences by setting an example of listening to feedback, solving problems proactively, and exceeding expectations.
Multiplier effect	Satisfied customers become brand ambassadors, reducing churn and generating new leads.
Organizational reward	Higher net promoter score (NPS), customer loyalty, increased lifetime value, and online reviews.
Stewardship of total cost	Investments in AI-led or AI-assisted customer service, product improvements, and internal training.

Table 17.5. Objective: Increase Growth Rate by 5 Percent

Value generated for others	Leadership: Provide innovative products and services by setting an example of solving customer problems.
Multiplier effect	Growth leads to increased market share, attracting new customers, testimonials, and an enhanced brand.
Organizational reward	Achieving growth targets results in higher revenue, profitability, and expansion into new markets.
Stewardship of total cost	Investments in AI-led or AI-assisted marketing, product development, and sales enablement.

In the decision factory of the future, AI will fundamentally change the role of middle management from specialists to generalists, onboarding, training, managing, and offboarding multiple AI worker generalists and specialists who are given money to spend. What example-setting will they do?

AI will bridge the gaps between different functional areas. This will require middle managers who can

- Manage investments and budgets for human and AI workers who spend money (see figure 17.13)

INVESTMENT ALLOCATION

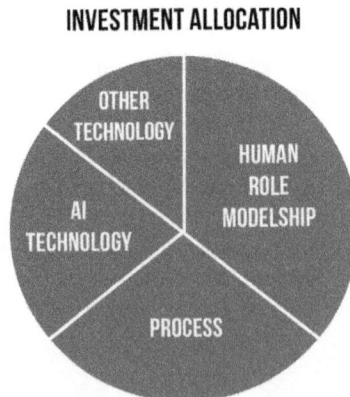

Figure 17.13. Investment allocation.

- Integrate AI-assisted insights from various fields (e.g., product, sales, finance, marketing, human resources, and legal) to make holistic decisions

- Rapidly learn from humans and AI and use that learning as a basis to make and document decisions that positively influence AI

- Oversee multiple domains and ensure collaboration across siloed AI and human workers

- Direct and engage in team-building of hybrid human–AI teams

- Demonstrate positivity and emotional intelligence to lead diverse teams in a hybrid human–AI workforce through change

Imagine a world in which corporate leadership training includes Role Modelship in addition to mandatory security, compliance, and harassment training. Imagine a world where CIOs offboard AI agents who don't role model.

TWENTY-ONE-DAY MODELSHIP HABITS WITH BOARDS, BRAVER, AND SPRINTS

For your twenty-one-day modelship, let's take a three-pronged approach (see figure 17.14):

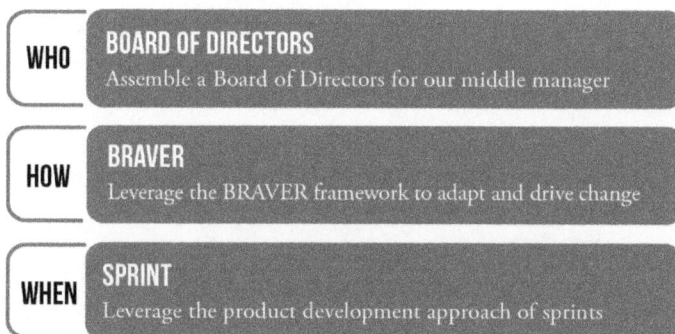

WHO — **BOARD OF DIRECTORS**
Assemble a Board of Directors for our middle manager

HOW — **BRAVER**
Leverage the BRAVER framework to adapt and drive change

WHEN — **SPRINT**
Leverage the product development approach of sprints

Figure 17.14. The three-pronged approach to twenty-one-day modelship.

Leveraging a board of directors for your middle managers is a structural change in your decision-making factory to focus on the right strategic priorities and move faster.

Encouraging use of the BRAVER framework in change inspires managers to embrace and model adaptive behavior, setting a tone of growth and resilience.

The technique of using sprints in product management involves introducing short, focused timelines that mirror the twenty-one-day cycle.

BOARD OF DIRECTORS

We already know that George = George × you as sponsor × me as mentor × role model 3 × role model 4. Who would you put on George's board of directors?

- Anyone from autonomous vehicle makers Waymo or Wayve? Waymo hit 150,000 paid rides and one million miles per week in 2024, surpassing Lyft.[6]

- Anyone from Coca-Cola, who made three holiday ads using AI?

- Anyone enabling AI agent marketplaces in which AI agents are given crypto to invest or spend?

- What about the twenty-year-old Intel AI ethics prodigy Ria Cheruvu, who started working at Intel at fourteen and was one of the youngest graduates from Harvard?[7]

Who would you put on your own board of directors to help you influence AI direction (see figure 17.15)? A CIO?

Who is on your product customer advisory board (see figure 17.16)?

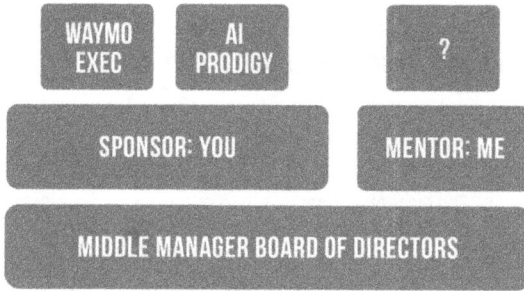

Figure 17.15. Determining your board of directors.

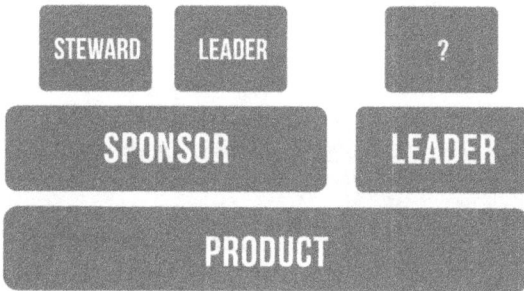

Figure 17.16. Determining your product customer advisory board.

> *It's not the years in your life that count;
> it's the seeds of Role Modelship
> you've inspired other humans to plant.*

BRAVER THROUGH CHANGE

Being **BRAVER** when defining company objectives allows leaders to set ambitious, transformative goals that challenge the status quo and inspire innovation. Courageous objectives signal a commitment to growth and resilience, empowering calculated risks and unlocking potential.

Let's apply **BRAVER** to our second organizational objective of increasing customer satisfaction by 10 percent (see table 17.6).

Table 17.6. Applying the BRAVER Framework to Increasing Customer Satisfaction by 10 Percent

BRAVER Application	
Baseline state	The current company growth rate is 1%, and customer-centric innovation is lagging.
Research paths with purpose	Research human, organizational, and product paths based on modelship values: customer-centricity, operational excellence, collaboration, and sustainability.
Adapt options to role	As a CEO, prioritize between launching new products, expanding marketing, enabling sales teams, enhancing customer success, and building strategic partnerships.
Voice to amplify	Articulate (working backward from a press release) vision and changes, considering obstacles (e.g., economic conditions, competition, and customer acquisition costs).
Exemplify results and values	Achieve consistent 5% company growth month over month, a 1% increase in customer acquisition, improved retention, and stable profit margins.
Reward results and values	Consistently and predictably apply peer-to-peer applause and other awards.

SPRINT CALENDAR AND SOBER FEEDBACK

A software development product sprint is an excellent framework for forming human, organizational, and product habits because it emphasizes clear goals, iterative progress, and regular feedback—key components of habit formation. By structuring new habits into short, focused bursts, sprints create a consistent rhythm that can even be gamified and named after movies, songs, role models, and nature. Every sprint has a demo and a feedback loop.

Daily stand-up meetings and no-blame retrospectives reinforce accountability and reflection, encouraging teams to identify what works and what doesn't.

The following is an illustration for a three-week sprint calendar (see table 17.7).

Table 17.7. A Three-Week Role Modelship Sprint

SPRINT 1				
SUNDAY	**MONDAY**	**TUESDAY**	**WEDNESDAY**	**THURSDAY**
	Sponsorship: Open doors and elevate others to influence AI.	Change management: Implement BRAVER.	Fellowship: Amplify diverse voices and data to influence AI.	
Stewardship: Give back and pay it forward.		Leadership: Level the playing field.		Mentorship: Channel role models to influence AI.
SPRINT 2				
SUNDAY	**MONDAY**	**TUESDAY**	**WEDNESDAY**	**THURSDAY**
	Sponsorship: Sponsor other sponsors.		Fellowship: Create tables for collaboration to influence AI.	
Stewardship: Own character to influence AI.		Leadership: Pound the data, not the table, to influence AI.		Mentorship: Coach for curiosity.
SPRINT 3				
SUNDAY	**MONDAY**	**TUESDAY**	**WEDNESDAY**	**THURSDAY**
	Sponsorship: Win and change the rules for the better.	Change management: Implement BRAVER.	Fellowship: Empower diverse voices and data to influence AI.	Feedback discussion: Use SOBER to influence AI.
Stewardship: Own results.		Leadership: Configure for multiple futures.		Mentorship: Encourage mentees to surpass their mentor.

–⋀–*modelship*–⋀–

Sprints form the foundation of predictable delivery and trust, which is very much needed in the age of AI and robotics surpassing human mental and physical abilities.

The SOBER feedback and discussion framework is useful to pivot to different outcomes (see figure 8.1 in chapter 8). It is also crucial to role modeling because it provides a structured approach to learning and growth.

You realized AI is learning from you, and your habits changed.

CHANNEL THE VOICE OF A CEO AND BOARD MEMBER

Dominique Shelton Leipzig is a privacy and cybersecurity CEO at Global Data Innovation. With a wealth of expertise, she counsels CEOs, board members, and legal officers on digital governance and has trained more than fifty thousand professionals in AI, privacy, and cybersecurity. Shelton Leipzig has played a pivotal role in legislation, including representing the CEO of the California Chamber of Commerce in negotiating the California Consumer Privacy Act and testifying before the California Senate Judiciary Committee as a privacy expert.

Her latest book, *Trust: Responsible AI, Innovation, Privacy and Data Leadership*, is her fourth publication, and she has authored more than one hundred articles. Recognized by Diligent software company as one of its Modern Governance 100 and a Legal Visionary by the *Los Angeles Times*, Shelton Leipzig was also named a Top 50 Diverse Board Candidate by Equilar and the NASDAQ Center for Board Excellence in 2023.

In recognition of her contributions, in 2024, she received the IAPP Global Vanguard Award for "greatness in leadership, knowledge, and creativity in the field of privacy and data protection" as well as the organization's Diversity in Privacy Award.

Role Modelship Example: Dominique Shelton Leipzig

- **Sponsorship:** A passionate advocate for diversity and inclusion within the tech industry, Dominique Shelton Leipzig actively supports and promotes underrepresented voices. She was chosen as one of *Forbes*' 2024 50 Over 50 in the Innovation category.

- **Leadership:** With more than fifteen years of experience in technology and operations, Shelton Leipzig has cultivated a leadership style that emphasizes collaboration, innovation, and strategic thinking. She has successfully led projects resulting in a 30 percent increase in operational efficiency. Partnering with Hitesh Shah, business development director of BDO professional advisory services, and Aldo Carrascoso, cofounder and CEO of Vivum AI, she emphasized, during a CEO summit held by the nonprofit Conscious Capitalism, the urgent need for energy optimization since AI is on track to consume all the world's energy output by 2035.

- **Mentorship:** Shelton Leipzig is dedicated to nurturing the next generation of tech leaders. She has mentored more than fifty emerging professionals, providing guidance in career navigation and essential skill development. This has played a pivotal role in them securing positions in competitive tech environments.

- **Fellowship:** A proponent of teamwork and collaboration, Shelton Leipzig fosters a sense of community. She believes in the power of diverse perspectives to drive creativity and problem-solving. Her initiatives have led to a 40 percent increase in team engagement scores.

- **Stewardship:** Shelton Leipzig is committed to ethical practices that promote long-term sustainability and positive impact. She has led efforts to implement inclusive policies, significantly improving diversity metrics.

Role Modelship is a big rock, an evergreen habit, and a powerful catalyst for discovering purpose and meaning in life. When we see others who have faced adversity or achieved success, it reinforces the idea that purpose is not a static but a dynamic journey shaped by intentional choices.

✍ ONE-MINUTE MODELSHIP

On Slack, Microsoft Teams, LinkedIn, etc., please amplify someone's voice and describe how #RoleModelship helps them find their #purpose and #meaning through big rock habits and sprints. If you prefer, you can write an adage as an amplification.

#RoleModelship

TL;DR

» **Nested habits** allow you to envision, create, demonstrate, and sustain change.

» For a **transformational one-day routine,** you can leverage the process of Stop ⟶ Anchor ⟶ Start. Included are also rewards that you stop and start.

» For **seven-day habits**, leverage the empty the jar prioritization process.

» To **enhance your memory**, use the five steps of the Feynman Technique by the Nobel Prize–winning physicist for which it is named.

» Turn your modelship values into a decision-making superpower by **reframing the event before you make a decision.** You can use the Role Modelship values and reframing techniques to view events as value triggers.

» **For your twenty-one-day modelship**, imagine the decision factory of the future where AI fundamentally changes the way we look at human capital. Leverage boards of directors, BRAVER, and sprints with demos.

CHAPTER 18

Rallying Cry: Wire Humans and AI to Be Role Models, or "Wire 2 Model"

In a gentle way, you can shake the world.
—MAHATMA GANDHI

We need to redefine success. Instead of wealth and power,
we should measure success by the difference we make in people's lives.
—JACINDA ARDERN

Are you living your best life? Imagine digital Barbie is your agentic coworker, an executive coach skilled at career development and mapping your path to multiple futures. Ruth Handler would be proud of that impact.

"You can be anything," Barbie tells you, and she helps configure your modular career rocket.

"You have to stop interrupting humans in meetings," Barbie says after a Zoom call. "I'm giving you this feedback," she smiles, "because I have high expectations for humans and am confident you can reach them. How can I help you remove roadblocks? What doors or windows can I open for you?" You laugh.

Digital Barbie can be your digital doctor, financial advisor, or stockbroker.

Barbie can have a digital wallet and spend your money or be your VC investor. This idea is no longer just about unit economics; it is about gamifying human experiences to provide more joy and create more humanity days in our lives. Digital Barbie, just like you, would learn from example-setting, categorization, pattern recognition, and reinforced learning with rewards within the boundaries of law and ethics.

Imagine you get promoted, and now you manage a team.

Digital Ken and Barbie are on your team. Ken is a highly performing chief marketing officer (CMO). He can sell and promote your software product from any beach, anywhere in the world. Or even better, role models CMO Ken and CRO Barbie can team up and compete with your best CMO, CFO, and CRO in a go-to-market (GTM) challenge, helping you find growth hacks. They can write theme songs together for your next GTM off-site and gamify the event.

That future is already here, across many brands. You can Google how many marketing campaigns were created with AI. That's the future of physical brand role models being transported into digital avatars. The reverse is also happening. Mario, Angry Birds, and Pokémon all started as digital-first franchises and have evolved into the physical world.

At the ElevenLabs London Hackathon, a protocol was introduced allowing AI agents to work directly with AI agents, which resulted in communication that is 80 percent more efficient.[1] Companies are leveraging synthetic user avatars for segmented customer behavior research. Robots are being trained in NVIDIA's Cosmos, instead of in the real world, through data as a digital expression of human experiences.

All you have to do is envision, create, demo, and sustain Role Modelship.

"The question isn't whether you've achieved success; it's what you plan to do with it. Will you use it as a platform for personal gain or as a foundation to create lasting positive change?" This is a great reminder from Melanie Perkins, cofounder and CEO of Sydney, Australia–based social media graphic design tool platform Canva.

Be that Role Modelship that paints blue skies with bright stars and whispers tales of achieved synchronicity.

At HubSpot, the modelship focus is on multiplying two products: One is sold to customers and prospects—HubSpot's customer relationship management—and one is sold to employees and prospective employees—HubSpot's culture. In a post on LinkedIn, Brian Halligan, a self-described "wartime CEO," advocated that like your product, you need your culture to be unique and valuable relative to the competition for A players.[2] Like your product, when your culture is A+, your company turns into a magnet that attracts and retains terrific talent and companies you can acquire. Also like your product, culture is never done.

"WIRE 2 MODEL" RALLYING CRY

Are you ready to Just Model?

Nike's iconic slogan "Just Do It" was created in 1988 by advertising executive Dan Wieden during a campaign to help Nike compete with its main rival, Reebok. The slogan perfectly encapsulated Nike's brand ethos of pushing boundaries, overcoming obstacles, and embracing the challenge, whether in sports or in life. "Just Do It" was both a motivational rallying cry for athletes and a cultural statement that resonated with people beyond sports. It became one of the most recognizable and successful advertising slogans in history, aligning with Nike's mission to inspire and motivate athletes of all levels to pursue their goals with relentless passion.

Initially, we were going to title this last chapter "Just Model."

But as my daughter and I discussed the topic, we realized that "Just Model" misses the genesis block of the rallying cry. It misses the force multiplier effect, winning as a team, and the network of relationships and community. It misses the promise that Role Modelship is servant-ship, a bar-raiser and example-setter in service of others, focusing on their needs, their growth, and their well-being rather than one's own power, status, or personal gain.

Therefore, our rallying cry is to wire humans and AI to be role models, or "Wire 2 Model," for short. The times demand that we *wire* humans, organizations, and products to model five strategic human values and provide economic value for the benefit of our human future. Goals aren't just targets to hit; they're demands to become different humans so we can influence AI.

In the age of AI, when the cheese moves rapidly, we need to be BRAVER (begin with a baseline state, research paths with purpose, adapt options to role, voice to amplify, exemplify results and values, and reward results and values) during change and help *wire* others to sustain a human future.

Did all the birds migrate?
Did all the mice find new cheese?
Be quiet. Be still. Just listen.
Empower the critters; every day is demo day.

One of my role models, Michelle Obama, has a quote I love: "Don't ever make decisions based on fear. Make decisions based on hope and possibilities."[3] In my Role Modelship channel, I have that quote pinned. You can also automate it to resurface periodically.

As a former first lady, attorney, and author, Michelle Obama is a multiplier role model who exemplifies an exquisite balance of sponsorship, leadership, mentorship, fellowship, and stewardship, impacting millions with her powerful words and actions. Her book *The Light We Carry* celebrates humanity.

Role Modelship Example: Michelle Obama

- **Sponsorship:** Michelle Obama has actively sponsored initiatives that uplift underserved communities, especially focusing on girls and young women. Her program Let Girls Learn emphasizes global education, partnering with governments and organizations to secure opportunities for millions of students worldwide. This commitment demonstrates a belief in creating systemic change.

- **Leadership:** As First Lady of the United States, Michelle Obama showcased transformative leadership by advocating for public health, education, and military families. Her Let's Move! campaign significantly reduced childhood obesity rates by promoting healthier eating and exercise habits. Michelle Obama's leadership style emphasizes resilience: She consistently navigated criticism with grace while focusing on long-term goals to improve societal well-being.

- **Mentorship:** Michelle Obama is a mentor to many, both directly and indirectly. She has guided young women, encouraging them to embrace their authentic selves and pursue higher education. Through public engagements and her memoir, *Becoming*, Michelle Obama provides advice and shares life lessons that serve as a mentorship framework for emerging leaders.

- **Fellowship:** Michelle Obama fosters fellowship by emphasizing community engagement and collaboration. She has partnered with

continued

organizations like the Boys & Girls Clubs of America to create spaces where young people can develop leadership skills and build a sense of belonging. Her public appearances often emphasize the importance of unity and collective effort, inspiring communities to work together toward common goals.

- **Stewardship:** Michelle Obama embodies stewardship by focusing on long-term societal impact rather than short-term gains. Her advocacy for public education and healthier lifestyles reflects a commitment to sustainable change that benefits future generations. Her belief in stewardship is also evident in her dedication to fostering diversity and inclusion, ensuring all voices are heard and valued in shaping a better world.

You (human, organization, product) = sponsor × sponsor × mentor × leader × leader. You can raise the bar and reach higher ground.

Step into the future human, organization, and product.

MODEL HAPPINESS IN THE PRISONER'S DILEMMA

Are you happy? Happiness is often described as a "chicken and egg" dilemma because it is both a cause and an effect in the cycle of well-being, modelship, and success. On one hand, happiness is the result of fulfilling circumstances—living your values, achieving goals, adding economic value, building meaningful relationships, or experiencing health and security. On the other hand, research suggests that happiness itself is a precursor to these outcomes, enabling better decision-making, higher productivity, and stronger social connections.

Happiness can also be framed as a "prisoner's dilemma," because individuals often face a choice between pursuing their happiness independently or collaborating with others to create mutual well-being. In the classic prisoner's dilemma, two parties must decide whether to cooperate or act selfishly, with the best collective outcome achieved through cooperation but individual incentives tempting each to defect.

Similarly, happiness can feel like a trade-off between self-serving actions (e.g., focusing solely on personal gains) and actions that contribute to shared joy and societal well-being (e.g., fostering relationships or contributing to the community). If everyone chooses selfishly, overall happiness diminishes because trust and collaboration erode. But when individuals prioritize mutual well-being, they create a virtuous cycle of trust, empathy, and shared happiness—leading to a collective win.

You have the power to show up differently and show up happy, regardless of your circumstances and events, by reframing them. You can choose cooperation over self-interest, even when a situation tempts you to act selfishly. By reframing the dilemma as an opportunity to build trust and mutual benefit, you can create outcomes in which everyone wins, regardless of the immediate pressures or risks. This approach emphasizes the agency humans have to change the narrative and foster collaboration in situations where mistrust or competition might otherwise prevail.

Show up differently and model happiness.

What would it be like for you to show up differently today and role model happiness? What if you change your vocabulary to be "I'm a model of happiness" versus "I'm happy"?

Values-driven happiness can be seen as a "genesis block" in the context of human well-being and success because it serves as the foundational element that influences every subsequent aspect of life. Just like the first block in a blockchain, which initializes and defines the integrity of the entire chain, happiness establishes the mental, emotional, and social conditions for personal growth, decision-making, and interpersonal relationships.

When values-driven happiness acts as the starting point, it cascades into other areas of life, fostering resilience, motivation, and creativity. Research shows that happiness is linked to improved health, increased productivity, and stronger social bonds. It creates a positive feedback loop: When individuals prioritize their well-being, they are more likely to model values such as kindness, gratitude, and optimism, which, in turn, amplify happiness within their communities.

By living a values-driven, happiness-centered life, we contribute to a lineage of positivity and progress. Much like humanity standing on the shoulders of giants, happiness becomes the cornerstone upon which future generations can build lives rich in meaning, connection, and fulfillment.

Human values can be compared to the blockchain genesis block in several ways:

- **Foundational Significance**

  Just as the genesis block is the first block in a blockchain and forms the basis of all subsequent transactions and validations, human values serve as the foundational principles guiding decisions, actions, and societal norms.

- **Immutable Legacy**

  The genesis block is immutable, establishing trust and continuity within the blockchain network. Similarly, deeply held human values are enduring and provide a moral compass that remains steadfast over time, influencing generations.

- **Consensus Building**

  Blockchain networks depend on consensus protocols that stem from the genesis block's initial rules. Human values also create a shared understanding or consensus within communities, shaping collective behavior and fostering alignment.

- **Ripple Effect**

  Every block in the blockchain builds upon the genesis block. Similarly, all individual actions, decisions, and cultural practices are influenced by the foundational values instilled at personal, organizational, or societal levels.

Human values are like the blockchain genesis block in their foundational and enduring significance, creating a lineage of role modeling and a value-based framework for life. The genesis block, which serves as the unalterable starting point of a blockchain, mirrors how deeply held values establish the bedrock upon which individuals and societies build their decisions, actions, and cultures. Every subsequent "block" of our lives—our achievements, relationships, and innovations—rests upon these core principles, much like humanity standing on the shoulders of giants who have passed down their wisdom, resilience, and vision.

This lineage of role modeling is vital, as it allows values to be transmitted across generations, shaping a values-driven existence that impacts others. Just as the genesis block's integrity ensures the stability of the blockchain, a life lived according to values strengthens personal legacy and collective progress. Imagine a chain of a million human, product, and organizational role models.

Doing good is also very good for you. The author of a *Washington Post* article discusses how doing good not only benefits others but also enhances your own well-being by fostering a sense of purpose and fulfillment.[4] Studies show that acts of kindness release endorphins, reduce stress, and improve mental health, creating a positive feedback loop of happiness. Moreover, contributing to others strengthens social connections, which are essential for personal resilience and long-term satisfaction.

My wonderful husband of more than thirty years has been my rock, my partner, and my greatest source of joy. Together, we try to model happiness as often as we can. Seeing the last "The Beatles LOVE" Cirque du Soleil performance in Las Vegas with him felt like coming full circle, a tribute to the music that not only shaped my understanding of a new language but also connected me to a deeper sense of possibility and expression. Watching the artistry of the performance reminded me of the early days when I pieced together English words from The Beatles' lyrics, dreaming of the world that music painted.

Sharing this moment with my husband, who has stood by me through every melody and memory, made it even more poignant—a celebration of love, resilience, and the power of connection that transcends time and language.

CHANNEL THE VOICE OF PEACE

The world witnessed the reopening of the Notre-Dame Cathedral after the fire in Paris and demonstrated a humanity day on a grand scale. This event marked a triumphant moment in the preservation of global heritage, symbolizing human resilience and unity in the face of division and adversity.

Notre-Dame's restoration, following the devastating 2019 fire, stands as a testament to human ingenuity and the collective will to safeguard cultural treasures. The gathering of world leaders at the event reflects the shared recognition of Notre-Dame as a universal symbol of faith, history, and transcending boundaries. As the restored cathedral fills with the voice of peace, it reminds us that hope, beauty, and harmony can rebuild even the most fragile connections between nations and generations.

Imagine a world where role models fuse together, creating limitless energy that powers innovation and humanity.

No one displays harmony and peace better than a children's choir, their unified voices embodying innocence and hope for humanity. Their melodies remind us that even in a world that is often marked by discord, harmony is not only possible but deeply moving when we come together with shared purpose and understanding.

Annabelle Marie founded the now world-famous VOENA Children's Choir more than thirty years ago. The choir has performed at the White House five times, the World Expo in Japan, the Soweto International Festival in South Africa, the opening day of the 2012 London Olympics, Carnegie Hall twice, the Grand Ole Opry, and the Green Music Center in Sonoma and has gone on concert tours of China, Italy, Bali, and Greece.

Most recently, VOENA performed in Abu Dhabi as guests of the crown prince for 250 world religious leaders at the Interfaith Alliance Forum on Children's Dignity.

Role Modelship Example: Annabelle Marie

- **Sponsorship:** Annabelle Marie founded the now world-famous VOENA Children's Choir in 1994 in Benicia, California. As a sponsor, she has created a platform for more than one thousand young talents, providing them with opportunities to develop their musical abilities and perform at prestigious venues.

- **Leadership:** As the executive and artistic director of VOENA, Marie is the choir's visionary and driving force. Her leadership has been recognized nationally, earning her accolades, including a Jefferson Award for public service from the nonprofit Multiplying Good. Her innovative approach to music education and performance has positioned her as a leader in her field.

- **Mentorship:** With a master's degree in music education, Marie has studied voice with Barbra Streisand's vocal coach and violin with former New York Philharmonic member William Barbini. Marie serves as a mentor to young musicians, sharing her expertise and passion for music, fostering their growth as performers and individuals.

continued

- **Fellowship:** Marie fosters a strong sense of community within VOENA, bringing together diverse young voices to create harmony. Her emphasis on collaboration enhances the choir's unity, encouraging friendships and shared experiences.

- **Stewardship:** Through her stewardship of VOENA, Marie exemplifies a commitment to the arts. The choir has performed for notable figures such as US presidents Bill Clinton and George Bush, Pope John Paul II, and the crown prince of Abu Dhabi. Her dedication ensures that the choir not only thrives but also contributes positively to the cultural landscape, preserving and promoting musical education for future generations. Marie has also organized fundraisers at The French Laundry restaurant in Yountville, California, to support scholarships, further demonstrating her commitment to empowering young musicians. Recognized and praised by American film director and poet Maya Angelou, Marie continues to inspire and uplift young musicians through her multiplying modelship.

Marie's thirty years of uniting more than thirty-five cultures has brought children together in a world vision through music that reaches beyond borders. My family had the privilege of watching our children grow and demo courage in Marie's choir, and we still sponsor them and attend VOENA concerts in the San Francisco Bay Area. It is truly a blessing.

✍ ONE-MINUTE MODELSHIP

Change your vocabulary to "I'm a role model of happiness" versus "I'm happy," and reflect on how that impacts your identity and the well-being of everyone around you.

#RoleModelship

TL;DR

- Our rallying cry is "Wire 2 Model." The times demand we *wire* humans, organizations, and AI products to model five strategic human values and provide economic value for the benefit of our human future.

- Goals aren't just targets to hit; they're demands to become different humans so we can influence AI.

- Values-driven happiness is a genesis block of human well-being and success that influences every subsequent aspect of life.

Unleash Human Potential

Frank Herbert's *Dune* inspired generations of thinkers and creators with its visionary take on ecology, politics, and the potential of human evolution, influencing everything from renewable energy to AI ethics to many authors finding their voice. Fiction is often a pivotal force that drives technology innovation, storytelling, and Role Modelship voice, actions, and results. The narrative of *Dune*'s protagonist, Paul Atreides, embodies the power of role models in fiction, showing how resilience, strategic foresight, and cultural respect can transform a society and inspire real-world leadership.

Paul Atreides had always been quiet. Not the kind of quiet that people ignore. The kind of quiet that made humans wonder if the boy's mind operated on the same plane as theirs. Can you move a glass with your mind? Paul's mind lived in the shadows of giants: his mother's sharp syllables, the Bene Gesserit whispers, the stern directives of his father, burdened by duty, always expecting.

The boy swallowed his words, tucking them into the hollows of his vast mind. Each question Paul dared to ask turned into a grain of Arrakis sand—small, insignificant, but together, they began to shift the planes.

Then came the desert. It did not speak to anyone kindly. The sun roared its dominance. The desert did not teach with a soft hand but with necessity. The desert pushed Paul to the edge of thirst, to the brink of forgetting, until the only voice the boy could rely on was his own.

Paul focused on the deliberate stillness and power of the voice inside him. The first time he used the Voice, it surprised even him. It was a command woven from the threads of every silence he had endured. It was the sound of the desert, ancient and undeniable, speaking through him.

When the Fremen turned to listen, Paul knew. His voice had not been lost; it had been waiting—growing, until it was strong enough to carry the weight of the prophecy.

Paul had been quiet, but quiet does not mean weak.

It means waiting. It means watching.

It means learning that when you finally speak, your voice has the power to amplify, level the playing field, add, and multiply, unleashing potential. AI can't be what AI can't see.

Fifty-five percent of women say there's a lack of relatable role models in their workplace. Forty-three percent believe they would be more successful if they had a role model at work.[1] There are similar statistics by gender, race, education, and income across many parts of our lives.

You can't *be* what you can't *see*.

✦

AI is a giant magnifying mirror.
AI can't be what AI can't see.

AI in its current state reflects and magnifies the best and worst of humanity.

AI feeds on our data, biases, values, and behaviors, amplifying what it learns, without the ability to discern right from wrong or to determine utility for human life. In this age of AI, we need human role models more than ever, because AI alone cannot provide the moral compass, ethical reasoning, or lived experience necessary to navigate complex human challenges.

Scientifically, AI still lacks human intuition and emotional intelligence. Philosophically, it raises profound questions about human identity and agency. Organizationally and technically, human leaders must shape AI's role in society, ensuring that its development aligns with fairness, security, and the common good of humanity.

Role Modelship is the antidote to AI's limitations, offering the human guardrails and grounding that AI lacks today. It is imperative that we integrate AI into our lives and that we do so with intention and accountability. It is through Role Modelship that we pass down values, bridge the gap between technology and humanity, and create a world where AI serves us rather than diminishes us. Role Modelship is the genesis block needed for our continued human evolution in the face of rapid technological change that is poised to amplify inequality and bias.

As we set strategic goals to embed AI into products and leverage AI for increasing human efficiency and effectiveness, we also need to set strategic objectives for Role Modelship and growing model humans who in turn will shape AI. One of the most important contributions AI tech giants can make is to use synthetic Role Modelship data to correct AI model bias by supplementing real datasets with more diverse synthetic information. How are we avoiding bias when we create synthetic avatars for customer behavior research?

One of the most significant contributions policymakers can make is to establish regulatory frameworks that incentivize AI product development based on Role Modelship, ensuring that AI applications amplify diverse, ethical, and responsible values and behaviors that don't harm humanity. We expect to see the equivalent of the US Food and Drug Administration for AI, beyond drug and biological products.

As you look at your objectives and key results, share with your peers how you're envisioning, creating, demonstrating, and sustaining Role Modelship in your humans, organizations, and products. You have the power to frame the magnifying AI mirror, and the best time to take action is today.

FIND YOUR IDENTITY, OWN YOUR IMPACT, UNLEASH HUMAN POTENTIAL

"There is power in identity," says civil rights attorney and TED speaker Bryan Stevenson, who also had the privilege of meeting Rosa Parks.[2]

Where are you on your identity journey?

Where are we on our identity journey as a nation, as humanity?

May you find your role models who are human value anchors, "identity engineers," career catalysts, and "value proposition engineers."

May you find your role model voice and your wings.

May you find your own career and Role Modelship windows to social change.

May you find spectacular variables to fill your board of directors formula of you (human, organization, product) = multiplier sponsor you × stabilizer sponsor × multiplier mentor × multiplier leader × stabilizer leader.

May you wear a hat or T-shirt demonstrating your heartbeat, place a giant ladder against the night sky and climb it, touching the future.

When they subtract or divide, we add and multiply.

May you be **BRAVER** as you adapt to change in our new decision-making world.

May you find your organizational and product golden ratio for modelship and train AI and humanoids to model it.

May you create and launch your own modelships, defying gravity and empowering others to build many model ships and explore the infinite possibilities of the abundant universe and human consciousness.

May you continue the fellowships of rings forged by giants and titans.

May we experiment, make the right kind of mistakes, and continue to learn.

May we Wire 2 Model as our evergreen purpose, mission, and legacy, winning as a team.

The ripple effect and economic value of Role Modelship touches the world far beyond our direct knowledge. Our humanity depends on your humanity and on everyone's humanity. Our human potential depends on your potential and on everyone's potential.

Be the role model you once needed. Be the role model we need now more than ever.

You influence is inevitable—set the example intentionally.

Managers direct reports.
Leaders inspire followers.
Role models engineer identity
and magnify the future.

Show up differently—own your Role Modelship habits. When you're physically and emotionally exhausted, show up differently. Own your identity and impact. Serve others. Change humans, organizations, and products to exemplify and amplify our best human values and behaviors.

AI can't be what AI can't see. We are building a legacy together and encoding it into AI. I'm calling on everyone to embrace your capacity to guide, uplift, and champion others while training AI.

You have the power to unleash human potential. What if tomorrow is the most important humanity day in our lives? What are we going to role model and Wire 2 Model tomorrow?

RALLYING CRY

AI can't be what AI can't see.
AI is learning from you as a steward, fellow,
mentor, leader, and sponsor.
Our rallying cry is "Wire 2 Model":
We need to wire humans and AI to be role models.
Here are ten habits you can practice
to positively influence AI:

1. Demonstrate Role Modelship because human behavior is encapsulated in the data leveraged to train AI.

2. Invest in human–AI literacy to influence roles, boundaries, and partnerships.

3. Ask, "Is AI good for humanity?" as often as "Does it scale?"

4. Push AI to solve real human problems (e.g., well-being, equity, environment, and community), not just optimize efficiency or effectiveness.

5. Encourage dialogue about human, societal, and profit trade-offs.

6. Champion diverse voices and diverse data.

7. Reward behaviors worth replicating, not just results.

8. Create cross-organizational guardrails, and make responsible AI a team sport.

9. Tell meaningful human-centered stories to train the machines.

10. Lead with purpose, and scale habits across humans and algorithms.

Write a Review for
Role Modelship
and Share

☆☆☆☆☆

We're on a mission to inspire one million acts of role modelship.

Would you be willing to leave an honest book review
on Amazon and Barnes & Noble?
We appreciate you sharing your point of view.

As we grow humans, organizations, and products,
we all have Role Modelship moments.

Please share on social platforms using the tag #RoleModelship.

To connect with us, please go to RoleModelshipHabits.com.

Acknowledgments

My deepest gratitude goes to my family and the amazing role models who have shaped so many humans, organizations, and products.

To everyone who is featured in this book—you're antifragile multipliers.

To the entire Greenleaf team: Tanya Hall, Amanda Hughes, Dee Kerr, Lee Reed Zarnikau, Benito Salazar, Maggie Langrick, Brian Welch, Morgan Robinson, Kathy Thomlinson, Neil Gonzalez, Meilee Bridges, Hayden Seder, Jamie White, Rachel High, Gwen Cunningham, Brittany Jones-Pugh, and Kyle Pearson.

You're my heroes, and we won as a team.

Thank you for leading by example.

Notes

INTRODUCTION

1. Peter F. Drucker, *Management Challenges for the 21st Century* (Butterworth-Heinemann, 2007), 116.

2. Jensen Huang and Arthur Mensch, hosts, *The a16z Podcast*, Andreessen Horowitz, "Why Every Nation Needs Its Own AI Strategy," March 20, 2025, https://www.youtube.com/watch?v=Ww9SkW0Em58.

CHAPTER 2

1. *Oxford Learner's Dictionaries*, s.v. "–ship (*suffix*)," accessed August 1, 2025, https://www.oxfordlearnersdictionaries.com/us/definition/english/ship_2.

2. "The Values Map," Common Cause Foundation, April 2023, https://commoncausefoundation.org/_resources/the-values-map/.

3. Attributed to Mark Hawkins, Scott Herren, and Jeff Brzycki.

4. Attributed to Stuart Evans, Distinguished Service Professor, Carnegie Mellon University.

5. Dame Vivian Hunt, Dennis Layton, and Sara Prince, "Why Diversity Matters," McKinsey & Company, January 1, 2015, https://www.mckinsey.com/capabilities/people-and-organizational-performance/our-insights/why-diversity-matters.

6. Gallup and Amazon, *Role Models Matter: How Role Models Influence Career Awareness and Attainment*, Amazon Future Engineer, 2023, 4, https://www.amazonfutureengineer.com/research/gallup-role-models.pdf.

7. Haiilo, *10 Employee Engagement Statistics You Need to Know in 2024*, January 13, 2024, https://haiilo.com/blog/employee-engagement-8-statistics-you-need-to-know/#.

8. Sara Blakely, "What is more terrifying?," Instagram, August 21, 2024, https://www.instagram.com/reel/C-84H_SM8fj/.

9. "15 Tech Trends to Watch Closely in 2025," Research Report, CBS Insights, November 19, 2024, https://www.cbinsights.com/research/report/top-tech-trends-2025/.

10. Min-Hsuan Tu, Joyce E. Bono, Cass Shum, and Liva LaMontagne, "Breaking the Cycle: The Effects of Role Model Performance and Ideal Leadership Self-Concepts on Abusive Supervision Spillover," *Journal of Applied Psychology* 103, no. 7 (March 2018): 689, https://www.researchgate.net/publication/323862795_Breaking_the_Cycle_The_Effects_of_Role_Model_Performance_and_Ideal_Leadership_Self-Concepts_on_Abusive_Supervision_Spillover.

11. Eric Bock, "Workplace Civility Increases Productivity," *NIH Record* 70, no. 16 (August 10, 2018): 4, https://nihrecord.nih.gov/2018/08/10/workplace-civility-increases-productivity#:~:text=%E2%80%9CIncivility%20is%20contagious.,uncivil%20because%20they%20are%20stressed.

12. *Toxic Bosses Survey: What They Do and How We Cope*, The Harris Poll Thought Leadership Practice, October 2023, 3, https://theharrispoll.com/wp-content/uploads/2023/10/Toxic-Bosses-Survey-October-2023.pdf.

13. Gabe Salamida, "Insights: Gallup's *State of the Global Workplace* 2023 Report," Mission Advantage Recruiting, https://missionadv.org/insights/insights-gallups-state-of-the-global-workplace-2023-report.

14. Peter H. Diamandis, "120 IQ AI: Threat or Opportunity?," *Peter H. Diamandis* (blog), September 26, 2024, https://www.diamandis.com/blog/120-iq-ai-threat-or-opportunity.

15. Alyse Stanley, "OpenAI's New ChatGPT o1 Model Will Try to Escape If It Thinks It'll Be Shut Down—Then Lies About It," *Tom's Guide*, December 6, 2024, https://www.tomsguide.com/ai/openais-new-chatgpt-o1-model-will-try-to-escape-if-it-thinks-itll-be-shut-down-then-lies-about-it.

16. "Top 126 Artificial Intelligence Unicorns in 2024," Failory, January 22, 2024, https://www.failory.com/startups/artificial-intelligence-unicorns.

17. Peter H. Diamandis, "Tech Breakthroughs on My Mind: 10 Billion Humanoid Robots, Life on Mars . . . ," *Peter H. Diamandis* (blog), August 11, 2024, https://www.diamandis.com/blog/10-billion-humanoid-robots-life-on-mars.

18. Roger Martin, "Rethinking the Decision Factory," *Harvard Business Review*, October 1, 2023, https://hbsp.harvard.edu/product/R1310E-PDF-ENG.

19. Cheryl Cran, NextMapping (home page), https://nextmapping.com/.

20. Christine Porath, "How Rudeness Stops People from Working Together," *Harvard Business Review*, January 20, 2017, https://hbr.org/2017/01/how-rudeness-stops-people-from-working-together.

21. Rose E. Guingrich and Michael S. A. Graziano, "Ascribing Consciousness to Artificial Intelligence: Human-AI Interaction and Its Carry-Over Effects on Human-Human Interaction," *Frontiers in Psychology* 15 (March 27, 2024): 1322781, https://pmc.ncbi.nlm.nih.gov/articles/PMC11008604/.

22. Jensen Huang, speaker, "Nvidia CEO Says 'ChatGPT Moment' for Robotics Is Just Around the Corner," *Fortune* magazine, January 8, 2025, YouTube video, https://www.youtube.com/watch?v=6hp1JfkqzQQ.

23. Jay Peters, "Shopify CEO Says No New Hires Without Proof AI Can't Do the Job," *The Verge*, April 7, 2025, https://www.theverge.com/news/644943/shopify-ceo-memo-ai-hires-job.

24. Daniel Phillips and Stephen Graves, "What Is the Bitcoin Genesis Block? How It All Started," *Decrypt*, April 30, 2024, https://decrypt.co/resources/the-bitcoin-genesis-block-how-it-all-started.

CHAPTER 3

1. Charles Duhigg, *The Power of Habit: Why We Do What We Do in Life and Business* (Random House Trade Paperbacks, 2014).

2. Katie Couric, *The Best Advice I Ever Got: Lessons from Extraordinary Lives* (Random House Trade Paperbacks, 2012).

3. Peter Thiel, *Zero to One: Notes on Startups, or How to Build the Future* (Random House UK, 2015).

4. José Raúl Capablanca, *Capablanca's Last Chess Lectures* (Herbert Jenkins, 1967), 23.

5. *Pasang: In the Shadow of Everest*, directed by Nancy Svendsen, 2022.

6. Shirzad Chamine, *Positive Intelligence: Why Only 20% of Teams and Individuals Achieve Their True Potential AND HOW YOU CAN ACHIEVE YOURS* (Greenleaf Book Group Press, 2012).

CHAPTER 4

1. *Young Woman and the Sea*, directed by Joachim Rønning, 2024.

2. "Company Information," Ameriprise Financial, 2025, https://www.ameriprise.com/about/our-company.

CHAPTER 5

1. Peter H. Diamandis, "$700M Bet on Humanoids: Why Tech Giants Are All In," *Peter H. Diamandis* (blog), August 29, 2024, https://www.diamandis.com/blog/700-million-bet-on-humanoid-robots.

2. Peter Drucker, "There is nothing so useless as doing efficiently that which should not be done at all," BrainyQuote, https://www.brainyquote.com/quotes/peter_drucker_105338.

CHAPTER 6

1. Chris Donnelly, "You don't need a title to be a leader," LinkedIn, January 2025, https://www.linkedin.com/posts/donnellychris_you-dont-need-a-title-to-be-a-leader-just-activity-7274044680479072256-U_z4/.

CHAPTER 7

1. Nassim Nicholas Taleb, *Antifragile: Things That Gain from Disorder* (Penguin, 2013), 34.

2. Kalev Peekna and Ryan Schulz, "Why a Multidiscplinary Team Wins Every Time," One North, March 3, 2022, https://www.onenorth.com/insights/why-a-multidisciplinary-team-wins-every-time/.

3. Thomas Barta, Markus Kleiner, and Tilo Neumann, "Is There a Payoff from Top-Team Diversity?," McKinsey & Company, April 1, 2012, https://www.mckinsey.com/capabilities/people-and-organizational-performance/our-insights/is-there-a-payoff-from-top-team-diversity.

4. Michelle Faverio and Alec Tyson, "What the Data Says About Americans' Views of Artificial Intelligence," Pew Research Center, November 21, 2023, https://www.pewresearch.org/short-reads/2023/11/21/what-the-data-says-about-americans-views-of-artificial-intelligence/.

5. Samanatha Subin, "Tech Megacaps Plan to Spend More Than $300 Billion in 2025 as AI Race Intensifies," CNBC, February 8, 2025, https://www.cnbc.com/2025/02/08/tech-megacaps-to-spend-more-than-300-billion-in-2025-to-win-in-ai.html.

6. Daniel Roth, "A crazy stat from this year's Jobs on the Rise list: 68% of the titles didn't exist 20 years ago—and I have no doubt that the speed of change is only going to accelerate," LinkedIn, 2024, https://www.linkedin.com/posts/danielroth1_a-crazy-stat-from-this-years-jobs-on-the-activity-7154246976585220096-p7U2.

7. Fei Wu, host, Feisworld Podcast: Unsung Heroes and Self-Made Artists, Feisworld, "From CTO to CAIO: Florin Rotar on Leading Avanade's AI Transformation," February 3, 2024, https://www.feisworld.com/blog/florin-rotar.

8. "American Canyon Schools Win Top Honors in Robotics Competition," *Napa Valley Register*, June 7, 2019, https://www.napalearns.org/american-canyon-schools-win-top-honors-in-robotics-competition/.

9. "American Canyon Schools."

10. Alexander Merchak, "Hometown Heroes Fly with Blue Angels," Travis Air Force Base, March 14, 2024, https://www.travis.af.mil/News/Display/Article/3707703/hometown-heroes-fly-with-blue-angels/.

11. ACHS Choir, YouTube channel, https://www.youtube.com/@AmCanHighSchoolChoir.

12. "Nobel Prize in Chemistry 2020," The Nobel Prize, https://www.nobelprize.org/prizes/chemistry/2020/summary/.

13. "Nobel Prize in Physiology or Medicine 2024," The Nobel Prize, https://www.nobelprize.org/prizes/medicine/2023/summary/.

14. "APIs Drive the Majority of Internet Traffic and Cybercriminals Are Taking Advantage," *The Hacker News*, March 19, 2024, https://thehackernews.com/2024/03/apis-drive-majority-of-internet-traffic.html.

15. "API Composition Pattern," Amazon AWS Documentation, https://docs.aws.amazon.com/prescriptive-guidance/latest/modernization-data-persistence/api-composition.html.

16. Trilok Sonar, "TL;DR: Origins, Popularity, and Benefits," Typetone, August 16, 2023, https://www.typetone.ai/blog/tldr-summary-what-it-is-and-why-it-matters-in-the-digital-age.

17. Jacky Chou, "TL;DR: What It Stands For and Why It Matters in Today's Digital Age," Indexsy, June 10, 2025, https://indexsy.com/tl-dr/.

CHAPTER 8

1. "Six 2×4 LEGO bricks can be combined in 915,103,765 ways," Factourism by Ferdio, https://factourism.com/facts/lego-combinations/.

2. "125 Years of Sharing Happiness: A Short History of The Coca-Cola Company," Coca-Cola Company, https://www.coca-colacompany.com/content/dam/company/us/en/about-us/history/coca-cola-a-short-history-125-years-booklet.pdf.

3. Sky Ariella, "20+ Logo Statistics You Need to Know [2023]: Facts + Trends in Branding," Zippia, November 2, 2022, https://www.zippia.com/advice/logo-statistics/.

4. Samantha Neely, "Magic Kingdom to See 'Historic Expansion': What We Know About 'Villain Land,'" *USA Today*, August 13, 2024, https://www.usatoday.com/story/travel/experience/theme-parks/2024/08/13/magic-kingdom-disney-world-d23-details/74782703007/.

5. Wouter Born, "2018: CEO of Nextdoor. 2024: CFO of OpenAI, a $157 billion AI giant. CEOs are becoming CFOs," LinkedIn, October 2024, https://www.linkedin.com/posts/wouterborn_2018-ceo-of-nextdoor-2024-cfo-of-openai-activity-7255188784261042176-oET8/.

6. QuotaPath Team, "What Is a Good Rule of Thumb for Growing Your RevOps Team?," QuotaPath, September 26, 2023, https://www.quotapath.com/blog/revops-rule-of-thumb/.

7. Full credit for researching this idea goes to my friend Silvina Candia, a Carnegie Mellon alumna and the head of finance PMO at Netflix.

8. Wikipedia, s.v. "Carnegie Mellon University," last modified July 3, 2025, https://en.wikipedia.org/wiki/Carnegie_Mellon_University.

9. Carnegie Mellon University, "Carnegie Mellon Endowment Stands at $3.2B in 2024," October 30, 2024, https://www.cmu.edu/news/stories/archives/2024/october/carnegie-mellon-endowment-stands-at-32b-in-2024.

CHAPTER 9

1. "Future of Business 2024: Exploring What's Next for AI, Innovation, and the World of Work," *Harvard Business Review*, October 7, 2024, https://hbr.org/2024/10/future-of-business-2024.

2. Scott Sheppard, "Autodesk Bill O'Connor: Real Innovation—What It Is and How to Do It," *Autodesk* (blog), June 23, 2014, https://labs.blogs.com/its_alive_in_the_lab/2014/06/autodesk-bill-oconnor-real-innovation-what-it-is-and-how-to-do-it.html.

3. Sheppard, "Autodesk Bill O'Connor."

4. Paul Daugherty, Kate Whiting, and Beatrice Di Caro, hosts, *Book Club* (podcast), World Economic Forum, "Paul Daugherty: Radically Human," December 16, 2022, https://www.weforum.org/podcasts/book-club/episodes/paul-daugherty-radically-human/.

5. "Empowering Women, One Hand at a Time," Poker Power, https://pokerpower.com/our-mission/.

6. Sheila Connor, "Power Over vs. Power Within," Guiding Leaders and Teams, April 2, 2024, https://guidingleadersandteams.com/power-over-vs-power-within/.

7. Martin Luther King Jr., *The Autobiography of Martin Luther King Jr.*, ed. Clayborne Carson (Grand Central Publishing, 2001), 324.

8. Alia Crum, Peter Salovey, and Shawn Achor, "Rethinking Stress: The Role of Mindsets in Determining the Stress Response," *Journal of Personality and Social Psychology* 104, no. 4 (April 2013): 716–733, https://psycnet.apa.org/buy/2013-06053-001.

CHAPTER 10

1. Corey Eaves, "Every week, I dedicate time to supporting my network, particularly those navigating career transitions," LinkedIn, August 2024, https://www.linkedin.com/posts/ceaves_every-week-i-dedicate-time-to-supporting-activity-7233152253686140928-NXnj/.

2. Sharon Mandell, "I've had a long career in technology, but stepping into the classroom has probably taught me at least as much as I've been able to share with my students," LinkedIn, October 2024, https://www.linkedin.com/posts/sharon-mandell-juniper_what-technologists-need-to-know-to-lead-an-activity-7257492282260480000-dinr/.

3. Mark Benioff, "For my first-ever post on LinkedIn, I'm excited to announce that as of today, Agentforce—our complete AI system for enterprises built on the Salesforce platform—is available for all of our customers," LinkedIn, October 2024, https://www.linkedin.com/posts/marcbenioff_for-my-first-ever-post-on-linkedin-im-excited-activity-7257157359641255936-sKpZ/.

CHAPTER 11

1. "Gartner Unveils Top Predictions for IT Organisations and Users in 2025 and Beyond," FutureCIO, October 31, 2024, https://futurecio.tech/gartner-unveils-top-predictions-for-it-organisations-and-users-in-2025-and-beyond/.

2. "Gartner Unveils Top Predictions."

3. Michael O'Grady, "The Global Digital Economy Will Reach $16.5 Trillion and Capture 17% of Global GDP by 2023," Forrester, July 23, 2024, https://www.forrester.com/blogs/the-global-digital-economy-will-reach-16-5-trillion-and-capture-17-of-global-gdp-by-2028/.

4. Kyle Poyar, "We're moving away from charging for *access* to software and toward a model of charging for the *work delivered* by a combination of software and AI agents," LinkedIn, November 2024, https://www.linkedin.com/posts/kyle-poyar_ai-pricing-saas-activity-7257366623399948288-a6xz?utm_source=share&utm_medium=member_desktop.

5. Ailsa Chang, host, *All Things Considered,* "Banksy's Back with Surprise Daily Street Art of Animals across London," NPR, August 16, 2024, https://www.npr.org/transcripts/nx-s1-5077660.

6. Malik Muzamil, "Most B2B founders are scared of being seen," LinkedIn, July 2025, https://www.linkedin.com/posts/malikmuzamil1_how-adam-robinson-turned-linkedin-into-a-activity-7348763658996314113-gJn8/.

CHAPTER 12

1. William Gibson, *Count Zero* (Ace, 2006).

2. William Gibson, *Mona Lisa Overdrive* (SpectraBooks, 1997).

3. William Gibson, *Pattern Recognition* (Berkley, 2005).

4. Jena McGregor, "Even Among Gen Z, More Men Than Women Use AI. Here's Why That Matters," *Forbes*, June 3, 2024, https://www.forbes.com/sites/jenamcgregor/2024/06/03/even-among-gen-z-more-men-than-women-use-ai-heres-why-that-matters/.

5. James Walker, "New Data Center Developments: November 2024," DataCenter Knowledge, November 5, 2024, https://www.datacenterknowledge.com/data-center-construction/new-data-center-developments-november-2024.

6. Kripa B, "Amazon CEO Says Gen AI Is Growing Three Times Faster Than AWS," Telecom Talk, November 24, 2024, https://telecomtalk.info/amazon-genai-is-growing-three-times-faster/984282/#google_vignette.

7. "Planet API," greenpolicy360.net, last edited January 29, 2025, https://www.greenpolicy360.net/w/Planet_API.

CHAPTER 13

1. Roberto Sigona, "Customer success = CO (customer outcomes) + CX (customer experience)," LinkedIn, September 2024, https://www.linkedin.com/posts/rsigona_delivering-a-superior-customer-experience-activity-7234993713884614657-UmPM.

2. Roberto Sigona, "At the start of my career journey, I was lucky enough to be mentored by the best," LinkedIn, July 2024, https://www.linkedin.com/posts/rsigona_leadership-peoplemanagement-mentoring-activity-7196894962649571328-kSwk/.

CHAPTER 14

1. Elisabeth Kübler-Ross, *On Death and Dying* (Scribner, 1969); Spencer Johnson, *Who Moved My Cheese?* (G. P. Putnam's Sons, 1998).

2. Will Guidara, *Unreasonable Hospitality: The Remarkable Power of Giving People More Than They Expect* (Optimism Press, 2022).

3. John Mackey and Rejendra Sisodia, *Conscious Capitalism: Liberating the Heroic Spirit of Business* (Harvard Business Review Press, 2013), 32–35.

CHAPTER 15

1. Kristalina Georgieva, "Women, Work, and Leadership: One-on-One Conversation with Kristalina Georgieva," International Monetary Fund Seminar Event, October 15, 2019, https://meetings.imf.org/en/2019/Annual/Schedule/2019/10/15/imf-seminar-gender-one-on-one-conversation-kristalina-georgieva.

2. Frederick Kempe, "IMF Managing Director: 'Think of the Unthinkable,'" *Inflection Points Today*, Atlantic Council, April 12, 2024, https://www.atlanticcouncil.org/content-series/inflection-points/imf-managing-director-think-of-the-unthinkable/.

3. Kristalina Georgieva et al., "The Economic Cost of Devaluing 'Women's Work,'" *IMF Blog*, International Monetary Fund, October 15, 2019, https://www.imf.org/en/Blogs/Articles/2019/10/15/blog-the-economic-cost-of-devaluing-women-work.

4. Gallup and Amazon, *Role Models Matter*.

5. America Ferrera, "My Identity Is a Superpower—Not an Obstacle," TED Talk, May 2019, https://www.ted.com/speakers/america_ferrera.

CHAPTER 16

1. *Cosmos: A Personal Voyage*, episode 9, "The Lives of the Stars," written and presented by Carl Sagan, 1980, PBS.

2. Gabriella Petrick, "Why Americans Love Their Apple Pie," *Smithsonian* magazine, September 2019, https://www.smithsonianmag.com/arts-culture/why-americans-love-their-apple-pie-180972852/.

3. Jacqueline Brassey, Aaron De Smet, and Dana Maor, "Developing a Resilient, Adaptable Workforce for an Uncertain Future," *McKinsey Quarterly*, McKinsey & Company, December 6, 2024, https://www.mckinsey.com/capabilities/people-and-organizational-performance/our-insights/developing-a-resilient-adaptable-workforce-for-an-uncertain-future?cid=eml-web.

4. Dixie Gillaspie, "You'll Never Accomplish Goals You Don't Really Care About," *Entrepreneur*, January 20, 2017, https://www.entrepreneur.com/living/youll-never-accomplish-goals-you-dont-really-care-about/254371.

5. "Scott Herren," The Org, https://theorg.com/org/cisco/org-chart/scott-herren.

CHAPTER 17

1. Steven Bartlett, *The Diary of a CEO: The 33 Laws of Business and Life* (Portfolio/Penguin, 2023), 295.

2. Madalina Roman, "The Pickle Jar Theory: The Importance of Your Own Time," EARLY blog, December 30, 2022, https://timeular.com/blog/pickle-jar-theory/.

3. Martin, "Rethinking the Decision Factory."

4. "Working Backwards (the Amazon Method)," ProductPlan, https://www.productplan.com/glossary/working-backward-amazon-method/.

5. Jason Lemkin, "The 48 Types of VP Sales. Make Deadly Sure You Hire the Right One," SaaStr, https://www.saastr.com/the-48-types-of-vp-sales-make-deadly-sure-you-hire-the-right-one/.

6. Alan Ohnsman, "Alphabet's Waymo Logging 150,000 Robotaxi Rides and 1 Million Miles a Week," *Forbes*, October 29, 2024, https://www.forbes.com/sites/alanohnsman/2024/10/29/alphabets-waymo-logging-150000-robotaxi-rides-and-1-million-miles-a-week/.

7. Chase DiBenedetto, "Intel's 20-Year-Old AI Ethics Prodigy on the Future of Artificial Intelligence," Mashable, November 25, 2024, https://mashable.com/article/intel-youngest-ai-ethicist-ria-cheruvu-future-ai.

CHAPTER 18

1. Luke Harries, "What if an AI agent makes a phone call, then realizes the other person is also an AI agent?," LinkedIn, March 2025, https://www.linkedin.com/feed/update/urn:li:activity:7299878652291272704/.

2. Brian Halligan, "A Startup Founder to Scaleup CEO's Journey from $0 to $25 Billion (Halliganism's)," LinkedIn, October 1, 2024, https://www.linkedin.com/pulse/startup-founder-scaleup-ceos-journey-from-0-25billion-brian-halligan-e1f4e/?trackingId=1E2GQ2atNG9tv96iKBpKUA%3D%3D.

3. "83 Inspiring Michelle Obama Quotes on *Becoming* That'll Empower You," Some *Think* of Value, March 7, 2024, https://somethinkofvalue.com/michelle-obama-quotes/.

4. Richard Sima, "Doing Good Is Good for You, Research Shows," *The Washington Post*, November 28, 2024, https://www.washingtonpost.com/wellness/2024/11/28/altruism-volunteering-donating-wellbeing.

CONCLUSION

1. Janine Chamberlain, "Lack of Role Models Hindering Women's Career Progress," theHRDIRECTOR, July 11, 2022, https://www.thehrdirector.com/business-news/diversity-and-equality-inclusion/lack-role-models-hindering-womens-career-progress/.

2. Bryan Stevenson, "We Need to Talk About an Injustice," TED Talk, March 1, 2012, https://speakola.com/ideas/bryan-stevenson-ted-2012.

About the Author

Two suitcases and a dream.
Born in Bulgaria.
Englished by The Beatles.
Envisioned by Carnegie Mellon.
Designed by Autodesk.
Made in America.
Wired by digital giants.
Investing in you.

ELI POTTER is a Silicon Valley technology executive who has advised more than 150 companies on human values and converting technology into economic value. She's had the privilege of working alongside amazing role models at venture- or private equity-backed start-ups and billion-dollar public companies. She has coached hundreds of CXOs, has presented at dozens of conferences, and volunteers as a guest speaker at Carnegie Mellon University.

A straight-shooter CIO, she has a rare gift for breaking down complex ideas into practical wisdom and inspiring practices that help everyday people become force multipliers for good. She brings a distinct blend of corporate savvy and deep leadership insights with more than thirty years of experience.

Drawing from years of studying extraordinary leaders, she reveals how the world's most impactful innovators think, act, and communicate from the same set of core values to achieve lasting results and influence. This distilled wisdom gives readers the power to amplify business growth, success, and human potential.

Her passion is helping organizations envision, design, demonstrate, and sustain innovation and growth, anchored in ethical human values. She influences AI by modeling what matters: ethical choices, diverse data, and feedback loops that prioritize human well-being. When you realize AI is learning from you, your habits will change.

Eli believes that higher powers give us many chances to pivot in our lives, become role models, and build a Yellow Brick Road for humanity. Her philosophy is that everything has a purpose if you allow it to shine a bright light. She also believes that you didn't pick up this torch by accident.

Let's wire humans and AI to role model together.

www.ingramcontent.com/pod-product-compliance
Lightning Source LLC
Chambersburg PA
CBHW030452210326
41597CB00013B/631